Selling Ben Cheever

Selling Ben Cheever

BACK TO SQUARE ONE IN A SERVICE ECONOMY

Benjamin Cheever

BLOOMSBURY

Published by Bloomsbury, New York and London
Distributed to the trade by St. Martin's Press

Library of Congress Cataloguing-in-Publication Data

Cheever, Benjamin, 1948–
Selling Ben Cheever : back to square one in a service economy / Benjamin Cheever.
p. cm.
ISBN 1-58234-158-3
1. Cheever, Benjamin, 1948– 2. Employees -- United States -- Biography. 3. Displaced
workers -- United States. 4. Working poor -- United States. 5. Career changes -- United
States -- Case Studies. 6. Industries -- United States. 7. United States -- Economic
conditions -- 1981–8. United States -- Social conditions -- 1980– I. Title.

HD8073.C5 A3 1001
813′.54--dc21
2001035124

First U.S. Edition

10 9 8 7 6 5 4 3 2 1

Typeset by Hewer Text Limited, Edinburgh
Printed in the United States of America by RR Donnelley & Sons, Harrisonburg

To my mother. She's as bewildered as I am by the discrepancy between admirable people and the people the world admires.

We are so apt, in our engrossing egotism, to consider all those accessories which are drawn around us by prosperity, as pertaining and belonging to our own persons, that the discovery of our unimportance, when left to our own proper resources, becomes inexpressibly mortifying.

– Sir Walter Scott, *Rob Roy*

The world has been kinder than I expected, but less just.

– Dr. Samuel Johnson

PRODUCT WARNING

The narrators of books are often superior characters. Biographers, for instance, are morally superior to their illustrious subjects. Political reporters have superior politics. Novelists have superior sensibilities. Not me. This is a book about failure, and I haven't even been consistently successful at that.

I first started this project in 1995. Since then I have read scads of books and articles, thrown myself into difficult, sometimes humiliating, situations. Six years have passed, but don't be too impressed. I have also spent an unconscionable amount of time in the kitchen, in my stockinged feet, pawing through catalogues, while I ate vanilla ice cream out of the container with a tablespoon. I'm not one of those paragons you run into on flap copy.

Nor is this book for everybody. I find the world slightly ridiculous. I come by this naturally. My father died of cancer. He was very funny about it. That's my model.

This is a book in which I take jobs I don't need, the kind of jobs others take out of necessity. If you think that this invalidates my experience, then nothing I write will convince you otherwise.

I believe in the victory of empathy. A woman can understand what it means to be a man, the rich what it means to be poor, the sick how it feels to be well. In the preface to the memoir about his conversion, *Surprised by Joy*, C. S. Lewis reports, 'I have been emboldened to write of it [his conversion] because I notice that a man seldom mentions what he had supposed to be his most idiosyncratic sensations without receiving from at least one (often more) of those present the reply, "What! Have you felt that too? I always thought I was the only one." '

I trust in the similarities we recognize between our secret selves

and others. I expect the shock of this recognition to shatter the walls
– stone walls of race, gender, and privilege that men and women
construct and also lovingly maintain.

CONTENTS

In January of 1997, when I was training to be a car salesman, another man and I used to spend the afternoon coffee break together. 'When you *want* to become a car salesman, does that mean you've hit the bottom of the barrel?' he said finally, without meeting my eye.

'No,' I said, 'it depends on what kind of salesman you turn out to be.' I still believe that. There was quality at the auto store, at CompUSA, and even at Nobody Beats the Wiz.

There were stinkers, too, of course, but they were also interesting to me. I was a stranger, a foreigner in the service economy. I've lived most of my life in Westchester County and on Manhattan Island, which is where I took the jobs for this book, and yet I feel that in my research I have traveled a great distance. I'd always stood on the other side of the counter. I'd always been the mark.

I was raised to disdain sales. When I went to work after college in 1970 as a reporter at the *Rockland Journal-News* in Nyack, New York, I looked down on the advertising salespeople, even though they worked upstairs. I started at $100 a week. I believe they started at $115, and earned more if they actually sold advertising.

So why did I finally step through the looking glass? How did I make the transition from senior editor at the *Reader's Digest* and a corner office in the Pan Am Building (now MetLife) to the wide-opened floors of commissioned sales?

Research? Yes and no.

I wanted to write. In 1988 I left my job at the *Reader's Digest*, set out on my own, and published a book of my father's letters.

I then wrote a novel, and for those of you who think nobody will turn down a book with *Cheever* at the top of the page, I'm here to tell you that they're out there. By the dozens. Ultimately, I cleared that hurdle, had one novel published, then a second. Three's the charm. The third would be my 'break-out book'.

My publisher was fired, and his imprint, Atheneum, was closed down. I was sorry, because Lee Goerner had become a friend, but I was not *that* sorry I was free now to go to any publisher I chose. The first two books had gotten a good deal of positive critical attention. And as long as I had a publisher, other publishers were *very* friendly, practically lascivious. 'If you are ever unhappy,' they said, 'give us a call.' Wink, wink.

Lucky them, I thought. *Lucky me*. I finished my third novel. It was sent out. There would certainly be a bidding war.

No bidding war ensued. Not a shot was fired. Not an offer made. Not one.

So maybe the book wasn't perfect. Some editor would roll up his sleeves, her sleeves. Working together, we'd make a masterpiece. That's what I thought. No sleeves were rolled. It's not as if they hadn't read my other books, either. They had. And it's not as if they didn't know what I could do. They did know what I could do. Some editors liked my first two novels and thought the third wasn't as good. Some editors didn't like any of my novels at all.

I'd strutted my stuff and left the world strangely unimpressed. I was reminded of the middle-aged flasher I'd seen in court when I was a reporter. He'd gone to the playground, flipped opened his raincoat. The teacher was alerted by the sound of children laughing.

Being a *Digest* editor had seemed foolish sometimes, but never this foolish. At least I hadn't been alone. There were dozens of *Digest* editors. You could see us in the cafeteria or in the parking lot at night. Failed novelists don't have a cafeteria. If you are a novelist who can't get published, are you really a novelist at all?

As a writer with a rejected novel, I was very much alone. As a man who'd spent decades preparing himself to do something unwanted, I was not. This was in 1995. Forty-three million jobs had been eliminated between 1979 and 1995, according to *The*

Downsizing of America, the book based on the 1996 *New York Times* series.

It was happening all over. Mike, the Pleasantville, New York, proprietor of I Can't Believe It's Yogurt, told me that he had been at Avon, then the post office. Now the yogurt store was failing as well. A man who had been a vice president when I was a junior editor at the *Digest* turned up to paint a mutual friend's condominium in Somers, New York.

So I put together a proposal. I'd write a book about downsizing. I'd play out everybody's worst nightmare, take entry-level jobs. While writing the proposal, I was a sidewalk Santa, trained to be a tax preparer for H & R Block, worked for Burns Security, and sold computers. *They're going to love this*, I thought. *I'm actually doing something now!*

Nobody liked the proposal.

'You're a writer,' they said. 'You're not out of work. Your distress isn't genuine.' They were wrong. My distress was genuine.

Some editors checked on the success of my two novels and found that, despite good reviews, the books hadn't sold very well. So apparently I was a failure as a writer, but I still wasn't out of work. Figure that one out and you win the Catch-22 John Yossarian Prize with gold-leaf cluster.

Finally, Adam Bellow – then at the Free Press – bought the proposal. (Yes, we knew each other. Two sons of famous writers. And yes, we were friends. About which I will have a good deal more to say later.)

Still, I was haunted by the comments of editors who hadn't liked the proposal. Was I qualified to write this thing? I'm not an authority. Nowadays we have respect for two sorts of authorities: those who are experts and those who are authentic.

I'm certainly not an expert. When I think of experts, though, I remember Dr. Stuart M. Berger. I met him only once and that was at a dinner party. He was hunched over an enormous bottle of Champagne – the type you see in the windows of liquor stores during the high holidays. The bottle came almost to my waist; it came to the doctor's knees. Berger was a tall man, more than six and a half feet. He was trying to get the cork out, but he was having difficulties because the smoke from the cigarette in his mouth was drifting up and into his eyes.

When I offered to help, Berger explained that he'd recently thrown out his back. The doctor, in case you've forgotten, was a famous health writer. He wrote a health column for the *New York Post*. His books included *The Southampton Diet* and *Dr. Berger's Immune Power Diet*. When the man who claimed to know how to live to be a hundred died at the age of forty, he weighed 365 pounds.

Don't get me wrong. I liked Dr. Berger. He gave me a couple of his cigarettes. Nor was he as anomalous as we might suppose. J. I. Rodale published health magazines and expected to live to be a hundred 'unless,' he said, 'I'm run down by a sugar-crazed taxi driver.' Rodale said this on *The Dick Cavett Show* and died right then and there of a heart attack. It's not just the diet gurus, either. When I was at the *Digest*, we employed a man who wrote compelling articles about how you could fall in love endlessly with the exact same woman: your wife. My then wife and I were exquisitely unhappy, so I took his teachings very much to heart. There were tricks and maxims, stirring tales from personal experience. I was shocked, therefore, when I met the writer and learned that he was on his fifth wife.

Certainly some experts do know what they're talking about, although few of them write best-selling books. In any case, I'm not an expert.

Am I authentic? It depends upon what you mean by *authentic*. Movie stars become authentic through struggles with drugs or alcohol. Writers often become authentic by recalling some harrowing or splendid 'true-life incident'.

The Education of Little Tree is the story of a boy brought up by Cherokee grandparents. First published in the 1970s, it was later reissued as an overlooked masterpiece. Schools interested in a window on Native-American culture made it required reading. 'A true story by Forrest Carter', reads the 1985 paperback, which I own. But it wasn't written by Forrest Carter. It was written by Asa Carter, an ex-Klansman. Probably he wasn't brought up by any Indians. Certainly not the Indians in that book. Why? Because those Indians are too good to be true.

Since I began this project, my third novel has been published, but I still have bragging rights as a failure. I'm a natural-born bust.

Perfect strangers praise me for the courage to allow my prose to be compared with that of my father. What, exactly, was my alternative?

I wanted to write. Do want to write. You have to run the race, don't you? Even if you're sure to lose.

My wife, a *New York Times* film and book critic, is also markedly successful. As is my sister, Susan Cheever. I'm haunted by the image of a knot of bored and restless people standing near a berm of freshly turned earth and beside an open grave. Head bowed, one mourner turns to another and whispers, 'Ben's life does seem to have been designed to excite unflattering comparisons.'

No, I'm not out of money − but I do know shame.

Besides which, work is about identity almost as much as it's about cash. People without jobs are people without status. The unemployment rate is universally accepted as a misery quotient.

When I began to hold jobs, I felt real again, a creature with weight and legitimate needs. When I was working, I was authentic.

Were my experiences on the job real? I think so. Plus, my financial security gave me the freedom to write about them. Had I actually roasted in economic hell, I might not have been willing to report on it. Shame is a central component of failure, and with shame comes silence. Nobody sends a letter to the alumni magazine to announce that he has failed to make partner. I have a number of acquaintances who lost jobs while I was writing this book. 'Tell me everything,' I always said to them. With few exceptions there would be radio silence, unbroken until the new position was landed. The dead waters, the interviews that didn't pan out, the sobriety jobs went unreported.

There certainly were fill-in jobs to be had in 1995. I saw them posted in the windows of the stores at which I shopped. I started walking into those stores and asking for job applications. This didn't feel good – like the first time you go to the hospital, and you're not bringing chocolates or flowers, you're bringing a suitcase with your very own pajamas in it.

Yes, yes, I told them who I am. Benjamin Cheever, former *Reader's Digest* editor, former novelist. Nobody ever said, 'You're too good for us.' Mostly they asked if I would work nights and weekends. And for a urine sample.

There seemed to be a lot of people starting again at square one, not because they were researching a book, but in an attempt to make a living and also to have some place to go in the morning. One of my colleagues in car sales was a former IBMer. When he was explaining why he lived so far north, he said, 'I moved there to get near my job. Then they fired me.' Then he laughed. We all laughed. It was funny.

I never held a job, for a month, for a day, that didn't alter my personality.

This is not to make myself out as a hero. It's difficult for a writer to be a hero, because he's always thinking, *Wait till the world hears how badly I was treated.* Punch a reporter in the face, and he'll think, *That's a Marine Corps ring he's hitting me with. The globe and anchor. Nice detail.* The heroes of this book are the ones who didn't expect to be written up.

The men and women who were kind to me on these jobs, they didn't do it for attention; they did it because they were kind. The ones who were cruel might not have been so cruel if they'd known I would write about it.

Was my approach underhanded? Yes and no.

I could have gone in and identified myself as a writer researching a book. Probably I wouldn't have been hired. Even if I had been hired, the story would have been entirely different.

Or I could have simply interviewed people. But that would have been a different story also. I would have had to ask permission. The people who want to be interviewed are a self-selected group and by no means representative.

When I was working at the *Rockland Journal-News* in the early 1970s, it was widely believed that economic conditions were so dire that senior citizens were eating dog food. Legislators, both local and national, would refer regularly to these old people and their irregular diet.

I had contacts in welfare rights and Legal Aid, so finding the local angle on the dog-food story didn't seem impossible. I got some tips, but the closest I came to a starving elder was a woman of about my own age who'd had her electricity shut off. She was living in subsidized housing, an apartment at least as comfortable as the one I was in then. She was good-looking, a single mom, taking college courses. There was an air conditioner in every window. She was allergic, it turned out, and her electric bill exceeded the utility allowance set by the Rockland County Department of Social Services.

I'm not an allergist, and it could well have been that her distress was completely genuine. Still, this wasn't a story they would run on the wires. It wasn't a story at all. I wanted some old gent with his grizzled chin three inches away from a bowl of Alpo.

Maybe there weren't any senior citizens eating dog food in the county. My guess is that if there were any, they didn't want their picture in the newspaper.

The lens of public attention attracts a certain brand of person – and in America, at least, those people seem unusually good at finding their own lunch.

Sometimes a subject will distort his story; sometimes the media does it for him. Often it's a collaboration. We had a photographer who carried a woman's high-heeled shoe in the trunk of his car. Fortunate enough to chance upon a ghastly auto crash, he'd put that shoe in the foreground before he took the picture.

He and I worked together once on an article about the local emergency food cupboard.

The photographer went out to take a picture of the cupboard. When he got there and opened the cupboard, it was crammed with food. So our photog, he turned to the woman who administered the program and said, 'Now this is a story about an empty cupboard. I'm going out to the car to get fresh film. When I come back, if the cupboard is empty, we'll have a picture and a story. If it's not empty, you got no picture and no story.'

Now there are some enormously talented interviewers, but these are rare. To complete a good interview is just about as easy as it is to take an oyster out of its shell, and still have a live oyster.

I'm not that talented. Besides which, the interviewer has to be tougher than I like to be. He must seem always to go along with his subject's vision of himself (usually heroic, always sympathetic) and yet be willing to present a more accurate picture.

'Every journalist who is not too stupid or too full of himself to notice what is going on knows that what he does is morally indefensible.' So wrote Janet Malcolm in her starkly honest book *The Journalist and the Murderer.*

There is another sort of information out there – and, no, it's not objective. Nor is it scientific. It's the kind of commonsense information we all get from simply living a life. When you're buying electronics, for example, watch for the 'spiff'; and if you're leasing a car, then multiply the monthly payments over the length of the contract. Always check the math yourself. And above all, remember what a friend told me on the floor at CompUSA: 'It's a small world, so don't make enemies.'

So instead of interviewing people about their troubles, I thought I'd share theirs with them and see what they'd say to a colleague.

This book's greatest failing is that it's turned into such a personal story. I'm the character I talk about most. So it seems as if I'm the only character who matters. Please know that this is not what I think. I'm selling Ben Cheever. Not because he's the best product. I'm selling Ben Cheever because he's all I've got. It wouldn't have been fair – or legally advisable – to reveal everybody else's life as if it were my own. Instead I've had to reveal my own life as if it were everybody else's.

The stories I found, like my own story, seem sad to me and funny. And yet the most shocking revelation is a cheering one, or at least I found it cheering. We like to pretend that *failure* and *extinction* are synonymous. People fired by the *Reader's Digest*, or even by the *Rockland Journal-News,* were referred to ever after as if they were dead. We didn't just lose contact with our colleagues; we lost sympathy. We lost interest.

'The opposite of love is not hate; the opposite of love is indifference,' according to Rollo May. We didn't damn our former colleagues to hell; we damned them into a state of unbeing.

Meanwhile those who succeeded became the subject of feverish curiosity. Cruelty, alcoholism, adultery, and the wildest eccentricities are beloved in the man or woman who rises through the ranks. Aberrations aren't just forgiven; they are cherished and sometimes even imitated.

Guess what. The failures haven't vanished in a puff of smoke. They're out there. Not always sad, either. Rarely repentant.

Failure is supposed to keep its chin clean. Failure is expected to know the forks. Failure should be solemn and upright – and silent. 'Really, if the lower orders can't set us a good example, what on earth is the use of them?' says Algernon of his servant, Lane, in *The Importance of Being Earnest.*

Oscar Wilde lived in England, you say. The English have a class system. And we don't? 'Class in America is a joke,' the poet Donald Hall once wrote, 'but it is not funny.'

So what I've been doing for the last five years is eating dog food in discreet little bites.

Almost three million people are laid off every year, according to Richard Nelson Bolles, whose book *What Color Is Your Parachute?* boasts more than six million copies in print. Eloquent testimony not just to the excellence of the text, but also to the seriousness of the problem.

Sundays, during 1995 and 1996, I often took my two sons to the

McDonald's in Thornwood, New York, for breakfast. When I began work on this project, I brought the *Tarrytown Daily News* along and read the classifieds. One day, having been back to the counter to complain about how my elder boy's Breakfast Burrito smelled, I returned to find a stranger collecting my newspaper. He was a small man with a moustache, in a short-sleeved wash-and-wear shirt, necktie, jacket, and hat. I told him that it was my newspaper, but that he could have it. 'All but this,' I said, and waved a hand at the want ads.

The man looked at me, then he laughed. It was a long laugh, dry and almost entirely without mirth. There I was in my expensive sweatshirt, with my blond boys, and I suppose he thought, *Maybe some day I will be his boss.* That's the American dream, then: half nightmare. The song: 'America the Beautiful'. The game: musical chairs. The tempo has never been so frantic.

Job security is a fixture of the past. The combination of a fluid global economy and the stock market's need for consistently high profitability will see nicely to that.

This book is written to honor those men and women who have been fired, and who dusted themselves off and got back into the ring, often with a dramatic reduction in status, frequently at a fraction of their previous wages.

It's also written in recognition of those people who have always worked hard for very little money. Twenty-eight and a half million workers nationwide earn less than eight dollars an hour. Only 37.6 million earn fifteen dollars or over, according to figures provided by the Economic Policy Institute, and printed in *The New York Times* in November of 1999.

America is an economic juggernaut, and I don't suppose an economic juggernaut can ever be entirely fair or just. You have to break eggs to make a revolution. Do you also need to break eggs to make a profit? Sometimes. Fine, but we've got to remember that no major faith I've ever heard of associates blessedness with gross income.

The poor are poor, but they are not damned until we damn

them. Which happens a lot. We live in an age in which some physicists think the photon may be a sentient being, and yet many of us assume that the clerks at Nobody Beats the Wiz are not sentient beings.

The woman behind the counter at Customer Service has trouble working the register – but remember, she probably took that job a week ago. Odds are good that she works nights somewhere else and is helping to support her mother. The American Express Platinum Card may guarantee easy credit, but it doesn't necessarily make you a quick study. I bet you'd have trouble with that register, too.

The heroism of the hourly worker (and no, I don't think *heroism* is too strong a word) is most dramatically illustrated in the downsized.

I once saw a former IBMer – not the one in car sales – work Easter Sunday to repair a customer's broken computer, a good deed, which, under the pay plan of his employer, actually cost him money. But even those who simply survive with grace are demonstrating a quiet and entirely admirable species of heroism. They are toeing the line in a race they have already lost.

They're all around you, these workers on the comeback trail. The new old faces behind the counter often have moving stories. This book is an acknowledgment of their numbers and a celebration of their resilience, their energy, and their humor. I have no doubt that without these silent divisions, the whole glorious front would collapse.

> And, behold, there are last who shall be first, and there
> are first who shall be last.
>
> > – Luke 13:30

Section One
The Framework

In democratic times enjoyments are more intense than in the ages of aristocracy, and the number of those who partake in them is vastly larger: but, on the other hand, it must be admitted that man's hopes and desires are oftener blasted, the soul is more stricken and perturbed, and care itself more keen.

  – *Democracy in America*, Alexis de Tocqueville (1840)

In the May 22, 2000, issue of *Time*, in an article titled 'What Will We Do for Work', consultant Tom Peters opened by saying, 'I believe that 90 per cent of white-collar jobs in the U.S. will be either destroyed or altered beyond recognition in the next ten to fifteen years. That's a catastrophic prediction, given that 90 per cent of us are engaged in white-collar work of one sort or another.'

Santa and the Underemployed

I PICKED UP MY RED CHENILLE SUIT, WIG, AND BEARD AT one P.M. on the Wednesday after Thanksgiving. 'Take 684 North from White Plains,' I was told, 'and get off at Exit 2.' The homeless shelter for which I was headed is on the grounds of the Westchester airport. In another life, I used to go there to catch Pegasus, the corporate plane that belonged to the *Reader's Digest*. There were never more than six of us aboard, and if you had a bag, the pilot would offer to carry it. I remember having jetted to Washington, D.C., for dinners with those in sympathy with the magazine. Former senator Sam Nunn, former representative Jack Kemp, and former secretary of the navy John Lehmann Jr. come immediately to mind. The *Digest* team would fly back that same night, drinking scotch and smoking Cuban cigars. I remember studying the profiles of the older men to see if they liked me, and if they didn't like me, to see what I could do about it. Their affection—if earned—might translate itself into cash and position. In the meantime, I enjoyed the free dinners and the richness of my surroundings. When I was anxious, the liquor helped.

The Eskimos have many words for snow, and the editors of the *Digest* had many names for the martini. It was a 'martin', a 'martoonis', a 'cold one', an 'eye-opener', 'the equalizer', and a 'silver bullet'. The team's refreshment was made of gin, never vodka, and wherever possible it was taken straight up.

The free meal at the homeless shelter, I noticed, was served without liquor of any sort, but then some of *these* men were probably alcoholics. When I arrived, the residents were waiting for a lunch, which, I was later informed, had been delayed by that day's light snow. 'So they're grumpy,' I was told. Passing the line on the way to the back room, where I was to meet the woman in charge of sidewalk Santas, I studied the faces. Nobody returned my gaze.

Rich and poor have often had to meet different standards. The acceptability of drunkenness is a vivid case in point. What's unusual about today's economy is that men and women get jostled out of comfortable berths with a good deal of regularity. It is possible to fall a long, long way in a very short time.

The office in which my contact worked had several Santa suits hanging from the sort of metal contraption glimpsed in museum cloakrooms or placed outside of Manhattan apartments by the catering service on the occasion of a large party.

The Santas who work for the Volunteers of America (VOA) are often recruited from the shelter. Outside help is also welcome. Still, it must have been unusual to have a perfect stranger pitch in. The woman who enlisted me was curious about my motives.

'Why did you want to do this?'

'I thought it would be fun,' I said apologetically.

'Do you have any experience with this sort of thing?'

You mean begging, I thought, but instead I said, 'No, not really.'

'You're not in sales?'

'No,' I said, and not without some satisfaction.

After I had been outfitted, a young man was called in to help me to the car with my gear. Along with my suit, hairpiece, false stomach, false beard, false puttees, and cowbell I had been given a make-believe chimney. (No, I didn't get a hat.) Made of wood, and painted to look like brick, the chimney was three and a half feet tall and weighed twenty pounds empty. It also came equipped with a sign attached to a narrow wooden post, which went into a bracket. Help Our Neediest Neighbors, it said. Screwed to the top of the chimney was a plaque: 'Designed and built through the ingenuity and volunteer efforts of the employees of the Consolidated Edison Company of New York and Local Union No. 1-2.' The device had wheels and a cleverly constructed retractable handle. Still, it was difficult to maneuver, particularly on stairs. Hauling it down to street level, the other man took hold of the sign, and its wooden post snapped. We established that the placard could be reinserted, and while the sign was no longer as far above the chimney, it did still stay in place. Grasping the device by its torso, we crossed the lot to my car. There was a padlock on the chimney's cash box to which I had not been given the combination. I guessed they were afraid I'd take in a few dollars and trade them immediately for some holiday cheer in the form of a pint of Four Roses.

After my friend and I had hoisted the chimney into the back of the Honda, I was asked politely if I had a cigarette. I didn't have a cigarette, although right then I could have used one. And also a drink.

Driving home, I wondered if it would be morally incorrect for me to hide the whole Santa getup in the basement for a week, and then just bring it back. By the time I reached our drive, my scalp had already begun to itch. I assumed I'd caught lice from the plastic hair of the wig when I'd tried it on and would now pass them on to my wife and sons. The sheets and pillowcases would be washed in poison, the house fumigated, while we stood ankle deep in the snow.

No, I didn't catch lice. The place to get them, apparently, is at private school. But I had taken my first uncertain step out of the upper middle class.

The brilliant trajectory of the immigrant poor to wealth and status has long been a central theme of the American myth. When I worked as a reporter in Rockland, there was a local politician who liked to say, 'When I came to this country, I was naked and alone, with twenty dollars in my pocket.' Of course he wound up rich and patriotic. His wording is unusual, the sentiment is not. We don't hear so much about it when the tide goes out. And yet the sudden and substantial loss of income among the members of the middle and upper middle class is one of the most prevalent – and least examined – socioeconomic stories of our time.

Technology and the marketplace change with blinding rapidity; perfectly good jobs vanish in a flash. Books & Things, our local independent, is gone. The Tarrytown GM plant – a source of prosperity for eight decades – has been shut and leveled. IBM is an outsized presence in Westchester County, and was, until very recently, a paradigm of corporate benevolence. However, the computer giant released 140,000 people in the seven years ending in 1993, according to Paul Carroll of the *Wall Street Journal*. In his book *Big Blues: The Unmaking of IBM*, Carroll writes that 'including spouses and children who were affected, those job losses disrupted the lives of perhaps 4,000,000 people – about the population of Pittsburgh.' Carroll reports that T-shirts appeared that had the IBM logo running down the left side, with the three letters acting as the start of the words *I've Been Misled*.

The company does seem to have struggled to keep up the tradition of generous management, during bad times as well as good. When I went to Manpower in White Plains in search of temporary work, I was told that I would not be hired by IBM. Why? Because IBM liked to give all its temporary jobs to people it had fired.

Still, some workers were outraged. John Dean Kleder, a former lab employee, drove his red Mustang through the plate-glass window of an IBM facility in California. The phrase *going postal* has been coined to cover the workers who are fired and then return to their place of employment armed and insane with rage. These are the exceptions. The huge majority go quietly.

Failure has long been underreported in this country. In *Falling from Grace: The Experience of Downward Mobility in the American Middle Class*, Katherine S. Newman quotes studies suggesting that during the 1970s, half of the population suffered reduced incomes, and almost one-third of them fell a long, long way.

'Under these circumstances, downward mobility ceases to be an exceptional experience and becomes a significant social problem,' she writes.

Newman goes on to report that a study of 33,000 civilian men during the 1970s showed 'that about one quarter (23.2 percent) of the respondents between twenty-one and fifty-three years old had slid down below their first jobs'.

There often used to be an understandable reason when somebody was fired. It meant he or she was incompetent. Or unlovable. Then, as payroll slashing grew more widespread, downsizing meant only that the victims were employed by a company that was in trouble.

Now the employee can work in a thriving corporation – and still get the axe. According to *NBC Nightly News*, 425,000 Americans were laid off in 1995 alone, while corporate profits were up 25 per cent.

In a Labor Day column in *The New York Times* (which ran in September 2000) Bob Herbert acknowledged a low unemployment – it was hovering at around 4 per cent at the time – but warned that 'families with children have had to work harder and harder over the past few decades to maintain a decent standard of living, and that phenomenon continues. The number of earners per family has increased, as have the average number of weeks worked per year, and the number of hours worked per week.'

Herbert referred to an Economic Policy Institute report *The State of Working America 2000–01*, published by Cornell University Press, which he said makes it clear that 'despite the rosy stock market stories of the past few years, the typical American family accumulated more debt in the 1990's than it made from the appreciation of stocks'.

'Meanwhile, the public profile of the poor has diminished almost to the point of invisibility. But they are still there,' Herbert writes.

Among these are the newly poor. In *What Color Is Your Parachute?* Richard Nelson Bolles describes a situation in which ruthless economic considerations trump loyalty and affection: 'While admittedly mergers or downsizings are used by employers to get rid of employees they wished to fire anyway, it is also true that loyal, effective employees, with ten, twenty years' devoted service, are getting unjustly discharged. In too many places, these include those employees who helped make the place run well, gave it heart, and caring. They are let go because downsizings demand every employee justify his or her existence, and their contribution was hard to measure *according to the bottom line*.'

When I got home with the Santa suit, I strapped on my padded abdomen and rang the cowbell. 'Ho, ho, ho,' I told my wife and children, 'Santa knows who's naughty and nice.' Then we read aloud from a Xeroxed credo:

> As a sidewalk Santa this I pledge
> To always honor this privilege,
> To never leave my chimney side,
> To let my honor be my guide.

The second page listed 'Santa Dos & Don'ts':

1. Eating, drinking, and smoking in the streets while in Santa suits is strongly discouraged.
2. Eating garlic prior to assuming your chimney post may drive down revenues for the day.
3. Keeping your suit and beard clean while on the streets is a good thing.
4. Drinking hot chocolate with whipped cream while wearing your beard may make a big mess.
5. Shaking hands with children is strongly encouraged. Picking them up, unless requested to do so by a parent, is not.

My wife wanted to know why I didn't have a hat.
John, my eldest son, wanted to know if I got to keep the money.

I said I didn't. Then he wanted to know if the people who sold hot dogs on the street got to keep the money. I said I thought so. Then he wanted to know how to get a hot-dog stand.

The dining room was to be painted the next day, and my wife was anxious to get me out of the house before the workmen arrived at eight A.M.

'What if they see you?' she asked.

'What are they going to do?' I asked. 'Not paint our house?'

Painters have their pride. Although painters can also be men on the way down. A couple of years ago, Eleanor Swink, a friend then still at the *Digest*, phoned me to report that Steve Smith, a former vice president, had showed up to paint her Heritage Hills town house.

'Is he doing this for a lark?' I asked. 'Is he on vacation? Does his brother own the business?'

'I don't think so. I think it's his real job.'

'Was he ashamed?'

'No, not really.'

'How does he look?'

'About the same.'

Steve and I used to drink at the Kittle House, which is the tavern nearest *Digest* headquarters in Chappaqua. He once played a round of liar's poker with my wife. She won, but Steve never showed me the serial number she was supposed to have won with, so I remember thinking that he'd engineered the victory in order to keep her interested. He had a lot of bravado. Late one night an attractive young woman, who also worked for the magazine, had left the Kittle House, but shortly returned to say that she had locked her keys in her Volkswagen. Nobody knew what to do. Nobody but Steve. He wrapped a towel around one hand, went outside, and smashed a window. I was not a vice president myself, nor slated to be one, and I remember thinking, *Oh, that's how a vice president acts*. Now I wondered if I'd gotten it wrong.

In any case Eleanor and I had fun talking about a great man brought low. It wasn't as much fun when the yogurt man went under. Mike had come out of a computer job at Avon, passed through a position at the post office, and then bet the farm on a couple of I Can't Believe It's Yogurt outlets, one of which was across from the railroad station in Pleasantville. Business was good. Five days a week, I ate his French vanilla for lunch. When my novels were published, and reporters came in from out of town, I'd meet them at the yogurt store.

I was there one evening when Art Carney's son came in. (I figure it's fair to call him Art Carney's son, because that's how he was introduced. Probably he thinks of me as John Cheever's son.) He's a handsome, popular man who works as a professional voice. Ask him and he'll recite the Dove soap commercial. Very convincing. Mike was thrilled. He had two celebrities, John Cheever's son and Art Carney's son. A virtual saloon. 'I get a lot of celebrities here,' Mike said.

My own youngest son, Andrew, idolizes Godzilla, and Mike's wife used to make Andrew a Godzilla cake out of frozen yogurt for his birthdays. Mike would try to give me the cake for free.

Then every deli in the area got a frozen-yogurt spigot, and Pleasantville has almost as many delicatessens as it does churches. Mike had to fire the high-school girls who worked in the store and put his family on staff full-time. He tried selling cookies, bagels, and finally Buffalo chicken wings. Towards the end, he was giving out a résumé with every small cone. 'I'll do anything,' he told me.

Mike wanted me to write a book about him. Once, when he was telling me what had happened, he began to cry. I looked away. 'We could lose the house,' he said. I told him that I wrote fiction. Humorous fiction. 'It's a great story,' he said. 'And if it weren't true, it would be funny.'

I balked. There would be some turning he'd taken, some disastrous decision he'd made. Mike wouldn't see it, but the reader would. Success can eat with her fingers. Success can fly by

the seat of her pants. Failure has to have a master plan. I suppose
we're afraid it's catching. Lord knows I might have caught the bug
from Mike.

Napoleon said, 'I have no sense of the ridiculous. Power is never
ridiculous.' Failure seems always to be. Dressed as Santa, I felt
ridiculous.

Unloading the car, I thought, *I'm insane.* And I wasn't using the
word in that complimentary way we used to use it when we were
in boarding school. *He's insane* meant 'he's irreverent, brilliant,
lucky'. I was thinking instead of the chronic and acute ward at
Boston State Mental Hospital in Mattapan, where I'd worked as an
attendant. I meant *insane,* as in a locked ward, the smell of urine,
mashed potatoes eaten with fingers from tin plates.

It was cold at the Pleasantville railroad station. I didn't have a hat.
The suit had no pockets, so I had to keep my car keys in my glove. I
set up my chimney at the top of the stairs to the platform and rang
my bell.

The first woman to appear gave me a dollar. 'Where's your hat?'
she wanted to know.

'I didn't get a hat,' I said.

Many people just put their heads down and raced by. Others
took a long time to give me a couple of dimes. Intense young men
and women in suits were the least apt to contribute, and when they
did so, they rarely made eye contact. This was admittedly a small
sample, but it seemed I got more money from women than men.
Black women often stopped.

The woman I know from the Pleasantville Pharmacy said,
'Merry Christmas, honey,' which cheered me briefly.

Then Art Carney's son appeared. Since our introduction at the
yogurt store, we've recognized each other several times at the
railroad station. He told me that when he was young, he damaged
his vocal cords trying to be a rock star, and that's why he's a
professional voice now.

'What are you doing here?' he said. 'And who does your
hair?'

'I didn't get a hat,' I said.

He nodded.

I rang my bell. 'Merry, Merry Christmas,' I said.

'I hope they're paying you a lot for this,' he said.

'Of course,' I said. 'Goodwill Santas make a lot of money.'

'No,' he said, 'how'd you get roped into this?'

I wouldn't say. Just smiled through my false whiskers and rang my bell.

'I have a friend who did a Metamucil ad,' he said. 'I said to him, "I hope they paid you a lot for that. I hope they paid you forty grand." '

'What did he do?' I asked.

'Oh, he eats the bran, he runs, he's this regular guy.'

'It wasn't flattering?'

'That's right,' Carney said. 'You do the Preparation H ad, maybe you get a lot of money, but you don't work for six months.'

Then he gave me a dollar. 'Now I want you to say, "Ho, ho, ho",' he said.

At 8:15 A.M. a woman came rushing into the station, muttering wildly about the 7:28. She asked me the time. I pulled back the fluffy white cuff of my suit so that I could see my watch. I told her it was 8:15. 'Then I haven't missed my train,' she said.

I didn't say anything. She flew down the stairs to the platform. A few minutes later, she came back up.

'Nobody's taking the train this morning?' she asked.

'One just left,' I said.

'But I didn't miss my train?' she asked.

'Not the next one,' said Santa cheerfully.

Then she seemed to remember that I'd said it was 8:15. Then she realized that 8:15 came *after* 7:28. Then she looked terribly sad.

She told me that her older boy had decided he didn't want to go to school. 'I was up early typing over his homework, making their breakfast, and now I've missed my train. He said he was sick. He wasn't sick. He didn't have a temperature. He wasn't throwing up. He just ate too many brownies last night. If I lose my job, who's going to suffer? They're going to suffer. I don't need clothes. I've stopped growing. Who's going to take care of them?'

I said it was hard but that she shouldn't be upset, because she'd done everything for her children. 'Because you love them,' I said. Which I figured was what a Santa was supposed to say.

'That's not love,' she said. 'That has nothing to do with love. That's guilt.'

She asked me when the next train left. I said 8:40.

She said that if she caught the 8:40, she'd probably miss her meeting. 'But then if I go home, and don't go to the meeting, the children will win.'

I tried to smile through my beard.

'I could stay home,' she said, 'but I don't have a phone at home.'

'It shouldn't be about the children,' I said through my white plastic whiskers. 'If it makes sense for you to go to your meeting, then go to it. If it doesn't make sense, then don't.'

At this point she walked away. Seemed she'd had enough advice from Santa.

But these are the high points. My Santa stint was a bore at best, at worst an embarrassment. When I worked the Tarrytown station, I had trouble finding a place to park. Most of the travelers just wanted me out of the way. When I told one friend what I was doing, he said he'd never humiliate himself like that. 'I'd leave town first,' he said.

I understood.

That very friend has since been to jail. The abyss is often closer than we think. Which may help explain why my neighbors didn't like to see me at their railroad station. Most people don't like being reminded of the need for charity. Even if it is associated with our number-one commercial holiday.

The cold looks hurt my feelings. I was a volunteer, though, so I had my righteousness to protect me. I can now see what a cowardly act it was, to make my first job a volunteer gig. Volunteers, after all, have status. People out of work do not.

Having left the *Digest* in 1988, I slammed the door on reentry by writing a piece for *The Nation* in which I chided then CEO George Grune for cutting off the free Thanksgiving turkey given to staff, while personally accepting millions of dollars in cash and stock. I compared Grune unfavorably to DeWitt Wallace, the company's founder.

I knew both men. Wallace was painfully polite, even shy. Once, when introduced to me for a second time, he said, 'I don't believe we've met.' I would have gone along with this, but I was afraid he'd learn the truth later and consider me a liar. So I said we had met. 'Oh, shit,' he said. He was clearly furious with himself for having forgotten my name.

Wallace had a chauffeur but liked to drive himself around, quite unreliably, in an undistinguished American car. Leaving the office, he'd pick up workers heading out to the bus stop. He'd drive them home, and on the way, he'd ask which department they worked in, and what they thought of their supervisor.

Grune, on the other hand, sometimes used to range around in the company cafeteria and eat lunch with people he didn't know. He once sat at a table with me.

The higher I rose in the ranks, the more I saw Grune. He was always cordial, and I never heard of his being cruel to an underling. And yet, since I left the company, he'd fired hundreds of people. Or had them fired.

Working as a reporter at the *Rockland Journal-News*, I was once sent to the school across the street from our Nyack offices to interview a convicted murderer. Released on a technicality, the man had been hired to work in the Head Start program, which was housed in that school. He and I talked about Nyack. We talked about the importance of early childhood education. But all the time I was in his presence, there were only three

questions I wanted to ask: Who did you kill? How did you do
it? Do you have trouble sleeping? I didn't ask. I was afraid to, of
course, but I also suspected that I wouldn't get a straight answer.
And yet I still wonder what it feels like to kill somebody, or to
have them fired. Not that firing is comparable to murder,
although some fired people suffer greatly, and a few die. I've
never seen a man or woman murdered; I have seen them fired.
I've heard them lie about it afterwards, telling me they left,
because 'life is too short' or 'I was tired of being a number'. And
I sympathize, because I know the fear. I have never held a job
for more than a month where I didn't sometimes wake up at
night in terror that I'd lose it.

Since I began this project in 1995, the economic climate has been
choice. Now in 2001 it doesn't look so good, but up or down, the
turmoil is here to stay. Among the billboards at the Pleasantville
railroad station in the fall of 2000, there were eight placards for
job-hunt-related Web sites, e.g., 'How was your day? Hotjobs.-
com'; 'When you love what you do, you're alive. Jobs.com.' It's
true these teases seem aimed at people moving up rather than
bouncing back – but then advertising has always been inclined to
accentuate the positive. *Who Moved My Cheese?* by Spencer
Johnson, M.D., had been the *Publishers Weekly* number-one
nonfiction best-seller for more than forty weeks. This book offers
consolation and guidance to people who have been fired or
otherwise marginalized. Sample chapter headings include 'If
You Do Not Change, You Can Become Extinct' and 'The
Quicker You Let Go of Old Cheese, the Sooner You Find
New Cheese'.

What's most alarming, perhaps, about the ferocious stirring of
the pot is that prosperity, where it does exist, seems not to trickle
down.

A September 1999 story in the *Washington Post* stated that
'despite the booming economy, the income gap between the
richest and poorest Americans has widened to a modern record,

as the nation's wealthiest households have enjoyed huge gains while the poorest still haven't caught up to the income they made in the late 1970's.'

The *Post* story referred to a controversial study released in 1999, which concluded that the income gap was the widest since the Congressional Budget Office (CBO) began collecting figures in 1977 and quite likely the widest since World War II.

'The top 1 percent of Americans have more wealth than the bottom 90 percent. . . . Crime strikes the poorest most of all,' writes Harold Evans in *The American Century*. 'America leads Europe and Japan in beggars, murders, and prisons per capita.'

Distinctions between rich and poor, always present in, for instance, airline travel, are being made in other areas of life. Injustices that one might hope to see fading in a mature democracy seem instead to be spreading. The troubled public-school system made the question of school vouchers a key issue in the presidential race of 2000. Both candidates, of course, had attended private high schools. As did I.

In a society geared to distinguish between haves and have-nots, faster computers working with ever-larger databases make it easier and easier to figure out who has the cheese. *Business Week*'s October 2000 cover story was titled 'Why Service Stinks: Companies know just how good a customer you are – and unless you're a high roller, they would rather lose you than fix your problem.'

'Welcome to the new consumer apartheid,' reports *Business Week*, hardly a radical publication. 'Those long lines and frustrating telephone trees aren't always the result of companies simply not caring about pleasing the customer anymore. Increasingly, companies have made a deliberate decision to give some people skimpy service because that's all their business is worth.'

Living on the wrong side of the tracks has always been risky. According to a piece titled 'For Good Health, It Helps to Be

Rich and Important,' which ran in *The New York Times* on June 1, 1999, social class 'is one of the most powerful predictors of health, more powerful than genetics, exposure to carcinogens, even smoking'.

Taking the jobs I held for this book has strengthened my own conviction that we live in a society increasingly segregated not by race or gender, but by class and income.

Burns Security: Bad Cop

THE GAP BETWEEN THE HAVES AND THE HAVE-NOTS, according to Harold Evans in *The American Century*, is shown in the increasing popularity of private schools, gated communities, and the growth of private police. Up until 1970, there were more public policemen than private. By 1989 private police outnumbered public by three to one.

BURNS SECURITY WANTS YOU!

18 YEARS OF AGE OR OVER?

EXPERIENCED, INEXPERIENCED, RETIRED?

NEED EXTRA MONEY?

IF YOU ARE INTERESTED IN WORKING FULL- OR PART-TIME

AS A SECURITY GUARD OR A SUPERVISOR,

<u>COME SEE US</u>

WE OFFER

*BENEFITS *FLEXIBLE WORK SCHEDULE

*PAID VACATION *TRAINING

BURNS INTERNATIONAL SECURITY SERVICES

1 WATER STREET

WHITE PLAINS, NY 10606

(914) 946–2022

INTERVIEWS WILL BE HELD MON–FRI, 9 A.M.–11:30 A.M.

EQUAL OPPORTUNITY EMPLOYER

WORK WITH THE LARGEST AND

BEST SECURITY FIRM IN THE WORLD!

'You're never going to see a security guard on TV or in the movies portrayed in a favorable light,' the former policeman told us during our special eight-hour training course. 'They are always fat old guys, falling asleep at their posts. They are always knocked over the head, tied up. They are always getting dead.'

The uniform is 100 per cent polyester. That's not just a promise, but a boast. I wore the straight blue, but the people hired in 1995 to work at the Westchester (the new mall in White Plains) wore pants that looked like flannel, and a green jacket with a *W* on the breast – as if they were students at a boarding school or members of a landlocked yacht club. (Burns has since been replaced at the Westchester by I.P.C. International. These guards dress as if on safari, with broad-brimmed hats made of, I believe, plastic.)

We were told never to wear our uniforms off duty, except when going to and from the job. But I'm getting ahead of myself. It took time to get the job.

When I showed up in the outer office at nine A.M. on Monday, September 15, I was wearing a blazer and a necktie. Most of the other applicants there were in jeans, and several had on sweatshirts that expressed their enthusiasm for beer or football. No former vice presidents here, and nobody asked to borrow my copy of *The New Yorker*. I filled out my application, which asked, early on, if I had any other names I'd been known by. The *Reader's Digest* hadn't posed this question, nor had the *Rockland Journal-News*. *Billy the Kid*, I thought, *Mort Zuckerman*. But I left the space blank and went back to my magazine. I'd been there for half an hour when a young man came in and started quarreling with the receptionist. He felt that he had been shorted on his paycheck. He said he was 'going to blow up this place'. He was called to the inner office, and when he came back out, he walked by us with a big smile. 'Better get out of here – save yourselves. Before the bomb goes.'

I knew it was silly, but I thought that maybe I should go across the street, have coffee. Probably there was no bomb. On the other hand, it would be ridiculous to die in an explosion while waiting for an interview for a job as a security officer. Still, I didn't want to lose my place in line. All the chairs were taken, and a number of men were standing. The economic tide had also risen. There were two or three men in suits, suits that would take months to replace on a Burns salary.

That morning I had put on a tie with dinosaurs. Janet thought this was a bad idea. 'You want to appear serious.'

'Dinosaurs are serious.'

I didn't get called until after eleven A.M. The young woman who interviewed me liked the dinosaurs. She said she liked trolls better, and that if I ever came upon a necktie with trolls on it, I should alert her.

Where the Burns application asked if I'd ever been convicted of any crime other than a minor traffic infraction, I wrote that I had been jailed twice, once for stealing road signs on Nantucket Island, and once for an antiwar protest in Cincinnati, Ohio.

The pleasant young interviewer smiled. 'Everybody did something like that.'

'I suppose. But I didn't want to hide it.'

'You did exactly the right thing,' she said. 'And I commend you for your honesty.'

Pleased and relaxed by the flattery, I went ahead and asked her how much I was going to earn. 'It depends on your post, and your experience,' I was told. 'But usually it's five to eight.'

Five to eight K, I thought. 'Dollars an hour?' I asked.

'Yup.'

There had been a section on the form for previous jobs, and in the space for my most recent experience, I'd put down that for the last seven years I had been writing books.

I suppose I was hoping that this might lead to an immediate promotion: 'Look, we also investigate the occasional murder, and we could use a man of your intelligence. In this case the victim was an editor, murdered by a novelist whose book she'd rejected.' I was also concerned that my personal excellence might jinx the deal altogether: 'I'm afraid, Mr. Cheever, that you're overqualified for this post. Besides which, we at Burns Security don't like to be written about.'

But all my interviewer wanted was 'some proof that you actually wrote books'.

I said that was easy. 'I'll bring the books in, show them to you.'

She said fine, and smiled, although I never did produce the books, nor were they mentioned again.

In order to work as a Burns security officer, I first had to take an eight-hour class and pass a test. Burns provides this class for free, although it's possible to pay to take a similar course elsewhere. At this point I'd already started on the tax preparer's course offered by H & R Block, which cost $250. The harder I studied, the more I appreciated the presidential platform of Stephen Forbes. In any case, I didn't have Block on Thursday, and that was the day of the Burns class. I had to bring in a driver's license, a Social Security card, or a passport. And also a check or money order for thirty-six dollars made out to the New York State Department of State. This was for the purchase of my license.

So when I came back on Thursday, I walked right through the waiting room and threaded my way down a corridor, which had a lot of walkie-talkies on the floor, their batteries being charged. And there was a classroom with desks, and people sitting at them.

When I was a kid, and classrooms were a given, I used to hate the way they looked and smelled. *Boredom*, I thought. Now that I'm an old guy, I love a classroom. *Rest*, I think.

The instructor was a handsome man, probably a good deal younger than I, but wearing a suit and necktie and with the posture of authority. He was fit but had what appeared to be the beginning of a gut. He seemed to be looking at me all day. Maybe he *was* looking at me. Or maybe he was like the oil paintings of Christ that I'd seen in Italy as a boy: Maybe he had eyes that fastened on every face in the room.

There will be a drug test at the end of the day, he told us. If we failed the drug test, he said, we wouldn't be hired. If we thought we might fail the drug test, we should probably leave directly, rather than waste the whole day. Nobody got up. I did notice, however, that not everybody came back from lunch.

Burns Security was founded in 1909 by William J. Burns, the first man to head the FBI. Why did we think he founded the company?

A man who had identified himself to me as a former phone-company executive raised his hand. 'To provide a service?' he asked.

Nope, we were told. Mr. Burns started the company to make money. And then we were asked, 'Isn't that the reason you're all here today?' We all raised our hands. All of us, except one young man with short hair, and a stud in one ear. He was a volunteer fireman. Also he was taking law-enforcement courses at Rockland Community College.

The ex-cop smiled. 'A buff,' he said. 'You're a buff. No offense intended, but most of us are here to make money.'

The function of a security officer, it turned out, was much the same as that of a scarecrow. If you could rig up a scarecrow that rolled around and had a videocamera in its head, you'd have the ideal security officer, but then you'd probably also have something that cost more than five dollars an hour to operate. A scarecrow couldn't think, of course, but security officers are not paid to think. 'Don't express an opinion,' we were told.

Could we arrest anyone? Sure we could. Anybody can make a citizen's arrest. You didn't have to be a Burns employee in order to make a citizen's arrest. 'If you want to, you can go out into the streets of White Plains and mark down the license plates of cars that are parked at expired meters and turn them in to the police. Anybody can do that,' we were told. And it was very clear that when he said *anybody*, he meant anybody without a brain in his head.

'The Burns policy is not to arrest.' Working at the Westchester, approached by a shopkeeper who says that such and such a person has just stolen something from her store, the prudent security officer would go with her and stand by while *she* made the arrest. Then the security officer could say to the person charged, 'Come with me now,' and lead him to the office. But don't touch him. If you so much as take his elbow like this, the teacher said (and made the motion that one might use to help an old lady across a patch of ice), and if he is not convicted of the crime he is charged with, then he can go after you for false arrest.

I was remembering now that the only time I had ever been with security guards before was when I was still in college and working as raw labor for Manpower in Boston. We were disassembling some sort of food show, and eating as we disassembled. Trouble was, not all of the food was precooked. A couple of resourceful security officers had located a hibachi, over which they were cooking tiny frankfurters, which they shared generously with the other workers.

This was clearly not the model I was meant to emulate. There was a guard who worked for Wrigley's, we were told, in a warehouse that stored the gum that had gone bad and had been slated for destruction. The security officer had taken a package of this gum, put a piece in his mouth, and put the rest in his pocket. This was caught on video, and he was fired. However insignificant it seemed, theft would not be tolerated.

Employee theft was clearly a central concern. Guarding an office building, we were there to check parcels in the morning and at the end of the day.

'You don't put your hands in somebody else's briefcase or purse. You ask them to move the objects around in there.' I'd wondered why the guards at the New York Public Library on Forty-second Street never would put a hand into my shoulder bag. I'd been rather hurt by this and thought maybe my shoulder bag was too disgusting to touch. I realized now that this, too, was done in response to legal considerations.

Despite our hands-off approach, we were supposed to be highly vigilant. We were told of a man who brought lunch to work, and every evening the security guard asked to look in the lunch box and saw that it was empty except for a thermos bottle. When the guard heard liquid sloshing around inside the thermos, the employee explained that he hadn't finished his coffee. But the thermos always had liquid in it, and finally after a year, the guard asked the man to open it for inspection. Aha! The thermos was full of motor oil. The employee had been smuggling out a quart of motor oil every day for a year.

The class was amazed. I wondered how the coffee must have tasted.

During the lunch break, our teacher got out a roll of paper towels and a spritzer of Formula 409 and began to work furiously on one of the empty chairs. When somebody asked him why, he said, 'We had an old guy in here yesterday who kept wetting his pants. Must've wet his pants four times.'

We were each given our blue Burns handbook. This was small enough to be carried on the job.

The Burns Promise
Burns promises to provide you
- Orientation to security
- Instruction on duties
- Appropriate and complete uniform
- Accurate and timely paycheck

Your part of the Promise
- Report to work on time.
- Report to work in full uniform.
- Know and perform security duties consistently.

The role of the security office is to DETECT, DETER, and REPORT.

In class we went over much of the same material, but in the idiom of daily conversation. And there were tips:

Turn off coffee machines.
Do not turn off computers.
Report burned-out lightbulbs.
Express no opinion.

In the incident report, note
  Who?
  What?
  How?
  Where?
  When?
  Why?

It was a lot like being a journalist. Only for even less money.

The drug test came late in the day, and afterwards the woman who had interviewed me said that it was our responsibility to also dispose of our samples.

So we each took our cup and went out into the hall in a long line. The door to the men's room was locked. A young guy in baggies was at the head of the line. He switched his plastic cup of urine from his right hand to his left and with his right hand he banged on the door. We were all lined up behind him with our cups of urine, laughing. He banged on the door again. 'What you doing in there?'

The door was opened by a young man still pulling up his pants, and we all pushed by, chuckling and holding our cups of urine in the air.

This was the only flash of humor all day. I guessed it would be wildly inappropriate to crack any of the sorts of jokes that immediately came to mind during class. I wanted to pass the course, and in fact I got 96 out of 100 on the test. I was clever. A very clever scarecrow.

At the time I took the Burns course, I was still struggling to qualify as a tax preparer for H & R Block. I'd taken Block's course because when I met the wife of an old running friend, she said that after her children had reached a certain age, she'd gotten back into the job market through the tax-prep chain. This somehow made that job thinkable. But then she'd been good at the work; I was not. I was getting up at five in the morning in order to finish my homework. So I put down that I was available for Burns only two days a week, from eight A.M. to four P.M. I waited a couple of weeks, but Burns never called.

I got a B on my midterm at Block. Even if I could have raised my grades substantially, it seemed highly unlikely that I would be hired that year to work for the agency. Too many people were getting the software and doing their own taxes, I was told. I wanted to hold as many different jobs as possible before I wrote the proposal for this book. So after the Block midterm, I dropped out. I then phoned Burns to say that I was now available any three days a week, from eight to four: 'I mean, if that's why I haven't been called.'

My change was duly noted, but the girl taking the information didn't seem at all sure that it was my limited availability that kept me off the force.

Then one Thursday afternoon, when I was sitting at my desk pretending to be a writer, Burns called. They wanted me. That night. From six P.M. to six A.M. 'Can you come right down now and pick up your uniform?'

Could I?

The mood in the Burns office that afternoon was ecstatic, or at least that's how I saw it. I wanted a job; they had a job to give me. I met my supervisor. There was a lot of touching. Everyone wished me good luck.

I was being given something precious. I am a diffident character, but it does seem to me that no career move is undertaken without a blessing given, and often as not, that blessing is undeserved.

In David Niven's 1972 autobiography, *The Moon's a Balloon*, he talks about getting his big break in pictures. It may have been easier to become an actor way back then than it is now, but it still wasn't easy, according to Niven. He reports that a sign outside central casting read, 'Don't try to become an actor. For every one we employ, we turn away a thousand.'

Niven was auditioning for a part in *Feather in Her Hat*, which was directed by Al Santell. Niven was so anxious that when he finally got on the set, he was spectacularly bad. 'I spilled somebody else's drink and said all the wrong lines to the wrong people, but, somehow, I staggered through to the end. Everyone on the set applauded. I couldn't believe my ears. Santell rushed up. "Hey, that's great, Dave! Just what I wanted . . . perfect! Now we have that one in the can, we'll just take another for safety. . . . Oh, this time don't hit the track, and watch out for the old dame's chair . . . one or two little changes. . . . Just clean it up a little . . . but it's great and we have it already – this one's a luxury." I sailed through the second take, loving every minute of it, completely relaxed.'

David Niven learned afterwards that Santell hadn't even had film in the camera for the first take, and he had told everybody to applaud.

The director knew that the only way to get the young man to act well was to tell him he already had acted well, to suspend critical judgement.

My first job at Burns was obviously not as propitious as Niven's acting role, but still my foolish little heart swelled. I felt that I was being trusted, given a chance I didn't deserve.

Outside, the light was failing. Inside, we were warm, and everybody seemed pleased. My instructor was there, and he beamed at me. I had blinked when I was photographed on the day of the class. So I needed a new picture for my identity card.

First I was given a woman's uniform, then the girl who loves trolls appeared and saw to it that I got the correct outfit. My new supervisor introduced himself, gave me directions and basic instructions.

Driving home, I felt as if my life as a novelist – even when the books were getting published – were somehow artificial, and that this was real. 'The building is locked and alarmed,' I was told. 'You'll sit outside in your car. They had a break-in last night. It's a perfume factory. I'll spell it for you: G–u–e–r–l–a–i–n. But don't ask me to pronounce it.'

I got home and discovered that the uniform pants were way too long. We didn't have any safety pins, and when I asked Janet to sew the hems, she was afraid that if she stopped stirring her white sauce, it would be ruined. 'I bet this happens a lot with security guards,' I said.

The boys were off on a play date. I hemmed the pants with straight pins. It was dark when I left. I passed the boys on the road. I beeped my horn but didn't get out. I didn't want to have to explain the uniform.

Flying north on the Saw Mill River Parkway, past the *Reader's Digest* headquarters, I wondered if I would be killed. It seems hysterical, but that's what I thought. I hail from the class and generation of American men in which adultery and automobile accidents have to pass for adventure. And of course there's getting fired. Don't forget getting fired.

The Guerlain plant I was hired to guard is across from JFK, the local Catholic high school, and the lights were on in the grottoes. I figured I was going to die for sure.

The man who met me at the plant was friendly in the extreme. The building stood in the center of thirty-two acres. He said the acres were wild. Staying there at night, he'd seen white deer. Albino deer. Had I ever seen an albino deer? I had not.

There was only one road into the facility grounds. The road was blocked with an automatic gate. The day before, they'd caught a couple of men who had a device they'd used to open the automatic gate. One man was from New Jersey, another from Staten Island. They both had rap sheets. They were driving decent cars. The police thought it might be the Mob.

I figured I'd park out in the single road. That way if I did fall asleep, anybody coming by would have to wake me.

'It's perfume, right? How serious can that be?'

'Get a truckload of this stuff, and it's worth a half a million dollars,' I was told.

'Yeah, sure, but who would think to do that?'

Well, actually, Guerlain had another facility in Canada, a small place, like the size of Mavis Tire, and that one had been held up, too. 'Men came in wearing masks and carrying shotguns, cleaned the place out.'

Did Burns know about this?

'I don't think we told them about that.'

So definitely, I wasn't going to park out in the middle of the road and fall asleep. I probably wasn't going to fall asleep at all.

I pulled the Honda into a space among a line of parked cars. I could watch, and if they did come, I'd be secret. There was a second building behind the main one with the generator in it. This second building also had a toilet and a phone. If anybody showed up, I was to go to this building, and call the state police. Call 911. Dial 9 first, to get an outside line. Fortunately I had a cell phone in my car. Having spotted a truckload of felons, I wouldn't want to have to scuttle off around the building, find a phone, and then dial 9 to get an outside line.

I was told to call the police if anybody showed up.

'Anybody?'

'Well, actually, the only person who might possibly come in is the vice president.'

'How will I know him?'

'You'll know him. He looks like a vice president.'

Then I was left alone. I didn't like it. I could easily imagine the ghostly truck slipping down the drive, three men in ski masks dropping to the ground as it moved. 'We'll take out the blue.'

And when I did sleep, I dreamt of big men in double-breasted suits, men with broken noses.

Finally, driven to distraction by boredom, and fear, and having grown quite cold, I turned on the car engine and read from Alfred Kazin's *Writing Was Everything*. I knew the light made me a more likely target, but I was very cold. Polyester doesn't hold the heat. Besides which, the outside lights were on. My reading light needn't attract attention.

Kazin quoted from Pascal's *Pensées:*

When I consider the short duration of my life, swallowed up in the eternity before and after, the little space that I fill and can even see . . .

Then the outside lights went off. It was about 4:30 A.M. Were the lights on a timer, or had somebody thrown a switch? I turned off the car engine. First I was frightened, then I was too tired to be frightened. When I was too cold to be tired, I'd turn the engine on for a few minutes. Nothing happened. At six A.M. I went home. Nobody called to say, 'The place was robbed, dummy. What were you doing out there, reading Pascal's *Pensées*?' Nobody called to say, 'You did good.' Nobody called at all.

That was Thursday. I didn't work again until Tuesday at midnight. Another officer had been at the plant since six P.M. We met at the electric gate. I got out of my car, he out of his. We both kept our lights on, our engines running. We stood out in the open night, showing our uniforms, like characters in a le Carré novel.

He was much older than I and seemed to be driving a Pinto, a car in which the body was one color and the doors another.

He complained to me about how on another job he'd been given a ticket by a policeman. 'He does the same work I do.'

The night wasn't nearly as bad as the first had been, although I was still scared. 'We're always getting tied up,' our instructor had said. 'We're always getting dead.'

I was off duty at 6 A.M. It was 5:55 A.M. Nothing had happened. Then the truck appeared. A truck, an actual truck. I couldn't believe it. The electric gate opened. The truck kept coming. That didn't mean anything. The criminals they'd caught knew how to operate the electric gate. I literally rubbed my eyes. The truck had its lights on. *This means it can't be a heist,* I thought, *or else they'd turn the lights off. Unless they kept the lights on to fool me into thinking it's not a heist.* I'd seen movies, knew what to expect. Two men and a woman in black clothes with ski masks would drop off the truck as it swung past. She'd be the one who insisted I be killed. After they'd covered my mouth with duct tape, she'd stay behind to pop a cap in my head.

I dialed 911.

'Nine-one-one,' the operator answered. 'What is your emergency?' and it was clear from his tone of voice that my operator was bored, that he sincerely doubted mine was a genuine emergency. Probably I was calling to ask how to get grape juice out of my linen tablecloth.

I told him I was a Burns security officer at the perfume plant in Somers, that a truck had just pulled in and no truck was supposed to pull in, and that I needed to talk with the state police.

'All right,' he said, 'I'll put you on hold.'

'Don't put me on hold!' I cried. But the sound on the other end of the phone was already different. I disconnected and redialed. 'Nine-one-one,' the operator said again, still bored despite my obvious peril. 'What's your emergency?'

I told him I had just called. I told him I was the Burns security officer. I was in Somers. I needed to talk to the state police.

I looked out the window. The truck was backing up to the loading dock. *Maybe they won't kill me*, I thought. *Maybe instead they'll just clean the place out, while I sit out here in full uniform and gab with the man at 911.*

I said that I needed to be connected to the state police. He told me he had been trying to connect me to the state police. The line went funny again, in the way it had gone funny before, but this time I didn't disconnect, and this time I got the state police. I started over, trying to keep the hysteria out of my voice. I told them about the truck. I told them I was told that nobody was supposed to be on the grounds. Nobody but a vice president, I said. I said the place had been cased recently by known criminals.

The policeman didn't seem as concerned as I was, but neither was he dismissive. Had I checked on the truck, to see who it was?

No, I said. I had not checked. I said that this same company I was guarding had been robbed in Canada. The company's plant had been held up by armed guys in masks. With shotguns. If I go out there and it's just somebody getting to work early, that'll be fine, I said. But if I go out there, and it's the Mob, I'm going to be in trouble.

The state policeman said it was okay. He'd send a car.

And they came. And they came quickly. Two enormous men in a large American car. With its lights out. I flashed my lights to show them where I was, and they pulled up to me. I told them I was the guy who had called them. 'I'm sorry to bother you, but I was told that nobody was supposed to come here. Except a vice president.'

The police sedan whipped over to the truck. There wasn't any gunfire. They came back. 'It's all right,' they told me. 'He has authority.'

'You sure?'

'Yeah, we are sure.'

'Thanks for coming, then.'

'It was nothing.' And they left.

So then I thought I'd better drive over myself. I had to talk to the man. Or men. What if the cops were wrong? And if they weren't wrong, I had to make a clean breast of it. So I pulled up to the truck. It was driven by a tall man, with long hair and glasses. He was on the back of his vehicle now, standing.

I looked up at him. 'Sorry to bother you,' I said. 'I was told to call the police.'

'There's never anyone here,' he said. 'I come here every Tuesday, and there's never anyone here. Where were you?'

'I was parked against the building,' I said, and pointed.

The man looked down at me from his own substantial height and from the height of his truck, which now had a load attached. When he spoke it was without malice. When he spoke it was without irony or sarcasm. He didn't sound angry, only amazed. After all, it was very early in the morning.

'So what did you think?' he asked. 'That some knucklehead was going to steal your garbage?'

I looked again at the back of the truck. The sky was going gray, and I could now see for sure that it had been a flatbed and that it had a load now. The load was a Dumpster.

The garbageman drove off. Then I drove off, leaving half a million dollars' worth of perfume unprotected. My mouth was dry. My heart was pounding.

Now it happened that an old red van had been parking at the end of our drive for a year or so. It had been coming in at about six in the morning, and staying there for at least an hour. I'd seen a man in it, and sometimes a woman. Often they sat in the van. Other times they climbed into the back and covered themselves with a blanket or quilt. I'd written down the license number, but I had not called the police. I didn't think about the van much, except when we were going away on vacation, and then it would worry me.

But this morning, after I got back from the Guerlain factory, I pulled into the garage and walked right back out to the van. I had my uniform on. Jacket and badge. The man in the driver's seat was awake. Reading the *Daily News*. He had on a nylon jacket that had *Vinny* written on the breast.

'Vinny?' I asked.

'No,' he said.

I said I didn't mind his parking there; I just wanted to know who he was. He nodded and called me sir. 'All right, Vinny,' I said, 'I just wanted to say hello.'

'Hello,' he said. 'I'm not Vinny.' He explained that he worked two jobs, that he lived in White Plains. 'I come here to sleep.'

'You can stay,' I said, and walked back to the house. When I came outside with the dog a couple of minutes later, he was gone.

While I was working for Burns, J and I went to dinner with another couple at a restaurant in Chappaqua. Driving out on Washington Avenue from Pleasantville, I very nearly hit a man in dark clothes, who was walking against traffic. He wasn't in the middle of the lane, but neither was he on the curb. It was raining, and the visibility was terrible. Ordinarily, I would have muttered something, and gone on, but now that I was a trained security officer, I felt differently. I felt responsible. 'He's going to be hit,' I told J. We turned around at the next intersection, and went back towards the man I'd seen walking in the dark. I stopped when I was abreast, put on my flashing hazard lights, and let down the window.

'Can I give you a ride?'

'No, thank you.'

'Look, I almost hit you driving out. It's pouring. The visibility is nil. You're in the road.'

'That's all right. I walk home every night.'

'But it's not like this every night. Let me give you a ride.'

'I said no, thank you.'

So I rolled up my window, went on to the next intersection, and turned around again. 'This time I will hit him,' I told J as we headed back. So I'd made the full transition from civilian to cop to bad cop. Took me less than a month.

Brooks Brothers: My Mother Tells Me I Went to the Wrong College

COMING OFF A LONG PATCH OF JOBLESSNESS, I WAS delighted when Brooks Brothers phoned back. My friend, the theatre critic Jacques le Sourde, had had a friend who worked at Brooks over the holidays. She had since died, but this was unrelated to her sales career, he told me. She'd enjoyed the job. Besides which, I liked the look of the notice that ran in *The New York Times*'s classified section:

Retail

Holiday Openings

at Brooks Brothers

America's most prestigious name in classic clothing for men and ladies
is now interviewing for seasonal opportunities in:

Sale Sales Support★ Customer Service
Seasonal schedules are 30–40 hours per week and include weekends.
Brooks Brothers offers a generous storewide discount on
merchandise for the holidays.

Please fax resume to (212) 309–7273, or apply in person
between 9 A.M. and 5 P.M. through Saturday.
Only qualified candidates will be contacted for an interview.

I had been contacted for an interview. So that was me, then, a qualified candidate. They hadn't even seen me yet, although I had applied in person at 346 Madison Avenue. I'd hoped that I could see somebody. I often make a better impression in person than on paper. (A vexing situation if you mean to be a writer.)

I hadn't been to the flagship store often since I'd gone there as a boy with my father. Unlike most places we'd visited together, the Brooks store on Madison Avenue had not been altered beyond recognition. The floors were still marble, the counters dark mahogany. I told a gentleman behind the necktie display that I was looking for a job. He sent me to the fifth floor.

Waiting for the elevator, I was touched on the shoulder by a stranger who beamed shyly down at me. 'Where are the bathrobes?' he asked. 'I don't know,' I said, and regretted my ignorance acutely. *It's not the Brooks suit that looks so damn good*, I thought, and not for the first time, *it's the Brooks man*. This one was holding one of those miniature baby-blue shopping bags from Tiffany. He stood erect with an easy bearing and had a full head of fine, straight hair going gray at the temples. His was an open countenance, not a mask of envy, guile, or sorrow. I recalled the wisdom of W. Somerset Maugham: 'It is not true that suffering ennobles the character. Happiness does that sometimes, but suffering for the most part makes men petty and vindictive.'

'You first,' he said when the lift arrived. Happiness seemed to have ennobled this man's character. Happiness and good fortune.

When I arrived at the fifth floor, there were two chairs out in the hall flanking a table which had a wooden tray with applications in it. One chair was empty; the other had a man in it, hunched over and writing with a Brobdingnagian fountain pen. I couldn't tell if it was a fake or a Mont Blanc, but the pen certainly was enormous. The man wielding it looked like a suit salesman. I didn't yet look like a suit salesman. The form was printed on rich cream-colored paper and asked not just which high school and college I'd attended, but also my grade-point average. I went to Antioch in 1966, I think, although I don't exactly remember the year. Antioch wasn't very good for my short-term memory. I went to college when, to quote Bob Dylan, 'the times they [were] a-changin'.

Revolution was in, authority was not in. Faculty members were reluctant to impose the notions of a failing and corrupt culture upon the magnificent ignorance of youth. Pass/Fail was the system, and if you thought you were going to fail, you could always get an incomplete. I'd garnered my share of incompletes.

The curriculum at Antioch would have been comical, if it hadn't been tragic. I took one course titled 'When Drawing Is Singing and Dancing.' If you intended to be a teacher, it was a requirement. The instructor used to like to sit silently at the front of the class. He had a chair. We all sat on the floor. Once in a while he'd say something meant to sound wise: 'The clock ticks. The rug covers the floor. Reading a newspaper every day is like eating.' Another offering was titled 'Shakespeare and Imperialism.' One woman fulfilled her physical-science requirements by having a baby. She got all fifteen credits and named the child Lenin.

So when Brooks Brothers asked for my grade-point average, I left the space blank. Maybe they'd think I'd just missed it. But I did fill out the rest of the form. In the service elevator to which I was afterwards directed, I heard one employee say to another, 'You're just a sales associate. You die out there on the floor, they step over the body, bring in somebody new.' I came out on to the street between Madison and Fifth, where the men who already had jobs at Brooks were smoking filtered cigarettes.

'Never, never, never give up.' That's what Winston Churchill said. So I marched uptown to the Polo Sport open house at Seventy-second Street. Applicants mobbed the door. When the door was opened and we were let in from the cold, we found a counter set with bread, cheese, grapes, Evian, seltzer with lime, and seltzer without lime.

'Help yourselves,' the Polo representative told us while passing out applications, 'I know you are all dying to be interviewed, but please eat.' He went on to violate the first law of contemporary fashion: 'Eating is good,' he said. Nobody touched the food. We were out of work, but that didn't make us idiots.

You could tell immediately – not just by what they were doing, but by how they looked – who already had a job at Polo Sport. Many of them were gorgeous, but they were not all gorgeous. Stylish is what they all were. Striking and mannered in a way that I imagine the members of a ballet troupe are striking and mannered.

Our forms were collected, and names from the pile were called for interviews. When the applicants passed back into the street, you could tell who had made it by what they said to their friends. Pretty soon you could figure out who was going to be hired and who not when they went in. Polo Sport was looking for beautiful, stylish people. Most of us were the ugly stepsisters.

So this ugly stepsister was delighted days later when Brooks phoned. There are jobs in this world with status and authority well beyond salary. The clergy come immediately to mind. Poets and cartoonists who have appeared in *The New Yorker*. Suit salesmen at Brooks Brothers.

'It makes sense,' I told friends. 'That's the way I was brought up – so that if all else failed, I could sell suits at Brooks Brothers.'

The interview was on October 17, and went beautifully, I thought. True, I was wearing my polo suit again. Cindy Werking, from Human Resources, didn't seem to mind.

I explained that when I was a boy my father used to bring me to Brooks almost every year to buy a suit. I didn't tell her how badly those suits had fit. 'We were in awe,' I said. 'So we lost you as a customer?' she said wistfully.

All is forgiven, I thought, gleefully taking my second ride on the service elevator. The hours were long, but I'd had retail jobs before. My wife and children were used to that.

As a boy I'd been frightened of the salesmen at Brooks. Now I would be one of them. So that was a progression. I would be a seasonal employee. But even so, the minimum was nine dollars an hour. The commission was 2.5 per cent.

I told everybody. Everybody was impressed. 'Brooks Brothers,' I said, 'at Christmas.'

Two days later, in the afternoon, my wife and I went for a walk together and then out to the end of the drive for the mail. Janet's face fell when she saw the envelope. She's smarter than I am. She knew what a thin envelope meant. I had to read the letter.

Dear Benjamin:

Thank you for meeting with me recently to discuss the position of Seasonal Sales in our Madison Avenue store.

We have now completed a review of all applicants and unfortunately do not have a position available for you at this time.

Once again, thank you for your interest in Brooks Brothers.

I was crushed. I phoned and left messages. Cindy wouldn't call me back. I don't blame her. Candor in this area can easily result in a lawsuit. The fact was, they hadn't liked me. They hadn't liked me enough.

I told everybody. Everybody was sad.

'Not still brooding about Brooks Brothers?' my mother said a week later, when I phoned her in the evening.

I allowed as how I was still brooding.

'You went to the wrong college,' she said.

Section Two:
Birth of a Salesman

I do wish the word *caste* were domesticated in the United States, because it nicely conveys the actual rigidity of class lines here, the difficulty of moving — either upward or downward — out of the place where you were nurtured.

— Paul Fussell

The great majority of us are required to live a life of constant duplicity. Your health is bound to be affected if day after day you say the opposite of what you feel. If you grovel before what you dislike and rejoice at what brings you nothing but misfortune. Our nervous system isn't just a fiction, it's a part of our physical body and our soul. It exists in space and is inside us like the teeth in our mouth. It cannot be forever violated with impunity.

— Boris Pasternak

CompUSA: 'Drugs are OK?'

'ARE YOU AN ENGINEER?' THE MAN ASKED ME WHEN HE CALLED.
'No.'
'Do you have any technical experience with computers?'
'No.'
I could hear him breathing on the other end of the phone line.
'I own a Macintosh,' I said.
More silence.
'I've had one since 1982. I love my Mac.'
Now I could hear him breathing again.
'Can you sell a Mac?' he asked.
'Yes,' I said, and that's how I finally got the job I wanted at CompUSA. This was in December of 1995. Setting up that simple phone conversation had taken a long, long time. And this despite the fact that there were help-wanted signs right inside the front door of the store I was aiming for, the one housed on the site of the former Conran's, hard by the County Center in White Plains, New York.

When talking to friends about the research for this book, I tend to skip over the many jobs I applied for and didn't get. On average, I must have tried for thirty in order to land one. Part of the problem is that I'm a novelist and therefore unqualified for even the most menial chores, but also I was always frightened. I don't like being rejected, and so I often failed to follow through.

I procrastinated. Which, apparently, is not uncommon. 'Studies have revealed the depressing fact that two-thirds of all job hunters spend only five hours a week (or less) hunting for a job!' writes

Richard Nelson Bolles in the 1999 edition of *What Color Is Your Parachute?*.

So I'd read the classifieds, and then if I could dream up any research, I'd do that. Finally, I'd make a phone call; if I got an answering machine, I'd heave a great sigh of relief. Now the ball was in their court.

Sometimes one phone call settled the matter. For instance, I seized on this item in the classified section of the New York *Daily News:*

Computer Repair Trainees

H.S. Grads ages 17–34 learn to repair state-of-the-art computers at our
expense and receive excellent salary benefits package.
For more info, call 1–800–262–8331.

There was a repair-school advertisement I'd been ogling in the *Times* classifieds. 'Build computers from scratch,' it said, but they were going to charge me one thousand dollars and when I visited the site, I was not impressed. The school was in Manhattan. The receptionist was very eager to take my money. The computers didn't look new. I liked the line 'from scratch', though. What were they going to do exactly? Drop me into the Maine wilderness with a bent pin, and two weeks later I'd come out carrying a laptop? The *Daily News* offering sounded much better. Plus, free. *They can't turn me down on the basis of age*, I thought. *It's against the law.*

'Hello, I'm phoning about your advertisement in the *Daily News* classifieds. Tell me about the job.'

'Thank you for calling,' I was told.

'Oh, you're welcome,' I said, 'but tell me about the job.'

'How are you doing today?' I was asked.

'Fine. I'm fine,' I said. 'Please tell me about the job.'

'Well, first of all,' the man said, and his voice fell, 'the job is with the U.S. Navy.'

'You mean I have to join the navy?' I asked, and my own voice trailed off.

'Well, yes.'

What about my family? I thought, but what I said was, 'I guess I'm too old for that.'

'How old are you?'

'I'm forty-eight.'

'Well, you don't sound forty-eight.'

'Well, I am forty-eight,' I said.

Other times I'd send off a résumé. When that happened, I felt as if I'd done something. I hadn't done much. If each résumé sent out is a bet against unemployment, your chances of getting a job are one in 1,470, according to *What Color Is Your Parachute?*. This sounds about right to me. I don't recall a single response to any of the many letters and résumé I sent off. Except in the case of schools, which were going to charge me, of course, or organizations offering 'investment opportunities'.

When I did tell friends how hard it was to land even a low-level job, they were incredulous. 'But you have qualifications,' they'd say.

'For instance?'

'Well, for instance, you can type.'

I tried that. 'There is no more telling sign about the state of the union than this one simple fact: Manpower, Inc. – the nationwide temp agency – has surpassed General Motors as the number-one employer in America.' So wrote Michael Moore in *Downsize This!*. So I went to the Manpower office in White Plains. When I'd signed up with the agency in Boston, during college, the jobs offered were manual. Now they seemed to be mostly clerical.

'I can type,' I said. So I was told I'd be tested and then my results would be sent to a placement officer. After that, I would meet with the placement officer.

I've always thought that if I typed faster, I would write faster, and perhaps with more freedom. I longed to escape the ominous, slow-footed suggestions of a highly self-conscious mind. I remember reading that Joyce Carol Oates types ninety words a minute. Although I seem also to have read that she writes in longhand. Dickens did train as a court reporter. That much I know. Jack Kerouac was supposed to have written *On the Road* on a single roll of paper, typing quickly and never going back. So there was the possibility that a faster typist would be a faster and also a more skillful writer.

Over the years I've bought a number of typing programs, and whenever I had a keyboard at hand and nothing else in particular to do, I'd type, 'The quick brown fox jumped over the lazy sleeping dog' or else, 'Now is the time for all good men to come to the aid of their country.'

When I was at the *Rockland Journal-News* and didn't need to take notes, I'd sometimes type in the background while I was on hold or while interviewing a dullard. Once, when I was typing away like that, the managing editor came into the newsroom and was impressed. 'Look at Cheever,' he said. 'See how hard he's working.'

What was I going to say? I nodded bravely and kept on typing.

'Bullshit!' said a friend, who was also in the newsroom. 'Look and see what he's typing.'

'He's working,' the managing editor said defensively. 'That's enough for me.'

'Do me a favor,' my colleague said to my boss, 'just look at what he's typing.'

This went on for a while, with me hammering furiously away at my keyboard and my friend taunting the managing editor, who stalwartly and quite uncharacteristically continued to take my side. Finally, the boss gave in; he came and looked over my shoulder. This was not my finest hour.

Yes, Bob Seltzer, the guy who turned me in, is still a friend. We eat lunch about once a year. He's now a CEO. You can draw your own conclusions.

In any case, you'd be surprised how quickly I can get through 'The quick brown fox jumped over the lazy sleeping dog.'

I hoped that that would be on the test. It wasn't on the test. I was used to typing my own thoughts. Apparently Manpower didn't particularly care about my own thoughts. I was put in a cubicle with a computer. I had to type a memo. This had been composed in longhand by some imaginary and cretinous boss. The document was larded with errors of every sort. Also, you had to set up an elaborate system of tabs. The space key kept sticking. I flailed away manfully until the time ran out.

When I met with my placement officer, he looked so sad that I wondered about my clothes. I was wearing chinos, a white dress shirt, and a sweater that was riddled with moth holes.

'The space bar kept sticking,' I explained.

My placement officer nodded at me and smiled.

'There are lots of jobs that don't require typing,' he said.

Several weeks later, Manpower did call me back, but I'd already landed the job I longed for at CompUSA. I adore computers, particularly Macs. I've spent hundreds of hours shopping for them. The 'Science' section of *The New York Times* is valued by me chiefly for the full-page advertisements placed by J&R Computer World.

I went to the CompUSA store on Route 119 in White Plains, handed in a résumé, and filled out a job application. Nobody called. So I went again, filled out a second job application, attached a second résumé. One evening when I was there with the kids, buying paper, I struck up a conversation with an employee of about my age who had a ponytail. I said I wanted to work at CompUSA. He said I should fill out an application. I said I'd filled in applications a couple of times. He asked if I'd spoken with the manager. I said no. He said I should do that. 'But I have the kids,' I said, backing up in a hurry. 'He likes kids,' said the guy with the ponytail. So we waited for fifteen minutes. The manager didn't show up. But before I left, Ponytail said, 'What you have to do is come back when the manager is here and talk with him.'

So the next day I drove to the store, went to Customer Service, and asked to see a manager. The girl at the desk got on the intercom; I heard a manager's name come over the P.A. and pretty soon one arrived. It turned out that there were several managers. This was a clean-cut, muscular young man in a crew-neck sweater, with a serious mien and a limp. He wanted to know if I'd filled out an application. 'Yes, I did,' I said, 'a couple of times.' He went over to a desk and shuffled idly through a pile of applications, then looked a little embarrassed. 'Would you mind filling out another application?' he asked. I said I wouldn't mind. 'Do that, and I'll talk with you,' he said.

He brought me to an empty room downstairs. I filled out my third job application. He came in, sat at a desk beside me, scanned my paperwork. 'We don't make anything on the hardware,' he said. 'So it's the software?' I asked. 'No, not really. It's the spiffs and the ESPs,' he said. 'That's what we look for. That's what we'll use to judge your performance.' I had no idea what he was talking about. I was just happy to be there.

Next, I was given an appointment at a doctor's office in Elmsford. I went there and spent half an hour in a waiting room in front of a table heaped with magazines for the weekend pilot. I thought that when I met the doctor, I could ask him about his airplane. I never met the doctor, though. A woman appeared and gave me a plastic beaker to piss into. She brought me to the bathroom, told me very apologetically that she'd have to turn off the water. She said she wasn't allowed to leave me alone with the taps opened. I said I didn't mind. She said she'd turn the water back on afterwards so that I could wash my hands.

I said that was OK. 'Tell me the minute you're through,' she said. 'I'll need to test the temperature.'

So I closed the door, produced my sample, and called out. The woman rushed in and pasted something on the cup of urine, which registered its temperature.

I'm speculating, but it seems likely that in the fall of 1995, addicts may have been using hot tap water to produce a passing urine sample. And sure as God made little green apples, addicts have a way around this system, too, by now. That is, if they didn't already have a way around it in 1995. A thermos full of clean urine? I wasn't frisked.

Where there's a will, there's a way. Where there's a need, there's a product. Researching a magazine piece on grass, I typed *marijuana* into the AOL search engine and found 'TestingFree.com – Pass Your Drug Test'. The site offered 'Our Most Frequently Ordered Products That Purify Your Body of Any Toxins with a Manufac- turer's Double Money Back Guarantee! Overnight Shipping Avail- able'. Products offered included '45 Minute Quick Chew: Emergency Flush Works in 45 Minutes! Sale price $44.95'. There was also a 'Dynamite Deal: 3 Rapid Screen Drug Tests for Only $49.99!!!! (2-Panel Marijuana and Cocaine Test Kit)'.

I passed my urine test. I always pass the urine tests. The other employment tests – and there will be other tests – I sometimes failed.

About a week later they called up to ask if I was an engineer; I told them how much I liked my Mac. They said I should come in. They asked me not to wear sneakers; to wear chinos, and a polo shirt as close to red as I had. 'We'll get you an official shirt soon.'

Later that afternoon, I was talking with a friend who writes screenplays. He told me he'd been eating lunch with a colleague who said he hated the movie business because everybody's on drugs. 'Let me get this straight,' I said. 'For eight dollars an hour, you have to be clean. But if you're earning, I don't know, like a million dollars, drugs are OK?'

CompUSA: 'People who have money are always assholes.'

MY IMMEDIATE SUPERVISOR, THE MAN IN CHARGE OF THE Macintosh section at CompUSA, was something of a legend. 'He would sell swampland to his mother,' I was told when I reported to the White Plains store early in December of 1995. 'He's sold two million computers.'

The uniform was a red polo shirt. They didn't have one in my size with the company logo, so I wore my own off-red polo shirt. The name tag identified me: CompUSA, it said. Then on the next line, The Computer Superstore. Below that on a strip of black label tape it said BEN.

My supervisor — let's call him Bill — wore a white dress shirt under a red sweater vest. On the latter he wore two pins. One was a likeness of the Macintosh apple, the other had the Intel chip. He was stocky, in his late fifties or early sixties, with jet-black hair combed neatly in a conventional part, and he wore glasses with black frames. He was with a customer when I first hit the floor.

I walked over and stood around the big cardboard boxes of Macintoshes and waited for prey. When a single customer appeared, I sidled up to him and asked, 'Can I help you?'

'Just looking,' he said, which is what I always say when a salesperson sidles up to me. 'If you do have any questions,' I said, 'I'm here to answer them.' Clearly, he was consumed with curiosity but also wanted to avoid getting into my sticky fingers. Several more customers came in. One of them actually said, 'I'm going to check out the computers here and then buy them from a catalogue.

They're cheaper that way.' I gave him my warmest smile. Another man was scouting out the territory for his brother, who was coming in the next day with the money. 'So I can't buy anything today. No way!'

Meantime, I noticed that Bill was making sales. One customer had come in and asked for him, which was an advantage I didn't have. When it came to picking prospects off the floor, customers also available to me, Bill seemed to have fabulous luck. Then I saw him selling a system to the guy who was just scouting for his brother. 'What about his brother?' I asked Bill later in the afternoon. 'What brother?' Bill said.

The Mac section of CompUSA was mostly selling the Performa that year, and there were several models running from just over one thousand to almost three thousand dollars. There was a CompUSA card you could apply for and charge with the same day, but most people used their own credit cards, although some paid with checks, and in a couple of cases I saw cash. It was a lot of money, or it seemed like a lot of money to me. Often the customer and I would get caught on the price, and he or she would leave the store. Bill's customers seemed universally better set than my own.

So whenever there was a break, I'd hang around him. I had lots of specific questions about the merchandise, but also I wanted to learn whatever I could about his style. I don't believe in magic, but what he did looked just like magic.

He wasn't a particularly attractive man – but boy, could he sparkle. What struck me first was that he wasn't at all slavish. I was slavish. If I caught a customer's eye, I would then do whatever was wanted. I'd rush to the warehouse to check on stock; I'd go to the manager to try for a better price; I'd ask them about their families, jobs, even hairstyles if the hairstyles were ugly enough. I moved quickly and sold slowly.

In order to make a difficult sale, you have to love the person you're selling to. You don't have to love him forever, but right then, you have to love him. You have to stop time.

One young woman came in who had a face that had been

dramatically disfigured. I asked her about it, and she said it was an automobile accident. She was intelligent and dignified, but I had trouble with her face. If we'd had more time, I could've gotten over it, but I couldn't manage it on the fly. I lost the sale.

Bill wouldn't have lost the sale. He moved slowly and sold quickly. Bill was both less anxious and more obviously empathetic.

If a customer tapped him on the shoulder, Bill would light right up, but if he was doing something else at the moment – finishing up another sale, for instance, or even rearranging products – he'd make his prospect wait. First he'd say something enticing like, 'I have precisely what you want, and I'll be with you in a minute.' You could virtually see the customer thinking, *Boy, am I glad I got this guy.*

When Bill did focus on the waiting customer, he often made the sale quickly, and also convinced his customer to buy the product insurance. We had a colorful little four-page foldout that painted the insurance plan in glowing terms.

The cost of protection was prorated, so that a five-hundred-dollar purchase could be insured for three years for $59.97, while it cost $599.97 in order to protect a five-thousand-dollar purchase for five years.

Now anybody who had ever leafed idly through *Consumer Reports* magazine knew that there was some reason this insurance wasn't any good. But when you worked at CompUSA, you had to believe in the insurance. Otherwise you were just a low-grade crook. Which nobody wants to be. So I believed. And pushed the insurance. And even gathered a couple of enabling anecdotes. My parents had a neighbor who had purchased a large-screen TV from Nobody Beats the Wiz, which went kerflooey before its service plan expired, and he got a new one. Free. Now there's a story I told over and over again.

But still, I almost never sold the coverage. Bill did. He sold it again and again.

I suppose all jobs are competitive to some extent. What had been debilitating at the *Reader's Digest*, for instance, was that judgments

of merit were so subjective and seemed often to have little to do
with actual performance.

In my haste to disdain sales, I'd completely overlooked the fact
that it's one of the rare areas of employment in which productivity
can easily be measured, and in terms that are very close to objective.
You could see who was good.

Bill was good, and you could see it on an hourly basis. He wasn't
a shark. I'd work with sharks later. A shark is a man who bullies and
shames the weak customer into making a purchase. There's a high
rate of returns with sharks. Nobody's entirely happy, but sales are
made.

Bill didn't coerce his customers. He acted as if each transaction
might easily blossom into a long and fruitful friendship. He talked
about where the customers lived, and where he lived, what
restaurants they enjoyed. It was the holiday season, and he invited
many people to a big party he was going to have in January. I never
got an actual invitation. I'm not even sure there was such a party.

One of my outside-world friends bought a computer from Bill
and was deeply snowed. He complained to me afterwards that
when he'd called Bill a second or third time, the salesman seemed
not to even remember his name. 'I thought we were friends.'

Bill turned this same charm on me, and I was intoxicated. He
wore cologne. I started to wear cologne. One day I even wore a
white dress shirt and red sweater vest. Nobody said anything, but I
got the distinct impression that I'd overstepped. The next day I
went back to the polo shirt. I sensed that Bill's geniality was
professional, but I still enjoyed it. I basked in the warmth of his
false amiability.

At night, after the store was closed, we'd move the big boxes
around on hand trucks, replenish and sometimes alter the displays.
We had a black manager, and he used to yell, 'Come on now, this
place looks like Harlem.' Bill and I worked together taking the
freight elevator back and forth to the stockroom, which was in the
basement. Bill was certainly not the first supervisor I'd ever sucked
up to, but he was one of the few whom I actually admired. He was

friendly and humorous. He gave me tons of useful advice and also the high points of his life story.

He hadn't actually 'hand-sold' two million computers – he'd owned a computer store. He sold the store and invested the profits in real estate. 'I expected to spend the rest of my life sailing and taking graduate courses.' The investments went south, and so he was working again as a salesman. He hadn't lost his touch.

When one of my customers went away without buying, and I asked Bill, 'Did I do anything wrong?' he'd say, 'You can't do anything wrong.' If I was stuck with a hard case, he'd give me a big, long wink. When I made a sale, he called it 'a home run', although technically it was not. I later learned that a home run is where you move the product and accessories and the insurance, or ESP, and convince the pigeon to put it all on the store credit card.

I'd been buying all my life, of course, but I'd rarely sold anything, which meant that I missed about half of what was going on. When I buy something, I'm always wondering if I'm being shrewd or stupid, if I'm paying too much. The personality of the salesman seems beside the point. I could see now that that's how many people buying computers felt about me. I could see, also, how mistaken they were. Our relationship, however brief, was intense and had a good deal to do with their final decision. Customers are dumb about sales personnel, because sales personnel want them dumb. A good salesman does a lot, but makes it seem as if he hasn't done a thing. I wasn't a good salesman yet, but I could see what it meant.

The one thing one mustn't do, I was told, was to antagonize a customer. 'Small world; don't make enemies,' Bill used to say. 'No black marks,' he said. He and the manager both told me that it didn't matter if the customer was right or wrong. What mattered was that the customer was happy.

How to avoid a black mark?

'The more difficult a case is, the more you have to flatter them,' Bill told me. This was the Christmas season – the most wretched time of year – and people came in looking like they needed to be sedated. They came in with the buttons on their shirts done up in the wrong order, with eyes that seemed to be red from sobbing, with hair tangled and makeup smudged. There were customers with chewing gum in their hair, and with screaming toddlers. One recently divorced man used to take two small, difficult children to the store for his weekly visitation. They'd knock things over, play computer games, go out for dinner, and then get dropped back with the mother.

One woman came over to the Mac section clutching a software package, and you could tell from twenty-five yards away that what she really wanted to do was to find out whom to blame for the general deterioration of civilization. Bill stepped out in front of me, took the software package from her with both hands, listened to her complaint, and then said, 'You're so smart to ask that question. That is the key question. Most people don't even know to ask that question. If we have what you're looking for, it's going to be right over by the rocket,' he said, and pointed to the large model of a rocket that we had set up at the far end of the software display. Off she went, to ruin somebody else's day.

This technique reminded me of something I'd been taught by another reporter at the *Journal-News*. When somebody is screaming, you mustn't hang up on them, because they'll call your boss right back, and they'll be much angrier. 'Uh-huh,' you say, 'uh-huh, uh-huh.' Make sympathetic noises, and wait until they're done with the tirade. Finally you start to talk to them, calmly, and as if you have a lot you want to say. Talk for about a minute and then in midsentence, you hang up on yourself. Half the time, they won't call back. If they do call back, they're going to be easier to deal with. Now they feel that you've both been wronged.

Of course I didn't know very much about computers, but I loved that job. I got to ogle the new Macs, sometimes even operate them. There was a canteen downstairs where you could buy and consume Diet Coke

I'd work from ten A.M. to ten P.M. and have the time of my life. Part of this was just escaping the highly solitary and humiliating position of the novelist, but also this was the first job I'd had in a long time that wasn't sedentary. I've always been drawn to the glamour of the writing/editing career, but what do you do mostly? You sit alone in a room. What do you get? Fat hips, weak eyes, and if you are lucky enough to be published, poisonous reviews.

Now I could move around and talk with people. Moving around and talking with people was actually essential to my job. Plus, I was useful. Are you wondering how? Often even those with sophisticated questions just wanted to be listened to. I'd stand there in perfect ignorance of the technical specifications they were struggling with and I'd say, 'Uh-huh. Uh-huh. Croton's a great town. I've heard that. It is a popular machine. You could certainly do that.'

Other customers knew even less than I did. Still others didn't want information at all. They wanted company. And for somebody to read to them.

I was a hardware salesman, but customers often came over from software with a box. 'This says Windows 95,' they'd say, 'but I don't have Windows 95. Will this run on my computer?' So I'd take the box from them, and I'd read the smaller print on the side where it said Windows 95/or Windows 3.2. Then I'd say, 'Do you have Windows 3.2?' and they'd say yes. 'This should work fine,' I'd say.

When they were in hardware, they'd go right up to a display model and ask, 'How many megahertz does this run at?' I'd lean into the display, put my finger under the line that gave the number of megahertz, and say, 'It runs at seventy-five megahertz.'

'Oh, and how much RAM does it come with?'

I'd move my finger down from the line that gave the megahertz to the one that mentioned RAM, and I'd read, 'Eight megs of RAM.'

At first I was uneasy about using my finger. I was afraid somebody would notice and think I was taunting them for not knowing how to read. This might have happened, if I'd ever had a genuine illiterate, but these people could read. Nobody was offended. The customers liked being read to.

It seems an absurd luxury for literate people to have computer specifications read out loud, but then don't we often hire lawyers to do our reading for us? And we pay them a lot more than we pay computer salesmen.

When there weren't any customers for Macs, I'd hang around the much larger PC section looking for people buying their first computer. In Westchester in December of 1995, there were a lot of people spending two thousand dollars on a computer that was going to be turned on on Christmas Day, and unless there was a game on it, it might never be turned on again. 'Doorstops,' we called them. I thought that if I sold these people a Mac, they might actually figure out how to use it.

I had a riff. I'd ask them if they wanted a Mac, and if they said no, I'd ask them why. If they said the machine had to be compatible with the one at the office, I'd back off. If they said there was not enough software for the Macintosh, I'd ask them what they wanted to do with the machine.

If they said they were going to research their family tree or keep a list of customers or even manage their money, I'd say that all of that could be done on the Mac. Same if they wanted to surf the Web. And when they said they wanted the choice of more software, I'd tell them gleefully that the number-one best-selling piece of software for PCs was called Remove-It.

'People buy all this fabulous software. It doesn't work. It conflicts with the software they do have. It slows down their machine. So what they have to do is get the brand-new software out of their machine. So they buy Remove-It. So that's at least two pieces of software you won't need if you get a Mac. Two pieces you won't miss, either.'

I'm not sure if Remove-It was actually ever *the* best-selling piece of PC software, but it was *a* best-selling piece of software. That's what it said on the box, anyway.

If they'd listen, I said that I bought my first computer . . . 'what, fifteen years ago? It cost two thousand dollars and had no hard disk. It was a basic Mac, and when I bought a hard disk for it, it had one meg. At that point a friend told me I had more memory than the Pentagon had had during the Second World War. It was a primitive machine, but I was holding a job at the *Reader's Digest* and working on a book proposal. My agent kept asking me to change the proposal. I'm one of those writers who can't go on to the next page until he's got the first one perfectly typed. The proposal was twenty pages long. If I hadn't had a computer, then every time my agent suggested a change, I would have had to type the whole document over again. I was doing this on weekends and evenings. Without the computer, I never would have gotten it done.'

People seemed impressed, and nobody had the indelicacy to say, 'So why's a hotshot writer like yourself working here?'

Asked if I still had the machine, I told them I had given it to my mother. 'And she wrote a book on it. She still uses it,' I'd say. All of which was true. I don't know why exactly, but when you're trying to sell something, it's always good to bring up your mother.

I made friends. First there was Bill, whose talents I stood in awe of and whose company I enjoyed immensely. Watching him close a sale was like watching a stunt pilot loop the loop. But Bill wasn't my only friend. Moving boxes, talking during the slow periods, complaining about the customers – there was a feeling among the floor salespeople that we were in this together. When one woman said she only had a moment and then took two hours to decide about the monitor, one of the other salespeople came up to me and squeezed my hand. 'It's not you,' he whispered.

Often a prospect would settle on a particular computer and there wouldn't be one on the floor. I'd beg Mr. Customer to wait, and rush down into the storeroom to see if we had such a computer in stock or, failing that, one that was comparable in price and specifications.

I don't know how many times I came booming down into the storeroom, having left a prospect loosely hooked up on the floor. 'Tell me please that we have Performa 6205,' I'd say, and some smiling kid would appear with it on a hand truck. The more computers I sold, the more money I earned. The stock people got nothing out of helping me, except that they were doing their jobs, and they were helping me.

At about the time I was working at CompUSA, I saw Bryant Gumbel declare on TV that everything in this country has a racial component. He seemed to imply that it was not possible for blacks and whites to work together. But we did.

Before I started on this book, the most recent prolonged conversation I'd had with a black man was at the dinner held by the headmaster of the Hackley School in Tarrytown, New York. We had two boys there at the time, and the dinner was for parents who had contributed at least one thousand dollars. The one black parent at our table was startlingly handsome, and I believe quite well off, but it was clear that we all regarded him as an exotic. He mentioned that he knew Mayor Dinkins. 'Oh,' said one of the other white diners, 'are you the one who plays golf with him?'

'No,' he said, 'I'm not *that* one.'

I encountered no such difficulties when at CompUSA. My great weakness as a salesman was an inability to work the computer terminals on which we were supposed to structure and then print out the terms of each sale. The software 'designed by morons,' according to Bill, was primitive and extremely difficult to master. I couldn't both work the machine and keep up the patter. I'd get absorbed in the software – and the customer would walk off. Or I'd be asking the customer, 'Where is that on the Cape?' and make the wrong keystroke.

Fortunately, there were also simple printed forms, called G tickets, for 'fast and dirty sales.' These were made out by hand and brought up to the register, where totals could be rung up and the sale completed in one step. Problem here was that you needed to enter the serial number and SKU, or identifying number, of each product (typically a computer and a printer), and I have terrible handwriting. Again and again I had my bacon saved for me by a cashier. Most of the cashiers were black women.

They didn't just complete the sales; they made certain that I got credit, and often fattened my paycheck. 'Do you need a printer for this?' they'd say to the customer. Or else, 'You want the insurance, don't you?' Plus, they called me sweetie or darling.

Being a computer salesman was a lot like fishing. It was fun to make a big sale, and it was also profitable. So that is one side of the equation. The other side is that we were like fish in a barrel. A customer could come in off the street and say whatever he wanted, and what the salesman had to say back to him was 'Thank you very much. Is there anything else I can do for you today?'

What hurt was when one customer caused you to lose a sale with another. This happened rarely to Bill, but often to me.

One afternoon a young woman came into the Mac section of the store, walked right up to me, and said, 'I know what I want. I want that one.' She pointed at one of the Performas.

'Great,' I said, and I meant it.

'Isn't it nice to have somebody come in who knows what they want?' she said.

'Yes, it is nice,' I said. 'Wait right here. I'll be back.' Then I rushed off in the direction of the carriages. There were large carriages, similar to grocery carts, on which we brought the computers up to the register. As I scuttled along, another young woman stepped out of the cable aisle and stopped me in my tracks. I would have had to knock her down in order to keep going.

'I'm so sorry,' I said, 'I'm in a hurry.'

'Well, so am I in a hurry,' she said.

'All right then. How can I help you?'

She wanted a cable for the monitor of her Macintosh. Did I know which cable she should buy?

The beauty of selling a Macintosh Performa was that everything came in one box. If the printer you bought was a Hewlett-Packard DeskJet, you needed a special cable, and I'd just learned which cable that was. Other than that one cable, the unit was self-contained and self-explanatory. About monitor cables, I knew nothing. Remember, I wasn't an engineer.

I said I didn't know.

'I just bought the computer,' she said.

'Didn't it come with a cable for the monitor?'

'Yes,' she gave me that. 'It's not really the cable I need,' she said. 'What I really need are the little screws.'

'Which little screws?'

'The ones that screw the cable into the back of the monitor.'

I took a deep breath. I said I was sorry, but I didn't think we sold any loose screws. Now I was in the cable aisle, and there was somebody else, a man this time, waiting to get my attention. He was looking at the woman and rolling his eyes. This made me like him.

'Well, actually,' she said, 'I don't really need the little screws. I need the sleeves that the screws go into. When I screw them in now, they don't hold.'

'How long ago did you buy the computer?'

'I just bought it.'

'You should call Apple.'

'I did call Apple. They told me to come here.'

'Apple told you to come here, to White Plains?'

'So you're not going to help me?'

'I'll help you,' I said, 'but we are a discount retailer. We only have the parts for which there's a large demand. I can't imagine we'd have that part.'

She was a blonde, with a good figure, and here she drew herself up with indignation. 'Well, I just met somebody else who had the same problem and is looking for the same part,' she said.

That's what the aroused consumer really likes to do. They like to catch you in an error. 'Ha.' That's what *they* consider a home run.

So then I asked if the other customer had found the part that he or she wanted.

'I don't know,' she said, as if I were wasting her time, and at my back I could almost hear that other sale going away, slipping from my grasp. By now I was too upset to really look for anything, but I went up and down the aisle, looking at what we had.

'I just bought the computer,' she said again, as if that increased the likelihood of our having the little screw sleeves.

'Well, then you should call Apple again,' I said. 'If it's under warranty, they'll fix it. They'll come to your house and fix it. You don't want to start fiddling with it yourself. You might violate the warranty.'

'But all I want,' she said, 'are the little things the screws go into. Do you have them, or not?'

I said I didn't know.

'Is there anyone in the store who might know?' she said, and now her voice was dripping with sarcasm.

I said I didn't know that, either, but that she was free also to ask another salesman. 'We're in the red shirts.'

So she stalked off, and the man who had been rolling his eyes at her moved in. He too wanted a monitor cable and was not sure which. I told him he'd have to look. He'd brought in the cable to which he wanted it to connect. 'That was smart,' I said, but I still couldn't tell just by looking at the packages which cable he wanted. I kept thinking, *I'm failing to make a two-thousand-dollar sale. These cables probably cost nineteen dollars, and I won't get credit for them anyway.* 'You're just as likely to find it as I am,' I said. He didn't like this. Since I'd lost his goodwill, I decided to cut my losses. I scooted out of the aisle and got the carriage and brought it back to the Mac section. My precious customer was nowhere to be seen. So I parked the carriage off to the side of the section. She showed up a few minutes later with a question about software, and I started gushing apologies about having been gone for so long. 'Oh, it's all right,' she said, 'I already bought the computer. I've been taken care of.'

The closer Christmas got, the more exciting the job was, and the worse the customers. The most trying cases were often the people who came right up to you with something like 'I've got the money here' or 'Let's just do it.'

It was snowing lightly at about ten A.M. on Saturday, December 16, when a garden-variety yuppie appeared with two kids in tow.

The morning had been slow. I was enjoying the carols, which were piped over the P.A. 'Deck the halls with boughs of holly . . .' The customer in question didn't look like me, but he was certainly a member of my economic cohort, wearing granny glasses, chinos, and a plaid shirt. I'd made the mistake of straying away from the Mac section, and that's where he caught me. He came right up to me, as if he were going to hand me a cocktail or a football. 'Let's do it,' he said.

'OK,' I said.

Central Park Computer had exactly the same computer we were selling but for two hundred dollars less, he told me, and he had the advertisement to prove it. 'Why is that?' he wanted to know. So I shrugged sadly. 'I don't know,' I said. 'Maybe it isn't exactly the same. In any case, we don't try to match their prices.'

'It's just exactly the same,' he said, waving the advertisement in my face, but not, incidentally, giving me time to read the specs.

'I think we're a better store,' I said.

'How much better can you be?' he said. 'Two hundred dollars better?'

'I don't know, maybe not,' I said.

'I should say not,' he said.

I looked around to make sure there wasn't a manager within hearing. 'Well, then maybe you'd better go buy from them,' I said in a harsh whisper. I thought recommending another store under any circumstances might have been a fireable offense.

In any case, Granny Glasses didn't take me up on it. 'I'd rather buy it from you,' he said.

'It's possible that we don't even have this machine,' I said. 'Before we go any further, I'd better check stock.'

Then I started to walk around the floor, looking for the PC he wanted. The Mac product line I had by heart, but not so the PCs. He followed me. 'You're not very good at this, are you?' he asked. I shrugged and kept walking. 'Wouldn't it be simpler if you knew where all the machines were?' he asked.

It wasn't at all unusual for a customer to expect a salesman to have an encyclopedic knowledge of the store and of computer technology. In the old days, when PCs first hit the general market, they were sold by computer boutiques, stores operated by people who did know the equipment and who had the time and background to help with technical problems. Everything was marked up by 20 per cent. By 1995 most of the little stores had gone under, the markup was gone, and so were the expert salesmen. The customers either didn't know about, or simply hadn't accepted, this change.

So there I was, walking up and down the aisles, checking boxes, with this man-hornet behind me. The machine Granny Glasses wanted had sixteen megs of RAM. I knew that there were suddenly a number of applications that either required or recommended sixteen megs of RAM, and that consequently those computers were going fast.

'You don't have to find it,' he said, 'because we need to settle on the price. They have this exact machine at Central Park Computer for two hundred dollars less.'

'The trouble is, I'm not even sure we have it,' I said. 'If I were in your position, I'd buy it from them.'

'Well, frankly,' he said, 'Central Park Computer is closed today. So I want to know what you can do for me.'

I said that if he was really serious, and if I could find the computer in our database, I would make up a sales form, bring it to a manager, and ask what the best possible price was. But really, I should probably check first, make sure we had the computer.

'If it's in your database, doesn't that mean you have one?'

'Not necessarily.'

'What kind of place is this?'

I shrugged again.

'Let's just see what you can do for me,' he said. 'I'll be in the store. But I want to do this. And I want to do it now. Today!'

So off he went with the kids, and I wrestled with the software. Meanwhile the Mac section was full of bewildered people, looking for a salesman. I had to do this. The guy was definitely capable of filing a complaint.

I got a sales form filled out. I tracked the customer down and asked if I could see the advertisement and show it to a manager. He said, 'No. Just tell him that the computer is available for two hundred dollars less than you're asking.' So I headed off to get a manager. Attracting a manager's attention was never easy. Attracting a manager's attention on a Saturday morning was like trying to get an autograph from a movie star. You had to stand in a crowd and wave your hands over your head. Finally, I had my turn with a manager. I said, 'I've got a guy who says he can get this for two hundred dollars less at Central Park Computer.' So the manager said, 'We don't honor Central Park Computer's offers.' I said, 'I know that. I told him that. But he wants to know what we can do for him on this computer.' I gave the manager the specs of the computer in question.

The manager went to a terminal and began to type. (Managers had a code that allowed them to see what the store had actually paid for a unit, and so to figure out precisely what price it made sense to sell it at.)

'What does he want?' the manager asked me when he'd gotten the unit up on the screen.

'Two hundred dollars off,' I said.

'No way,' said the manager. 'We don't have any room at all. Tell him to buy it for the price it's listed at. Tell him we'll give him a break on the ESP.'

So I went back to Granny Glasses and said, 'My manager says we don't have any room. We'll give you a break on the ESP.'

'Wait a minute,' he said. 'You mean you're not authorized to give me any breaks? You mean you have to ask your manager to lower the price for you?'

I said that was right.

'So why don't I just skip a step and go straight to the manager?' he asked. I said, 'You could skip a step and go right to the manager, if you wanted.'

So then he nodded, grabbed his kids, and left the store.

I'd forgotten about him, and was talking with another customer, when Granny Glasses reappeared. 'Let's do it,' he said. So I said, 'You want that computer?' He nodded. 'You want it at the price we're offering?' He said, 'No, I've got an ad here from the Wiz. Says they have that exact machine for three hundred dollars less.'

I said that I had already spoken with the manager, who'd told me that they had no room on the price. 'He said we can't go down on that price.'

'You do recognize the Wiz as a legitimate competitor?'

'Yes, we do. But he says we can't go down on that price.'

'That's where you're wrong,' he said. 'He didn't know about this advertisement.'

'No,' I agreed, 'he didn't.'

'So ask him again.'

'All right,' I said, 'but give me the advertisement.'

So I took the advertisement and glanced at it. It did look like the same computer. I hunted down the manager I'd talked to earlier. 'This that same jerk?' he asked when I got my turn. I nodded. He scowled at me. Then he looked at the advertisement. 'That's without the monitor,' he said. 'Tell him if he buys the ESP, we'll give him a good price.'

So I went back to the man in the granny glasses. 'He said this is without the monitor,' I told him, and gave him back the advertisement.

'Now you're wrong!' said the customer, and he was angry. 'It's not without the monitor.'

'OK, OK,' I said, 'I don't know if it has the monitor or not, but I do know that my manager is not going to reduce the price on this computer, assuming we have one. Buy it from the Wiz.'

'I want to buy it from you, now.'

'You don't want to save three hundred dollars.'

'Well, frankly,' he said, 'the Wiz is out of stock.'

'OK,' I said.

'What about upgrading me to a seventeen-inch monitor?'

'I can't do that.'

'Why not?'

'That's a big upgrade.'

'Shouldn't you go ask the manager?'

'No, I shouldn't go ask my manager,' I said.

'All right,' he said, 'let's do it.'

I couldn't believe my ears. 'You want to buy that same computer?'

'Yup.'

'At our price?'

'No, I don't want to,' he said, and smiled at me as if this had all
been great fun, 'but I will.'

'OK,' I said. 'Now let's see if we have one.' And of course we
didn't, nor did we have a comparable machine. Outside of Packard
Bell (Packard Bell had a bad reputation that year) we had nothing
with sixteen megs. Now he was furious. 'You fucked up,' he said.

I said I was sorry.

'I want to speak to a manager,' he said.

'OK,' I said.

'Tell me who's a manager,' he said.

So I pointed over to the manager I had tracked down twice on
his behalf. 'That guy's a manager,' I said.

'All right,' the customer said. 'And what's your name?' So I stood
still and let him read my name off my chest while he wrote it down
on the copy he had of the Wiz advertisement. Then he left.

By this time I was trembling with suppressed rage. A large,
phlegmatic man came up and patted me on the shoulder. 'Are you
busy?' he asked. I said no, and wagged my head. 'I'd like to buy this
computer,' he said. He pointed to a box. I nodded. I got out a G
ticket and tried to write up the serial number, but I found that my
hand was trembling so violently that I couldn't write.

So the customer took the pen from my hand and wrote the serial
number down himself. By then I was sufficiently composed to
record the SKU and his name and address.

I never heard from the manager. I never saw Granny Glasses
again.

The action late on a Saturday afternoon was feverish, and the level of ignorance was high on both sides of many transactions. One man came in and asked for a word processor. 'You mean the software?'

'I don't know.'

'You have a computer?'

'No.'

'So then you need to buy a computer first, and then get the word processor. Or else you could buy a typewriter.'

'I don't want to buy a typewriter. I don't want to buy a computer. I just want a word processor.'

We had nothing of the kind for sale.

At one point a gnarled older man, who looked as if he'd spent his life as a manual laborer, popped out of the modem aisle. He was wearing work clothes still dusted with what looked like cement. He seemed to have memorized his question, which was both technical and specific. Something about opening the case to his desktop and installing a modem. Nothing I would attempt myself.

I had no idea.

He repeated the question. I still had no idea. 'Read the boxes the modems come in,' I said. Then he reached forward, grabbed me by the collar, and twisted my red polo shirt angrily in his hand. 'You are the worst salesman!' he said, and there was real anguish in his voice.

I stood there with a blank look on my face. Completely relaxed, mimicking a hiker in the mouth of a bear. The man let go and walked off.

I understood his unhappiness. But I wondered if he would have been willing to go to a store with qualified sales personnel and pay 20 per cent more.

Since I was in White Plains, former colleagues and acquaintances showed up from time to time. Those who didn't know about the jobs book seemed to accept my downward mobility with wonderful equanimity. 'Oh, so you're into this now,' said a woman who had been a editor with me at the *Reader's Digest*. I can't know, but I thought from the way she worked her face that she was thinking, *Ben never was all that smart.*

She bought a Macintosh Performa for her daughter, telling the girl that I was a nice man. (*Nice* in our culture is often code for 'sap'.) I sold another Performa to a man who had taken a picture of me and my Labrador retriever when my first novel was published. He recognized my name when I was making up the quote for his purchases on the terminal in the Mac section. He had his daughter with him, seated in one of the grocery cart-like carriages.

He said he was disappointed in the picture of me because the dog came out solid black without any of its features visible. I said I thought it was a fine picture. I also remembered that he'd been having trouble with his contact lenses that day. I think he may have been keeping one or both of them in the bottom of a cup he'd taken from a deli. He was surprised and pleased that my recollections of him were so complete.

None of this manifested itself in special treatment for the novelist manqué. The photographer carried an advertisement from another store, which entitled him to a lower price on the printer. I had to hunt up a manager to get this confirmed. The photog was reluctant to buy the service plan. This was one of my first closings, and Bill tried to help. My colleague explained that while Apple provided one-year coverage (dial 1–800 SOS Apple and drop the *e*), the ESP is better, because the line isn't busy. The photographer said he might buy the ESP, but he had to call his wife first. He went out into the store entrance to do this. When he returned, he said he was going to stick with Apple. My mentor tried one last time. 'The line will be busy,' he said. 'No, it won't,' said the photographer. 'I just called them. They picked right up.' Then we all smiled. I felt like I'd just been made to chug a bottle of bitter cough medicine. And yet he chatted amiably with me about his daughter while I helped him out to the car with the Performa. I said she was beautiful, and she was beautiful. He agreed. 'I tell people she's the best thing I've done,' he said. I nodded. 'Maybe I'll take your picture when your next novel comes out,' he said.

The Mac section was directly behind the software section and the woman in charge of software seemed to have a cold the entire time we worked together. She thought I was naive. Once I told her that when I was trying to sell the ESP, I'd acknowledge that most consumer magazines were against it, before I argued about how good it was.

'Don't you ever give a customer ammunition like that,' she said. 'Get caught saying anything negative about a product or service, and you'll be looking for a job so fast.'

Which made me not like her, but it also made me wonder how smart it was for me to go around telling everybody what a bad writer I am.

One evening, I was summoned to the software aisle by a young woman with her arms full of boxes. She said she was buying a whole new system and wanted to know which programs to get with it.

So I asked her which computer she was buying. She told me. I knew that this particular computer came with a hard disk loaded with free software.

I told her she should wait until she'd mastered the software she already had before she bought more. I suggested she might want to buy a word processor but that otherwise the machine was going to come well-equipped. I looked at the boxes she had. I picked out the ones I knew duplicated those already installed. She didn't seem to welcome this advice, but she surrendered the software and thanked me for my integrity. I put the software back in the displays from which it had been taken.

That night at eleven P.M., when we were cleaning up the store, I came upon another pile of software, almost identical to the one I'd relieved this woman of. Apparently, she'd again gathered up the boxes I had separated her from and then put them all back down in a heap. When the software manager came by, I complained. 'I told this woman she probably didn't need heaps of software if she was buying a new computer with a load of software in it. It was her first computer. And I helped her put the stuff back. Now she's obviously gathered it all up again and put it down in a different part of the store so that I have to put it away a second time.'

'That's awful,' the software manager said, and I thought I was going to get some sympathy at last. 'Never ever tell anybody not to buy anything. Not if you want to keep your job.'

But this hostility was quite uncharacteristic. Mostly we got along. Mostly we got along famously.

There were customers who sensed or knew how to treat a salesperson with dignity. A kindly speech therapist from Rockland came in for a long talk, left the store without buying anything, but then came back and sought me out. After I'd loaded the computer into the back of his car and put the printer on the front passenger seat, he thrust ten dollars into my hand. I was flushed with thankfulness at first, and then shame. I like to think of myself as a generous tipper. But apparently I also like to think of myself as the one who tips.

When I met H. Cabot Lodge, he'd already picked out the Performa he wanted. He had it in a carriage. I asked if I could help him. He asked if it would help me to help him. I said yes; he said OK. So I took down his statistics, pausing at the name. He lived in Bedford. I was dying to tell him that my father was a famous writer, my wife a film critic for *The New York Times*. Instead I said that I'd been driving through Bedford that weekend and saw a lot of cars parked outside the movie theater, which was playing *Nixon*. 'My wife said that's because it's Bedford,' I told him. 'Are there still a lot of Nixon supporters in Bedford?'

H. Cabot said he'd like to see the movie. 'My grandfather ran for office with Nixon,' he said. 'My grandmother couldn't bear him.'

Writing my own name on the G ticket, I said, 'I also have a famous name.' H. Cabot Lodge didn't even blink. On the other hand, he was genuinely courteous throughout, and when I left him at the register, he called me Ben in a way that made me feel that I had been honored rather than sullied.

One dear woman who'd heard me give a reading from one of my two published novels came in with a question about modems, and then looked into my face. 'You're Ben Cheever. You're a writer. You don't belong here.'

'Yes, I do,' I said. But I wanted to cover her with kisses.

Christmas Eve was the best, of course. People actually were buying, although we were almost completely out of machines with sufficient megs of RAM. During hasty Diet Cokes in the canteen, I'd had a long conversation with another salesman with whom I'd become friendly. He was a big white guy who had another job, sold computers for extra cash. He'd been in and out of retail for years. I said it was terrible that so few of the machines had sufficient RAM. 'They come in here wanting to buy. I tell them it's insane to buy anything with less than eight megs of RAM. Really they should go sixteen. Then they ask what we have with sixteen megs of RAM. I show them the Packard Bell. They don't want the Packard Bell. What else do we have with sixteen megs? Nothing. I've spoiled Christmas.'

'Let them buy,' he said.

'What do you mean?'

'Just don't get into it about the RAM. They can always upgrade. You're giving them too much information.'

I wasn't sure he was right. I liked my new friend, though. We traded jokes. Then we talked about first marriages, how bad – and second ones, how surprisingly good. 'It's embarrassing to admit,' I told him, 'but I love my wife. I've got a good deal.' He said, 'Me too.' He told me that since it was Christmas Eve, his wife was going to pick him up. 'I want you to meet her,' he said. So when they were closing up the store, I went up to the front door. At first I didn't see anyone outside. Then I saw that there was a gorgeous black woman out there waiting for somebody.

'I'm Ben,' I said, and shook her hand. 'I've heard a lot about you.'

'I've heard a lot about you too,' she said.

'He's a good husband,' I said.

'He's a good salesman,' she said.

'Did you get the warranty?' I asked, and she laughed.

A couple of days into the New Year, I finally got my official polo shirt. I also had my interview with the man in charge of personnel. I said how much I loved the job. I did love the job. 'But you hate the customers, right?' my manager said. I agreed that I hated the customers. 'Why do I hate the customers?' I asked. 'It's because it's Westchester,' he said, 'and they're all rich. People who have money are always assholes.'

Modeling: A Very Handsome Man

THE AD COPY THAT FIRST CAUGHT MY EYE WAS IN THE
Pennysaver and actually began with the question 'Has anyone ever
said you should model?' The classified I responded to was in the
Tarrytown Daily News, then our local daily.

'Models/Actors Earn top $$' was the heading: 'N.Y.'s leading
int'l Model Scout featured in Glamour & Cosmo specializes in
developing and promoting new talent for print, video, commercial
& runway, needed for placement in N.Y., L.A., Paris & Tokyo. No
experience necessary. Please call: MODEL U.' And then there was
a phone number.

That's how I wound up at Model U's Manhattan offices. The
building needed a paint job, and the carpeting on the stairs was badly
worn, but I was greeted eagerly enough, given a form to fill out, and
a place to sit while I wrote. If you're a woman, you have to put down
your bust, waist, and hip measurements. If you're a man – and I'm
one of those – they only want your suit size and inseam. From where
I sat, I could see a desk. There was a very unprepossessing young man
working there. He was thin and had extremely short hair. Was this a
new fashion, or lice? With him was a woman. Quite an attractive
woman. They were both smoking cigarettes.

When I'd finished the form, another woman appeared, another
beautiful woman, and led me to a desk. Let's call her Samantha
Slim. Sam and her sister (I'll call her Billie) had started the agency.
Samatha seemed tired. She lit up a cigarette and asked why I was
considering modeling. I had a copy of the ad with me. I held it up.
"'Earn top dollars,'" I quoted. "'No experience necessary.'"

Samantha smiled weakly. 'Well, it's not that simple,' she said.

I said, 'I know. Or rather, I had guessed.'

Then she got out an album with pictures of gorgeous people in it. She said that she could send me to a photographer and a stylist. She said that for $250 they'd fix me up and then take pictures. For another fifty dollars, I'd have an oversized postcard made up. The card would be a sort of triptych, with me in three poses, three different outfits. Me in a tuxedo, me in jeans and paddling in a canoe, me in a Speedo bathing suit. She showed me a series of postcards with people in them. Handsome men, fetching women. I didn't look anything like the people she showed me. After my triptych had been finished, she said, it would be sent out. 'And probably you'll get called for auditions.'

I was leaning forward at this point. Entranced. I could smell her scent in the air between us. 'But there are no guarantees,' she said. 'You might not be hired at all.'

'Thank you,' I said, 'for your honesty.'

Samantha bowed her head slightly. 'I hate to have people mad at me,' she said.

I nodded. A couple of beats went by. 'I think I'll wait on this,' I said. Then Samantha took a long drag on her cigarette. 'You're a very handsome man,' she said. 'Otherwise you'd, like, be out the door.'

Times like this you wish you still smoked. I could have had a cigarette. Savored the moment. Instead I had to say something, get out. I stood up. I said I'd wait − but leaving the agency, I was walking on air. I'd had a beautiful woman tell me that I was 'a very handsome man'.

Of course I suspected her motives. I toyed with the idea of calling up my ugliest friend, sending him in for an interview. I wondered what Samantha would say to someone truly ugly.

Still, I was high as a kite. But also I could see the bankruptcy of my entire life plan.

When I was seven years old, I fell hopelessly in love with my beautiful mother. She was in love with my father. He was a writer.

So naturally I concluded that the way to get a beautiful woman to be in love with you was to be a writer. Of course I'd have to learn to read first. Then to type. Then write stories. I'd type stories, send them out into the world, and if I was extremely lucky, one of them would be published. Then a beautiful woman grazing out on the veldt somewhere would be deeply moved. Slain by the force and precision of my prose.

I therefore planned to be an artist, a choice for which I was uniquely ill-equipped. Artists – people like my father – are mavericks, brilliant and with a clear individual moral identity. I was quite an ordinary child. A little melancholic, perhaps, but really I just wanted to get along, fit in with the crowd. Plus, I was a very slow reader. I couldn't spell.

In any event, it took me decades to get published. I worked at newspapers and a magazine, spent my weekends sending out precious little stories. These were bluntly rejected, etching a deep line of bitterness in what might otherwise have been a contented man.

The modeling agency showed me what an ass I'd been. If I had wanted to meet beautiful women then, I should have gone to work at a modeling agency. I wouldn't have had to have my stories rejected. I could have smoked at work. I wouldn't even have had to learn to read. I would have been there in an office, among dozens of gorgeous women. They would have just loved an ordinary guy like the one I used to be.

Was it too late? Did Samantha really think I was 'a very handsome man'? Should I cough up three hundred dollars? But then I didn't look anything like the people in those pictures.

Back home in the suburbs, I studied the literature I'd been given. Billie had 'launched the careers of many superstar models including Kathy Ireland and Andie MacDowell.' Was Samantha going to catch up with her sister by launching me?

A week later I got a postcard:

It was a pleasure meeting with you today. As discussed I feel you have strong potential to work in the modeling industry, and I would be very interested in working with you. Give me a call when you're ready to get started, or if you merely have any questions. Looking forward to hearing from you.

And it was signed 'Sam.'

Sure, the note was stiff, but probably Samantha wasn't a natural writer. I pictured her alone in the office at night, smoking, typing out the message with one finger.

A week later I got a second copy of the same postcard. The exact same postcard.

Then I got the letter:

Within the last few months, you were in to see us and we suggested that you consider scheduling a testshoot with a leading fashion photography team so you can be marketed to the major agencies. We quoted you a price of over $300. Like you, many people who we are interested in working with have been unable to schedule a testshoot because of the cost. . . . We have appealed to the studio team, the creative staff of photographers, the hair and makeup people, and the stylists to reduce their rates, so we can offer **you** a substantial savings.

As a 'SPRING BREAK SPECIAL,' they are reducing the price of the regular Package, for 8 weeks only, to select individuals, at $225 + tax − a tremendous savings. . . .

This letter wasn't even signed.

Nobody Beats the Wiz: 'What do people fear more than death?'

WHEN I WAS TRAINING FOR A JOB AT NOBODY BEATS THE Wiz, I went one evening to see my wife participate in a panel discussion at the 92nd Street Y. Leonard Lopate moderated, and the panel's topic was 'The Critics and the Criticized'. The director Arthur Penn (*Bonnie and Clyde, Little Big Man*) was also on the panel and seemed notable for having missed the part in his artistic development where one learns arrogance and bad manners. From the audience, I could see Penn cheerfully deprecating himself and pouring everybody's water. The screenwriter Lorenzo Semple Jr. brought up a quotation from one of Janet's reviews, which he recited as an example of what he didn't like in critics. He was witty, but his voice was distorted by anger. He wouldn't sit up straight, nor would he pull his chair into the table.

After the last question from the audience, there was a rush for the stage. One of the people who came up had seen Janet on another panel. 'That was a great night for film,' he said. Then he pumped his arm in the air. He was wearing a wash-and-wear shirt buttoned to the throat. No necktie. 'I love *Taxi Driver*,' he said. 'What a great movie! What a greeeaat movie!'

After most of the crowd and some of the panelists had departed, Lopate suggested that the rest of us go out for a drink. By this time a stranger had attached himself to Janet. He was wearing a leather jacket, scarf, and black jeans. Everything torn. He had his face about two and a half inches away from hers. I heard him say that he was an actor. I believe he had a screenplay with him. 'I'm just trying to talk to Mizz Maselin,' he said when somebody suggested that he might not join us for a drink.

Lopate was accompanied by a female producer who remembered me from the time I was on his radio show for one of my novels. 'I was the person who read the book,' she said. She was strikingly attractive, with hair just streaking gray. Remember when gray hair meant a woman was old? Now gray hair is apt to be a sign of vitality. The producer had a pleasant boyfriend; he had cigarettes. As a backsliding former smoker I was enjoying myself immensely, walking along the sidewalk, talking and smoking, but I was worried about Janet. The actor didn't seem to be quieting down at all. I expressed my concern. The producer said that if I wanted, she could help Janet. 'Could you?' I asked. 'That's my job,' she said. So she sailed up to the actor, and words were exchanged. The next thing I knew, the actor had backed away and was violently giving both women the finger. 'You don't need to diss me,' he said, 'I only wanted to talk to Mizz Maselin.' Lopate interjected himself. Then I introduced myself to the actor as Janet's husband. We shook hands. I seem to have said something about how we were all human beings.

At this point it was decided that maybe a drink wasn't such a grand idea, and we all headed off in different directions.

I mention this only because the next day, when I showed up for class at the Nobody Beats the Wiz building at Thirty-first Street and Sixth Avenue, I saw the same actor. I looked away immediately and afterwards never allowed eye contact. I heard him ask if they were accepting applications. He and I got in the elevator together. I kept my face to the wall. Since I was already in class, and he was just applying for a job, we would head off in different directions when we got out of the elevator. I was terrified he'd recognize me before we reached our floors. He didn't. Nor did I ever see him again.

Status changes the way we see. And yet status changes quickly, and can be willfully disguised. When I first started the process of applying for the Wiz job at a different store in Scarsdale, New York, the entrance through which I walked was being swept furiously with a push broom by a man with black hair to his shoulders. I later learned that he was the manager of the entire store and presumably took down a fabulous salary, since Scarsdale was always among the top three for volume in a chain which then had fifty retail units.

I was beginning to get some idea of how little I was actually worth on the open market. New to me still, though, was the promise of riches.

I remember one evening when a man in his late fifties came and stopped at the stairs leading down into Home Office, the Wiz department where I ended up. He stood there like a bull elephant on a ridge, apparently expecting to be admired. A colleague grabbed my arm, pointed up at the stranger. 'He earned a hundred and fifty thousand dollars last year,' I was told in a hushed whisper.

'Selling what?' I whispered back.

'Home theatres.'

But I'm getting ahead of myself. The sensation I remember most vividly the day I moved past the manager with the push broom and into the bowels of the Scarsdale branch was of having my pupils dilate violently. The surfaces in the building were covered with black velvet, or something designed to look like black velvet. The lighting was markedly subdued, as if this were a cave, or the lair of a college student and follower of the Grateful Dead.

I found a woman in a dark business suit with a cell phone in one hand and a sheaf of papers in the other. When she got off the phone, I gave her my résumé.

'You wrote two novels?' she asked.

'Yes.'

'What were they?'

'You won't have heard of them. I'm not John Grisham.'

'No,' she said. 'What were they about? I might have heard.'

''Bout life,' I said, and shrugged.

'All right, then,' she said, losing interest. 'What's the difference between SVGA and VGS?'

'I don't know.'

'If you're talking about a computer,' she asked, without giving me a chance to recover, 'what's a high-speed bus?'

'Some computers have them, and some don't,' I said. 'I think the better ones have them.'

'What can we can do with a person who doesn't even know the fundamentals?' she said, and sighed.

I bristled. I told her I'd already sold computers for CompUSA. 'I can answer the questions asked by nine out of ten customers,' I said.

She backed away into the shadows. Moments later a young man appeared, also in a dark business suit, also with a cell phone. I was given twenty minutes in which to take a multiple-choice test. Then I was presented with a series of forms to fill out, including a schedule. On a sheet titled 'Days and Hours You Can Work' I filled in a twenty-hour week with both Saturday and Sunday left blank.

The man in the suit took my papers away, then returned and said that my projected schedule wasn't going to work.

'But these are the hours I want,' I said.

He went away into the darkness. When he returned, he said that in order to qualify for the special eight-day training program, I needed to put down that I planned to be available for a forty-hour week. Once I was out of training, he said, I could cut the job down to twenty hours a week. I'd need to work the precise schedule out with my manager.

I nodded dumbly. Then he filled out a fresh sheet, writing, 'Open' for the schedule. And in the section titled 'Days and Hours When You Are Unable to Work (Please provide reasons)' he wrote, 'None'.

I signed this along with several other forms. In one I promised to show up fifteen minutes early for each shift and not to sign out until the shift was over. I also vowed not to wear jeans or sneakers.

As the man who had interviewed and tested me gathered up my papers, he was given a form filled out by another applicant. 'Souflé!' he exclaimed loudly. 'I'm not talking with anybody named Souflé. What kind of name is that?'

Walking out of the building, I could hear the woman with the cell phone catechizing a new prospect: 'What's the difference between SVGA and VGS?' Then from the darkness, I heard a faint, uncertain voice intensely reminiscent of my own. 'I don't know,' it said.

Which must not have mattered frightfully, because I at least was given an appointment for a urine test, and enrolled in the coveted eight-day training program.

My reluctance to work weekends and holidays was related to the fact that this book had not yet been sold. The proposal, which I had expected to have publishers fighting over like dogs over a steak sandwich, had been turned down repeatedly. I'd transformed myself from an author who couldn't get his third novel published into a hack who also couldn't sell nonfiction, and was spoiling his family life by holding a variety of humiliating and low-paying jobs that took him away from home on weekends and holidays. I figured I'd soldier on, but if possible, I'd contain the time I spent working so that I could still be of some use to my wife and children, the only people who seemed truly interested in my services.

So a couple of weeks after my interview, I showed up for classes, which were held on the fourth floor of the Wiz store at Thirty-first Street and Sixth Avenue in Manhattan. 'Gentlemen must wear a suit, or sport jacket with tie, and dress slacks at all times,' my form had said.

In place of a sport jacket, many of the other students had worn leather jackets. I, of course, was bibbed and tuckered, wearing a blue blazer and button-down shirt. The room in which we met had a man at a desk in front. The job candidates collected in chairs facing him. The man at the front of the room had me down as 'Ben Cheves'. I was given a time card and taught how to swipe in. There were about twenty of us; more than half of the men wore pagers. A third of the students were women. I was in my mid-forties at the time, and a good fifteen years older than everybody else in the class.

The room was freshly painted, with posters on the wall of Bruce Springsteen, Darth Vader, and a Sports Sony Walkman. There was a Poland Springs water dispenser. Shortly after I arrived, another employee showed up for whom they didn't have a time card. 'You're fucked,' he was told cheerfully, but he sat with us and waited.

When the instructor appeared, we followed him into another, larger room, with chairs, tables, and a green blackboard. There were windows all along one wall. I learned that most of the women would be in the group briefly and then go on to specialized schooling as cashiers. Some of the men would also drop out early, since they were preparing to work in the stockroom. Only the sales counselors, the RAF of the Wiz, would be together for the full eight days.

Our instructor was a slender man of indeterminate age with bright eyes and a weak chin. He seemed keen on the program, but he also carried an aura of sorrow. He was enthusiastic about the Wiz, but I thought I could tell that he'd been enthusiastic about other employers in the past. Other, different employers. Ultimately it was this sorrow, and an irony I suspected but couldn't exactly locate, that made his positive attitude so difficult to resist.

'Welcome to Nobody Beats the Wiz, new-hire training,' he told us after everybody found a seat. 'Benefits start after three months. After two months you're entitled to ten per cent off on Wiz merchandise.

'Two things we ask you to do,' he said, and turned to write on the board:

1. Take responsibility
2. Have fun

'You need to get seventy per cent to pass,' he said. 'I haven't lost anybody yet. The thought of firing anybody makes me break out.'

Ask questions, he told us. 'The only question that's stupid,' he said, 'is the one that doesn't get asked.

'Your training is important, because *you* are important. Because you're going to come in contact with the most valuable people at the Wiz: our customers.'

He then passed around a sheet which had the words *Icebreaker* at the top followed by some statements. We were to sign our names next to the statements that applied to us. These included:

Has visited Niagara Falls
Owns an exotic pet
Views Rush Limbaugh
Knows what the acronym 'SNAFU' stands for
Worked as a commissioned salesperson

We all scribbled away dutifully and then handed the form up to the front of the room.

Reading from it, the teacher told us that one man had a fruit bat, one woman owned a boa constrictor, and another man had a snake.

'What sort of snake?' he was asked.

'Just a regular snake,' he said.

I got my name mentioned for having known what *SNAFU* stood for: 'Situation Normal. All Fucked Up.'

The instructor wanted to know if I'd been in the military.

I said that no, I had not.

I was sitting immediately to the right of a black kid in his late teens or early twenties. After I'd admitted missing military service, he tapped me on the shoulder. 'But you do watch Rush Limbaugh?' he asked.

'No.'

'You look like you'd watch him for sure,' he said then, but without any edge to it.

'Thanks,' I said, but without any edge to it.

Then the teacher, I'll call him Paul, asked which of us spoke a second language. Some hands went up. 'English counts,' he said, which got a laugh. 'But, seriously, you all speak a second language,' he said. 'We all speak the language of the body.'

The first thing we had to learn was the Wiz credo. The

mnemonic acronym for it was ICER. The credo: Integrity, Customer, Excellence, and Respect.

> Integrity: To be totally honest with our customer, fellow workers, company, and yourself. Customer: To do whatever it takes to satisfy our customer. Excellence: To strive for excellence in everything we do. Respect: To respect our customer, fellow workers, company, and yourself. Give respect, and you will receive it in return.

Paul told us the Wiz was spending three thousand dollars on each of us for schooling. He said that philosophy was always important. When he'd worked at Neiman-Marcus, everybody had had to read *Minding the Store* by Stanley Marcus.

I asked if there was a book Wiz employees needed to read. Not really, he said. There would be texts handed out at the end of the day. And a training film called *The Wizard of Oz*, he said. I took this to be a joke.

He showed us how the initials *ICER* had been worked into the logo which was etched or painted at several places on the fourth floor.

We learned that the company had started in 1976 with a single store on Fulton Street in Brooklyn. Nobody Beats the Wiz was founded by Norman Jemal. Apparently, Norman Jemal's favorite Broadway show had been *The Wiz*. Norman had owned a construction company called Namron. *Namron* was Norman spelled backwards. Norman had since died, but the CEO of the Wiz was a man named Lawrence Jemal. The executive vice president was named Marvin Jemal. Stephen Jemal was head of Namron, which did all Wiz construction.

Paul handed out a sheet titled 'Company Hierarchy'. He told us the Jemals were 'good people'. He said we should remember how to spell their names. When this got a titter, he said, 'It will be on the final.'

This was in the early spring of 1996, and we were told that the

Wiz was the largest regional home-electronics chain in the United States of America. 'The goal of the company is to become a nationwide retailer,' Paul told us.

Paul wrote '*FUD*' on the board. Then he wrote, 'Fears, Uncertainties, Doubts'. He told us that we must learn how to deal with our customers' FUDs.

The reason nobody beats the Wiz, we were told, is that we don't let them. If a customer has proof that a recognized competitor has a lower price, the salesperson should take the Wiz price, subtract the competitor's price from it, and multiply the difference by 25 per cent, or divide it by four. Then add a dollar. Subtract that total from the competitor's price, and that's the price you sell at.

So if the Wiz was selling something for one hundred dollars and a customer produced proof that a recognized competitor was selling it for ninety, then the customer could buy the product from the Wiz for $86.50.

We were told that there was a thirty-three-day price guarantee, and for that time customers were entitled to a refund, except for camcorders, which must be returned within five days. 'Why?' Paul asked us.

Nobody knew.

'Vacations ordinarily last seven days,' he told us. People would film their vacation, then return the camera. TVs with a screen larger than thirty inches also could not be returned. Why? Because customers were regularly buying huge projection-screen TVs and returning them on Super Bowl Monday with the rings from beer cans still on the housing, potato-chip crumbs in the speaker fabric.

'Not that we should criticize customers, ever,' Paul said. Nor should we disparage the competition. 'I refer to them as "the enemy",' Paul said, and smiled, 'but we shouldn't ever bad-mouth them to a customer.' Another appliance chain called Tops had put up Wiz and P. C. Richards logos in their toilets, and the Wiz and P. C. Richards sued them. The case was settled out of court for twenty-five thousand dollars, Paul told us, which was given to charity.

Our role as employees could not be overestimated, Paul said. Word of mouth was a vital element in the business. Studies had shown that a satisfied customer tells three other people about his experience. A dissatisfied customer tells ten to twenty people.

'Forget the Golden Rule,' Paul told us. 'Learn instead the Platinum Rule: "Do unto others as they would have you do unto them".'

A store loses 15 per cent of customers over a year. One per cent die. We couldn't do anything about them, but 58 per cent of those lost attribute their change to poor customer service.

We would be tested on the Five Cs of customer service. These were:

1. Caring
2. Considerate
3. Creative
4. Committed
5. Courteous

For those of us who spoke Spanish, the second letter of words two, three, and four provided a useful mnemonic: *oro*, the Spanish word for 'gold'. We could remember it by using the phrase 'The customer is gold to me'.

We had fifteen-minute break, and I went out of the building with the young black man who had taken me for a Limbaugh fan, a dittohead. He had his hair laid flat against his head in cornrows. I thought that this might be an expression of hostility, or at least of an unwillingness to mingle with white folk, but he seemed happy to speak with me. He had a bright, open face. He was trying for a job in the stockroom, he told me, and I automatically felt a little smarter than he was. Employees in the stockroom earned a flat salary, while sale counselors were entitled to commissions.

Paul was out in the street smoking, too. He had his sleeves rolled up and one arm displayed the tattoo 'Jumpmaster'.

He did not boast, but when questioned, he admitted that he had been an army paratrooper. He talked a little about night drops. He told about how he had been specifically warned never to jump a certain way when leaving the helicopter – and so of course he tried it.

'When you're young . . .' he said, and wagged his head.

Going back into the building, I asked him why none of the women were training to be sales counselors. He said that was an interesting question. He said that for some reason, they preferred to be cashiers. When they did become sales counselors, he told me, they often performed well.

I asked him how they selected people for the program. He said they kept out people who didn't speak English, or if 'a guy comes up to me and says, "I sell more drugs than anybody else on the block."'

Back in the classroom, Paul told us that *The Wizard of Oz* could count as a training film because Dorothy could never have made it to Oz without the lion, the tin man, and the scarecrow. Teamwork was essential to Dorothy, he said, and would be essential to us.

He asked us what we thought teamwork was. Nobody seemed certain. 'A team,' he told us, 'is a group of people working together for a common goal.' He said we'd be tested on this.

The requirements for teamwork, he told us, were:

1. Communication
2. Cooperation
3. Consideration
4. Responsibility

To remember, he said, we should think of *co* and *tion* three times, and then *responsibility*.

We were each given stapled textbooks from which to study. These texts should be used for review, we were told. Anything on which we were going to be tested would be covered in class.

Right before we left that evening, Paul played *The Wizard of Oz* for us on a VCR. He made a point of showing us the part in the film where a stagehand kills himself. I saw only shadows, which I was told represented a man climbing a stepladder, putting a noose around his neck, and jumping off.

The next day I showed up early and there was a lot of complaining about all the homework. One of the white students said that when somebody else in his family saw him doing all the paperwork, they figured he must be applying for welfare.

It developed that the one thing we all had in common was a devotion to electronics. Many of us had worked in computer stores before, and we all had systems and gadgets that exceeded any practical need. One of the other 'cadets' had taken the one-thousand-dollar course whose classified I'd been ogling. The course promised to teach students to 'build a computer from scratch'. He'd gone to work at CompUSA afterwards as a techie, installing memory upgrades and the like.

He told me that people would buy computers, remove the innards, and then try to return them. There was another cadet from the Manhattan CompUSA. He spoke of a customer who used to come in every day and buy a different computer.

When I asked why anybody would do that, my new friend smiled. 'I guess he just likes computers a lot.'

'So if you have technical know-how, what are you doing here?' I asked the one who had taken the course, and he shrugged.

There was some discussion of the pay plan. As I understood it, we were being paid a lesser wage during training, but when we hit the stores we'd be entitled to a draw of seven dollars an hour. This was against unearned commissions. Our commissions were 1 per cent of sales. If we consistently failed to meet the draw, we'd be fired.

There were rumors of salespeople who had done very well at the Wiz. One of the other cadets had been working at a different computer store where there was no draw. 'So, in other

words, you could get dressed up, go to work – and earn nothing?'
I asked.

'Yup,' I was told.

Then there was talk of commissions at other establishments.
Barney's, I was told, gave the salesperson 40 per cent. 'So if you sell
a guy a shirt for one hundred dollars, you make forty dollars?' I
asked.

'A job at Barney's,' I was told, 'is like winning the lottery.'

When Paul arrived, the chatter stopped. He told us that Lawrence Jemal was in the building. Paul suggested that we might want
to straighten our neckties. I noticed that nobody straightened his
necktie.

That morning we were given our first test. I was sitting next to
the black guy who thought I must watch Rush Limbaugh, the
one who wanted to work in the stockroom. The exam was
multiple choice. Almost immediately my new friend began to
make noises of distress. He rolled his eyes, smacked his forehead
with the back of his hand. I thought, *He's going to fail. He doesn't
even have the ambition to try to be a sales counselor, but he's still going
to wash out.*

I was tempted to lean over and give hints on some of the harder
questions. I was afraid that I'd get caught, though, and I had no
doubt that Paul would throw me out for cheating. I kept my mouth
shut.

These black kids may be nice, I thought, *but they haven't had my
advantages.*

After the morning break, the tests were handed back, but folded,
so that we couldn't see each other's marks, which were written at
the top of the first page. I peeked and saw that I had gotten 98
points out of 100. After my friend had looked at his test, and
screwed up his face with dismay, I reached over with my left hand
and gave him a conciliatory pat on the shoulder. I wanted him to
know that whatever grade he'd gotten on the test, I still considered
him a splendid human being.

First Paul asked the class if anybody had a perfect score, and sure enough, a beautiful young cashier-in-training had gotten 100. Nobody had 99. I had raised my hand when he asked about 98s. Had anyone gotten 97? Several hands shot up, including that of my young stockroom friend, the one I had been so sure would fail.

Ask me today if I'm a racist, and I'll deny it still, but since that morning, I've been a little less passionate in my refutations.

There was a certain amount of product knowledge stirred into the second day of training, but there was also a good deal about body language. When dealing with customers, we were not to put our hands in our pockets. 'If you put your hand in your pocket, you look as if you're concealing something,' we were told.

I remembered reading of a young doctor who had studied at a Boston hospital early in the last century under an administration that insisted that all doctors-in-training sew their pockets closed.

We must listen, Paul told us. Most people don't listen, he said. Studies showed that adults spend 70 per cent of each day in verbal communication. Forty-five per cent of the time, they're listening, he said. 'You do the math.'

People speak at a rate of two hundred words a minutes, think at the rate of two thousand, we were told. So the listeners go on ahead and lose interest. Words account for less than 10 per cent of the message we get across, Paul told us. Not a cheering statistic if you mean to be a writer.

Paul wrote the word *yo* on the chalkboard and showed us with various inflections how that single word could be made to mean:

1. Yes.
2. No.
3. Hello.
4. Hello!
5. Stop that!
6. That's a pretty girl.
7. That's a bad idea.

While we must be acutely aware of the messages our posture, clothing, and tone of voice gave off, we should also be careful never to dismiss customers because of their posture or an unpromising wardrobe, Paul said. He told of a man who had come into the Neiman-Marcus at closing one day, looking like he'd been sleeping in the streets. Just to glance at him, you'd practically expect the guy to ask for a dollar, Paul told us, but instead this individual had gone over to the jewelry display, pulled out twenty-nine one-thousand-dollar bills, and made a purchase.

'Richard Gere shops in our NoHo store all the time. He looks like a hobo.'

Which didn't mean, Paul told us again, that we could be sloppy ourselves. We should be neatly dressed and always equipped with pens, worksheets, measuring tapes, and a generous supply of mints. Bad breath was bad for business, he told us. 'If you stink, you can't sell.'

That afternoon we watched again the section of *The Wizard of Oz* in which the stagehand is supposed to hang himself in the background. I still couldn't see it.

By the end of the second day I was enthusiastic about the job. I liked Paul enormously. He was a gifted teacher. When a friend referred to the Wiz jokingly as 'Everybody Beats the Wiz', I got quite sore. I was pleased to remember having gotten this email from another friend, when I was working at CompUSA and concerned with the morality of pushing the insurance:

Well, I can say that our Wiz purchase of a big screen (in Nov. 1989) with an insurance policy, which raised the total outlay to about $3,500, was a bargain. Now, 6+ years later, the set works fine, but we did have one catastrophic failure, just before the policy ran out. And the innards were repaired at no cost.

The keystone of faith in an electronics store is the insurance. The Wiz policy at the time was called Performance Plus and administered by Independent Dealer Services, Inc. If you believe the insurance offered by your store is good, you can believe in your job. I believed in my job.

In order to get to the classroom, you had to walk into the store downstairs. You could take the elevator from the first floor or climb the stairs up through the store. I was truly shocked one afternoon in the second week, when I saw the Casio watch I wore then on display and selling for a hundred dollars. It was the first G shock that lit up—'electroluminescence,' they called it. I'd bought the watch at Caldor. This was two years beforehand, and it cost seventy-six dollars at the time. Electronics are supposed to go down in price, not up.

Back in the classroom, we were briefed about the electronic-product industry. There was an amazingly high level of technical knowledge among the students. The computer, we were told, stores everything in terms of a zero or a one. *Zero* represents 'off'/ 'false'/'no'. *One* represents 'on'/'true'/'yes'.

I don't quite know what the great fascination for gadgets is, but apparently the passion is basic to the species. I was cheered during my reading to discover that Samuel Pepys, that famous seven-teenth-century diarist, was enraptured with his first pocket watch, a costly instrument that rarely kept the correct time.

The appetite has grown feverish as the gadgets have gotten better and also cheaper. The Wiz cadets seemed to share a belief that these infinitely clever creations would not only make us more efficient, but also improve the very essence of our lives.

During the 1990s, Paul told us, computer speed will double, storage requirements triple, and memory quadruple every eighteen months.

Each class had a name, Paul told us, and we would be the ice men, because, he said, 'When I'm done with you, you'll be able to sell ice to Eskimos.' He broke us into groups, had us interact, with one student as salesperson, one as prospect.

Never ask a customer what he or she wants to spend. 'You've

painted yourself into a corner.' If possible, give a demonstration. 'Demo the demo' was a slogan we learned to repeat.

Never, ever ask a customer, 'Can I help you?' He's always going to say, 'No.' Be less threatening and more specific. 'What features are you interested in?'

We were told how to focus on a 'tie-down', a particular feature of a product, and then encourage the customer to imagine enjoying that feature. The new TVs with the picture-in-picture capacity were the favored example. Learn from the customer when he might want to know what was going on on two stations simultaneously and then let him inhabit that scene. Maybe he's interested in two different football games. Let Mr. Customer visualize himself sitting in a chair, with the control in his hand. Draw him into a reverie, then shut up.

We also learned about the 'TO', or 'takeover'. If you've got a customer to the point where he or she seems almost ready to buy, but it has become a war of wills, a stalemate, then you signal another salesman to come in. If this can be done smoothly, the intervention of a second, enthusiastic witness is enough to ensure a sale.

'Hey, John, would you come over here for a second? Show Mr. Customer how the picture-in-picture works. Don't you have one of these sets at home?'

Paul also told us about spiffs. *The New Shorter Oxford English Dictionary* defines a spiff as 'a money bonus given to an employee for selling old or unwanted stock'. I knew from working at CompUSA that there were spiffs on some products. For instance, we'd had a particularly slow-moving computer: It was a desktop that had the Mac operating system, but it wasn't manufactured by Apple. If you sold one of these computers, the manufacturer gave the salesperson a direct bonus of two hundred dollars. Outside of this particular item, I had not been aware of spiffs while at CompUSA. At Nobody Beats the Wiz most items had spiffs. There were too many to recall, but this didn't matter, because at the Wiz the spiffs were written right into the product number, which was displayed

near the item on sale. The spiff began after the first seven digits of
the number and and ended before the last five. So the salesperson,
looking at a long number with a trained eye, might see 25000 in the
middle of it and know he was entitled to a cash bonus of $250 if he
moved this particular turkey.

Paul asked if anybody had ever gone into a TV showroom and
seen a Sony and a Panasonic and a brand you'd never heard of, and
the Sony and Panasonic had horrible pictures, while Brand X had a
picture that was crystal clear. That's because Brand X has a high
spiff, he told us. So the salespeople in those stores have carefully
adjusted the color and reception on the other TVs so that they look
horrible.

He certainly didn't want us to do anything of the sort at the Wiz.
We were nevertheless encouraged to know our spiffs. During an
informal conversation I had with Paul after one of our breaks, he
told me that a Sony representative had come into one of the stores
and tried to buy a Sony. Sony, because of its excellent reputation,
has low spiffs, or no spiffs at all, and so the salesman was determined
not to sell a Sony to the man from Sony. In fact, he went on at
considerable length and in detail about how weak the Sony line
was. As a result, Sony was so angry at the Wiz that they threatened
to withdraw their brand, Paul said.

One evening, our assignment was to shop the competition and
take notes. The prize for best quote retrieved was given to the cadet
who had asked a salesman a second question about a product at a
competing store and was asked angrily, 'Who do you think you are?
John Gotti?'

Back in the classroom, we were given our numerical targets.
Three out of ten customers should buy an insurance policy.
Accessories should constitute 8 per cent of the total spent.

'This guy is going to do well,' Paul said, pointing at me, after
we'd been playacting. 'He has charisma.' I was genuinely pleased. I
also thought, *Maybe I will do well.*

'Will you be using your Wiz card today?' is a question we were
supposed to ask every customer. Wiz cards, which were obtainable

at the moment of purchase, should be used in 35 per cent of transactions. When selling a Wiz card, we should also sell Wiz Guard. Wiz Guard was an insurance policy that cost seventy-five cents for every hundred dollars the customer spent and guaranteed that if the customer was killed or incapacitated or lost his job while he still owed on his purchase, the minimum payment would be made. The specter to be raised here, Paul explained, was that of unemployment.

'What do people fear more than death?' Paul asked us.

'Public speaking,' I said.

Nope. 'Recent studies show that the greatest fear felt by American voters today is that they will lose their job.'

Nobody Beats the Wiz: Easter Sunday

AFTER DINNER ON THE EVE OF MY FIRST DAY OF ACTUAL work at the Wiz, I drove to Scarsdale in order to introduce myself to my manager and establish a schedule for the week ahead. I brought my two sons. 'Why are we going out now?' one of the boys wanted to know. 'They sell electronics,' I said. 'How bad can it be? Give your mother some time alone. Maybe we'll buy something.'

The inside of the store looked better after dark, almost festive. Objects bathed in a golden light. I led the way downstairs into Home Office. I asked the first man in a Wiz vest where the manager was. He didn't know. 'He might have gone home,' he said. The second person I asked led me over to the counter and pointed to a young man who was speaking with a customer. I waited silently until this exchange was completed, then introduced myself.

'Hi, I'm Ben Cheever. I'm coming to work here tomorrow,' I said, and thrust out my hand.

It's impossible now to recall exactly how my new manager must have impressed me, as he took my hand. The resentment I grew to feel for this young man has wiped out this picture, but looking back, straining a memory which doesn't like to acknowledge positive characteristics in this man, I think he was actually quite handsome. He was certainly slender, had light hair, and he was wearing a suit. I believe the suit was green, although it was always difficult to determine the true color of anything once inside that store. I introduced my boys. Andrew

was six at the time; John was ten. I believe the manager smiled
down at the children. He may even have tousled Andrew's
hair.

Standing there with my hand on Andrew's shoulder, I said that I
wanted to work twenty hours a week, and if possible, no weekends.
'I heard nothing about that,' the manager said. 'Retail *is* weekends,'
he said. I said that when I'd applied for the job, I'd explained how I
wanted to work twenty hours a week. 'I don't mean to be negative
about you,' he said. 'I have you down for tomorrow from two to
ten P.M., Friday from two P.M. to ten P.M., and Saturday from ten to
six P.M.'

'And Easter Sunday?' I asked, remembering how I'd promised
the family that this job would be different, and thinking of how
disappointed the children would be if I wasn't home.

'Oh, Easter?' he said. 'I'm not certain what the store's hours will
be, but I have you down Easter from open to close.'

I said I'd call the man who had hired me and try to get this
straightened out. He said he'd call him, too. 'I don't mean to be
negative about you,' he said again.

'Let's give it a try,' I said. 'See how we get along. I'll come in
tomorrow.'

Then the boys and I retreated. We didn't buy anything. We
didn't even look. 'You're still a writer?' Andrew asked as we drove
home.

'Sure I am,' I said, the bluff being a basic parental move.

When I got home, I called the cell-phone number of the man
who had hired me, and left a message. He didn't call back. I phoned
him again. I phoned him a third time. He never returned my call.
The next day I showed up fifteen minutes early. 'I'm here to work,'
I said to the first salesman I met on the floor. 'Where's the
manager?'

'You mean Asshole?' he asked.

'I guess,' I said. 'He's in the storeroom,' I was told, and a finger
was pointed towards a door in the wall. Through that door I found
the manager. 'Here I am,' I said. He was on the phone. He nodded

at me, kept on talking. I stood while he finished his call. He put the phone down, told me to 'wait here', and strode off.

He came back a couple of minutes later and looked at me as if I were something he thought he should recognize but couldn't quite place. He gave me a hand signal and disappeared again. Five minutes later, he came back, this time holding a folded vest. 'It may not fit exactly,' he said. 'It's the only one we've got right now.' I wear a size 38 suit. The vest was size 44 and missing the two middle buttons. I put it on.

'Button it up,' he told me.

'But it's missing its buttons,' I said.

'Button it up anyway,' he said. 'You've got to keep it buttoned when you're on the floor.'

So I buttoned the top button and also the bottom button. I felt like a man in a clown suit. The vest kept flapping open in the middle, revealing the bright snarl of my red-and-blue necktie.

Then I left the storeroom and went out on to the floor. One of the other salesmen was standing with his back against the glass counter that held the watches and electronic organizers. He was a big man, more than six feet, and broad across the shoulders. Joe. Let's call him Joe. I went and stood beside Joe. A customer came down the stairs. I walked out towards the customer.

'Can I help you?' I asked.

'Nope,' the customer said.

I returned to the counter, got back in position next to Joe.

Joe didn't look at me. 'Don't ever ask them that,' he said.

'I know,' I said. 'I know.'

I let a decent period of time pass, then said, 'There isn't much business.'

Joe cocked his head to one side. 'There will be,' he said. 'We're light.'

'Light?'

'We lost four people.'

'They didn't sell enough?'

Joe wagged his head. 'No. They were keeping the imprints of

customers' credit cards and letting their friends use them to buy computers.'

I tried to imagine how Paul would react to this news. ICER. *I* is for 'Integrity'. *C* is for 'Credit-card Fraud.'

An hour or so later, the manager gave me my number and password. When you rang a sale up at the register, you had to type in a password and also your sales number. When you wrote a sale up and sent the customer to the registers upstairs, you put your sales number on the slip. In this way the store kept a record of your productivity, and it was on the basis of this record that you were paid.

Home Office sold computers, printers, faxes, items of relatively high value. We also sold telephones, watches, and answering machines. This small-ticket merchandise ate time without earning substantial commissions.

Souflé, the man whose name had caused a sensation on the day I first applied, also turned out to be working in the department. He was a tidy, polite black man said to be both a certified public accountant and an ordained minister. His vest fit much better than did my own.

For reasons that remain unclear to me, Souflé was detested by one of the older salesmen, a man I'll call Ralph. Ralph Palmer had muttonchop whiskers. Not ordinarily profane, Ralph always called Souflé Shit-for-brains Souflé. I didn't dislike Souflé. In fact, I was thankful to him for keeping me from being the most despised sales counselor on the floor.

I was certainly one of the least productive. Souflé sold three computers before I sold one. When I mentioned Souflé's success to Ralph, he was not impressed. 'He's not a salesman,' he told me disdainfully, 'he's a clerk.' A 'clerk', I learned, is somebody who will only deal with 'lay-downs'. A clerk sells a customer what he or she had intended to buy for what he or she had intended to pay. A salesman, on the other hand, sells the customer more than he or she meant to buy, for more than he or she had expected to pay. A home run at Nobody Beats the Wiz meant not only the sale of the highest-priced product possible, but also the accessories, the insurance, and the store credit card.

Ralph thought that someday I might be a salesman myself. Clearly it hadn't happened yet, but he had hopes. As did I.

Outside of his mysterious detestation of Souflé, Ralph was a decent, friendly guy. He told me that he had worked for years at Radio Shack and at Radio Shack they actually calculated the dollars-an-hour earned by every salesman. Ralph said that he had held the title for most dollars an hour. He told me he'd earned fifty thousand dollars a year.

Ralph warned me never to ask Angelo for help. Angelo was the department shark. He had the stride and manner of a high-school football star. He swaggered through the store. He was the best, or that's what he told me. 'I'm the best.' He wore brown double-knit slacks. He had a bit of a gut, a neatly trimmed beard, and a face that looked like something Disney cartoonists might have dreamed up for the Sheriff of Nottingham.

When a customer came on to the floor, Angelo would virtually grab him by the ear, sell something, or frighten him out of the department.

Most of the time I couldn't get close enough to hear what Angelo said to his victims, but it appeared to me that he actually bullied people into buying, and buying fast.

I was both horrified and fascinated by his technique, since I have never fully understood how to make anybody do anything against his or her will, much less spend money.

Ralph told me that Angelo's figures weren't as good as they looked because a lot of people simply returned the merchandise he frightened them into buying. This was wishful thinking on Ralph's part, since Angelo's statistics were some of the best in the store.

Ralph was correct about his warning, though. Caught with a customer whose questions I couldn't answer, I called on Angelo once. The big man came right in, answered the question, and then closed the sale with *his* sales number.

I had been thrilled to work at CompUSA. I hated working at the

Wiz. I've read *Death of a Salesman*, and I know there's something terribly wrong with Willy Loman's injunction to be well liked, but barring larger issues — and they have to be very large — I'm with Willy on this one. I want to be well liked.

At CompUSA I was well liked. I carried heavy boxes, got in early, left late, helped my colleagues, and beamed at those who helped me. I didn't care how low I was on the hierarchy, as long as I fit in. At the Wiz, I couldn't find my level.

Everybody in Home Office was suspicious of everybody else in Home Office. 'What did you do before this?' Joe asked me. I said I'd worked at CompUSA.

'In White Plains?'

'Yeah. Right near the County Center.'

'Why'd you leave?'

'To get the training here.'

'Before CompUSA?'

'I was a magazine editor.'

'And now you're working for Nobody Beats the Wiz?'

I nodded. 'Soufflé's a certified public accountant.'

'But here?' Joe asked again.

'I've had a checkered career,' I said.

Joe was companionable, but nobody was friendly, because we were all competing against one another. Sales totals were posted every evening, and each individual got a printout of his sales history every day.

Since there were only so many customers, and since we had little to do with bringing them in, this created a sort of anti-utopia. I first realized how bad it was when a customer came in and asked for a cordless telephone that I needed to go into the storeroom to find. When I asked one of the other salesmen where the cordless phones were kept, he wouldn't tell me. I repeated my question. He still wouldn't tell me.

It took me a couple of minutes to figure this out. The longer I spent in the storeroom, the more likely the other salesman was to rack up sales.

There had been a lot of talk about teamwork at Nobody Beats the Wiz University, but in fact, the system of payment was designed to discourage teamwork. Or decency of any sort.

And yet I'm such a chameleon that I grew loyal to the place. When one customer said she was checking us out and then planned to shop at CompUSA, I joined another salesman who was sneering at her.

'I worked there once,' I told her. 'Those people aren't trained.'

The rap on CompUSA among the sales staff in general was that the pay plan at my old employer was not as directly tied to commissions. 'You want to work for eight dollars an hour?' Of course our draw was seven dollars an hour, although we could earn a good deal more with commissions and spiffs. But you can also earn money in Atlantic City.

As the writer, I'm tempted to portray myself as the hero of this story. I didn't stay long enough to develop truly pernicious habits, but I wasn't a hero, either, and we had a hero. Let's call him Steve. I didn't much like Steve. He was a short man, with a limp and buckteeth. He'd been with IBM for years and then got shed during the great bloodletting. 'But they gave you a good package?' I said.

'I can't complain,' he said.

Steve actually tried to help the customers. I had a friend at the time who'd called the Wiz to ask about buying a laptop, and Steve told him, 'You don't want to buy a laptop here.'

Twigging to this uncharacteristic honesty, my friend immediately said, 'Sure I do. What's your name? How long will you be there?'

Steve listened to customers, gave them reasonable advice. For this he was known. People would come in and ask for Steve. If he wasn't there, they'd leave. They wouldn't buy from me. Steve really did care about the customer, although often as not, he wasn't compensated for his troubles.

We had a cell-phone station in the basement, and this was operated by two very cool dudes, one of whom I'll call Ron Dee.

Ron Dee wore a beret. Ron Dee was friendly but also acutely aware of his high status. I don't know what you had to do to get assigned to cell phones, but it couldn't have been easy because we all wanted the job. The phones were big-ticket items, and the department moved a lot of them.

Joe was allowed to fill in sometimes when both of the black men were out, and he confided in me that he expected to become a full-time cell-phone salesman someday. 'It's a gimmee post,' he said. 'You sit there, and you say, "Gimmee, gimmee," and the customers give you money.'

You got a post like that by pleasing the management. My attempts to please the management seemed ill-starred. When business slowed down after nine P.M. on my first night, I offered to wipe down the glass cases with paper towels and Windex. Anxious to do something right, I was very sparing with the Windex, so Asshole said I could use more. 'We buy it in bulk,' he said. So on the next glass panel, I sprayed the Windex more generously. 'But you don't need to waste it, either,' he said.

It was 9:45 P.M. I was wearing a ridiculous vest. I was almost fifty years old, down on my knees, cleaning glass. *This must be a joke*, I thought, but when I looked up, Asshole was not smiling. There was a flicker of movement above his mouth, but this could as easily have been sadism as mirth.

Everything was new to me, and I never worked the register or wrote a ticket or even unloaded stock in our stockroom – where were all those stock guys I had expected to look down on? – without wondering if I'd done it exactly right.

Noting the cowlike pleading in my eyes, and being a man with many responsibilities, Asshole made himself unavailable for questions. His training technique was to wait until I'd done something, allow time to pass, then tap me on the shoulder, and say, 'You did that wrong. Not that it matters, but I wanted you to know that you did that wrong.' There followed the specific advice: 'Always,

always point them towards the most expensive purchase . . . Put all the cordless in the middle aisle of the stockroom . . . Don't ever let a customer wait . . .'

Tips that might have been welcome, if they'd come before the mistake, served only as barbs. I didn't recall the specifics but internalized a growing sense of despair. The injunctions I did recall were often difficult to live up to. For instance, 'Never let a customer wait!'

What if you had two customers? One afternoon I got a woman who said she wanted to buy 'your cheapest telephone'. 'Nothing fancy'. Her voice was high and strident. I couldn't tell for sure if she was angry at the moment, but it looked as if she'd been furious when she put her makeup on, either very upset or standing in the back of a violently swaying bus.

I directed her to our cheapest, simplest telephone. *This is going to be easy*, I thought, because the cheapest models were stacked out on the floor, whereas many of the more costly phones had only the demos on the floor, and the ones for selling were in the storeroom. She didn't like the color of the first phone I showed her. I showed it to her in another color. She didn't like that color, either. She selected a slightly more costly model. I went into the storeroom and got her the box. While she studied the information printed on the box, a trim Asian woman appeared holding a boxed telephone in her hands. Could I help her? There were no other salesmen around at the moment, so I said I'd help her the moment I was free. The woman who wanted the cheap, simple phone decided she didn't like the one I'd gotten her. She selected a different model, a model which also happened not to be on the floor. I went off to the storeroom to retrieve this. When I came back, she needed to study the box.

The Asian woman was still standing there, politely, the phone she wanted to buy held out to me in both hands.

The woman with the sloppy makeup didn't like the second phone I'd gotten her, either. She picked out a third model and asked me to fetch it.

When I reappeared with the third phone, the Asian woman was still standing there, still waiting.

So while my first customer was reading the specifications on the new box, I asked, 'Can I just help this woman for a moment while you decide?'

My first customer didn't say anything, so I turned to the second woman. 'Is there a volume control on the ringer?' she wanted to know.

'I don't know,' I said, 'let's see.' But I hadn't had a chance to look on the box, before the first woman tapped me on the shoulder. 'I guess I'll take this one, then,' she said, but she said it angrily, as if this were the very last straw.

'Can I write it up?' I asked.

'Do you have to? Can I just pay for it upstairs?'

'You can pay for it upstairs, but I wish you wouldn't,' I said.

'I will,' she said, and headed upstairs.

Now I turned back to the Asian woman. *She's on my side*, I thought. *After all, she's the one I got in trouble for.*

Desperate for affirmation, I said, 'Some people are nice. Some people are not nice.' I didn't look at the second woman when I said this. I said it calmly. I said it quietly. I said it to the room in general.

Instantly, I could feel the woman beside me stiffen. Her face went rigid. Not only was she not sympathetic, she was actually angry, too. At me.

'Is this the phone you want?' I asked.

Now she wanted to punish me. 'I need to open the box,' she said.

'It's a sealed box,' I said.

'I'm giving it as a gift,' she said. 'I need to open the box.'

I breathed deeply. Together we took the telephone out of the box. Together we checked the contents, pulling each item out of its little waxy paper bag and turning it over, examining it for possible shortcomings.

I figured she'd get every part out of the box, and then ask for a different telephone. This happens. I could imagine Asshole saying,

'You did that wrong!' Fortunately, this woman was a victim of her own neatness. She wanted me punished, but she couldn't resist the need to wrap the phone back up. She also let me write her up, but believe me, it was a close thing. I'd done something terribly wrong.

What had I done? I'd acted like a person who was entitled to his feelings.

Looking back on my printouts of sales, I can see that the cordless phone the Asian customer bought cost $79.98. Since the first woman didn't let me fill out a slip at all, my total commission for that agonizing forty-five minutes was eighty-eight cents. The spiff was one dollar.

The main thing, of course, was to sell the insurance. The performance guarantee, it was called. Selling the performance guarantee was called getting the bagel, as in 'I sold a Performa and got the bagel'. I wasn't enthusiastic about the insurance any-more. I didn't trust the place. And getting the bagel wasn't the end of it. First, you were supposed to direct your prospect toward the most expensive item, then get the bagel, sell the accessories, and if possible, put it all on the Wiz card.

I helped a sweet guy who bought a cordless phone for $299.98. He wanted the expensive nine-hundred-megahertz model because he liked to talk on the phone while he had his dogs in the yard. That wasn't my fault. But I told him I had a dog, and how much I liked my dog. Then I sold him the two-year insurance policy on the phone for $29.98. 'And will you be using your Wiz card today?' I asked him. So then he applied for and got a Wiz card, and also Wiz Guard, so that if he died, the dogs wouldn't have the phone taken away.

This was the one time Asshole was pleased with me. 'Good job,' he said. 'Home run.' Afterwards I kept thinking, *If he has a yard for his dogs, he can't be that desperate. But then if he has money, why would he want to buy a three-hundred-dollar telephone on time?*

I felt wretched about this. My spiffs on the transaction totaled $8.50. My commission was $3.30.

The moral unpleasantness of the job was heightened by the physical unpleasantness. There was no bathroom in the department, and the nearest toilet was upstairs just to the left of the entrance door. This was the same toilet used by the customers. In order to go there, you had to ask permission. Asshole would look around. If the department was empty, you could go. If there were customers on the floor, he'd say, 'Ask me later.'

Often as not, you'd get upstairs and find the bathroom locked, with a customer inside, or another salesman. If this person took too long to finish up, you were supposed to go back to the floor and work for a while before you asked again.

April was 'Founder's Month' at Nobody Beats the Wiz, and there was a poster-sized picture of Norman Jemal on one of the bathroom walls.

Sometimes I could make a bridge to a customer, slow time down, give them enough information, and get a smile of gratitude at the point of purchase. I sold a fax to a man who hadn't seen me before.

'You're new here?'

I nodded.

'You were out of work?'

I nodded.

'I was out of work once. That's no good.' And then after we'd completed the sale, he said, 'Thanks. I'll be back. I'll ask for you. You made this transaction a pleasure.' He actually said that.

Ordinarily, I wouldn't have minded being asked to spend an hour cleaning out the storeroom, but when I realized that this was time in which I could earn no commissions, the chore rankled. Same with the injunction that we arrive at work fifteen minutes before our shift started. This was volunteer time, unpaid.

Saturdays, the entire staff had to come in an hour early for the weekly meeting. We all sat on the floor, and after Asshole had taken attendance, he went up to the store's main office to get our productivity figures.

There was a sort of pulpit in the section, used during business hours for the sale of cell phones, but which Asshole preempted, Caesar-like, if he needed to speak to the entire department.

While Asshole was upstairs, Ron Dee, the cool guy, got up behind the pulpit, cleared his throat, and said, 'I can save some time here, by telling you now that you all suuuuck!'

A couple of people laughed. I didn't laugh. I didn't get it.

Asshole came down the stairs a few minutes later, with a manila folder in which he had everybody's statistics. The amount of numbers crunching that went on at that store was extraordinary. Everybody's sales were documented, of course, the names and addresses of everybody we'd sold anything to, and also our productivity was broken down. What percentage of our total gross was attributable to the sale of insurance? How much did we make selling accessories?

First, Asshole gave us all a general pep talk. 'I thank you, and my pockets thank you,' he said again and again. Then he went over the performance of each employee in the department. 'I can't live with that,' he kept saying.

Ron Dee's joke was suddenly funny. Then funnier. Surprise! Surprise! In one category or another, we all sucked.

I was concerned about Easter. It seemed that most everybody was working on Easter Sunday. Except Angelo, the shark. 'Are you working Easter?' I asked him. 'When hell freezes over,' he said. 'That's when I'll work on Easter Sunday.'

Saturday was busy, but there were additional, sharp salesmen who only worked Saturday, and so the increased volume did not manifest itself in increased sales for me. I was at the store from 8:45 until 6 P.M. (I was entitled to a half hour off for lunch, which I could only take after it had been approved by Asshole. The half hour was deducted if you took it off, and also if you didn't take it off.)

At the end of the day, I was way down on the salesmen's roll of honor. My sales totaled $991.87 for a total commission of $10.28 with $16 in spiffs.

Easter Sunday started badly. I got up later than I had expected. I thought I'd make everybody a celebratory breakfast of scrambled eggs. I had the butter in the skillet, when I remembered that the clock had moved overnight. Then I remembered the jingle: Spring forward, fall back. I checked the front page of the *Times*. My heart stopped. I turned off the frying pan, ran around the house kissing everybody.

I knew it was going to rain, but I was afraid to bring a coat. There were no lockers, and I assumed a good coat would be stolen. I jumped into my car and raced to work. When I got there I found that I had two dollars in my wallet.

I swiped in, put on the dreadful vest, and hit the floor, still breathing heavily. *Nothing* was going on. *Nothing*. Three of the salesmen had computers turned on and were playing solitaire.

It was an hour before the first customer arrived. He was furious. He'd bought a laser printer for his old IBM. When he had attempted to install the printer software, he'd caused the whole machine to freeze. He came in with the printer (which he intended to return for a full refund), his computer, and a box full of software.

Steve had sold him the printer, so Steve set up a table in the back of the department and started trying to get the computer to work again.

Outside of this lone customer, there were no civilians on the floor. None. I thought, *Good. They'll close early*. But the store didn't close, and pretty soon we got the after-church crowd – the women in their Easter bonnets, the girls in those bright patent-leather shoes that are supposed to be so pleasing to God.

I had my hopes. How long could this go on? Easter Sunday. And very little business.

Then the phone rang.

'Nobody Beats the Wiz,' I said, 'Ben speaking. How can I help you?'

The woman who was calling wanted to know if we carried plain-paper faxes. I told her we did. 'And how late are you open?' she asked.

'I don't know for sure,' I said. 'We may close at three.'

'Oh, no,' she said, 'you're open until seven.'

'How do you know that?' I asked, my spirits falling.

'It's right here in the ad,' she said.

So if it was right there in the ad, how come Asshole hadn't known?

Other than in my unrealistic expectations, Easter was a day like any other – except that I felt bad for missing the family celebration. It was raining too hard to go out for the half-hour lunch break I was entitled to, and charged for. I lost both dollars in the vending machine.

There was a big rush, of course, at 7 P.M. I heard one customer complaining loudly that he thought we were going to be open until 9 P.M.

Finally, just before closing, Steve got his customer's computer working again, packed the software into the box, and helped him haul everything out to the parking lot. He came back inside and pitched in with the cleanup.

I'd had it bad, but Steve had had it worse. He'd had the price of the returned printer knocked off his previous day's total, and Sunday he sold nothing.

Plus, he spent all day peforming intricate computer repairs with a furious customer leaning over his shoulder.

I sold $1,355.32 worth of merchandise. Which earned me a commission of $12.63. My spiffs totaled $26.85. So I'd earned $39.48 for the day. I was paid $7 an hour, but I'd *earned* $39.48. Sooner or later there would be a reckoning.

It had been busy, and the sense of relief was considerable when the outside doors were finally locked. Asshole went upstairs for the last time. We gathered together, like a defeated football team huddling around the ball. Steve settled down on a box and began to pare his fingernails with a penknife.

'You spent all day fixing that one computer?' I asked.

He nodded.

'You fixed it,' I said.

He shrugged.

'I don't know if it'll stay fixed,' he said.

'I bet it does,' I said.

And then the man who had spent his adult life selling and fixing computers heaved a bitter, little sigh. 'Probably not,' he said. 'When you get inside one of those things, it's amazing that any of them work at all. Ever.'

The key to selling happily at an electronics store wasn't a belief in the products, though – since products are varied and they change. The key was to have faith in the store and in the insurance we also sold.

When I worked at CompUSA, I'd been a true believer. Bill wouldn't lie to me, and Bill had said that if you buy an expensive item without the extended warranty, 'you'll wind up in repair-shop hell'.

When friends who knew I'd sold electronics asked me if they should buy the insurance, I urged them to do so. Was I sure? they'd ask me. 'I'm sure,' I'd say.

Nobody Beats the Wiz had hurt my faith. Did we ever do anything that was not designed to turn a profit? Was buying the bagel really a good idea? I wondered.

So I went to the Tops Appliance City that was then located ten minutes from my house and paid $57.97 for a Sony Sports Walkman, and when the young salesman started in about the insurance package, I listened.

'It's a delicate instrument,' he explained. 'They break, they get stolen, lost. Buy the insurance, and you're entitled to a full refund.'

'No matter what?' I asked.

'No matter what,' he said.

So I paid another eleven dollars for two years of insurance.

Now I'm an audiobook addict. I always have a Walkman attached to my belt. The canary-yellow cable runs from belt to head. The little speakers are in my ears. Fall into a canal when I am strolling or jogging by, scream to me for help, and I won't hear you. I'm listening to a book.

When I fall down running and scrape my knees and palms, they bleed and then get better. The Sony Walkman, however, doesn't bleed when it hits the ground. Nor does it heal itself. I'm clearing the dishes after dinner, and the yellow earphone-cord gets caught on the knob of a cabinet. I move suddenly away; the Walkman is yanked out of my belt, and the floor is terra-cotta.

Eleven dollars seemed a lot to pay for insurance on a device that cost $57.97, but that was for two years' coverage. No matter what. 'Even if it's stolen,' he told me.

'Even if the little rubber seal comes out,' I asked, 'and so it's not waterproof, and I have trouble closing the case?'

'Even if the little rubber seal comes out,' he confirmed.

So three months later, the little rubber seal came partway out of the groove in which it was set. Ordinarily, I would have put on my reading glasses and worked a screwdriver to try to get it back in the groove, but not this time. This time I was covered. I'd put the receipt for the insurance in the glove compartment of my car. I retrieved my papers and sat down at the phone. I had an hour to lose.

This all took place in 1996 and phone menus weren't yet developed to the maddening extent that they are now. But they had Hold buttons at Tops, and they had piped-in music. Even in those high and far-off times, it wasn't easy to get an actual human being on the line, however rude.

And sure enough, the first woman I spoke to was a rude one. She didn't actually say I was a liar, but she did say that my name wasn't in the computer and that my documentation failed to prove that I had purchased the 'defective equipment' at her store. I bleated with rage and indignation. 'I spent eleven dollars insuring a fifty-seven-dollar Walkman, and now you're not going to cover me?'

For this I was put on hold. There was music, Frank Sinatra doing it his way. Not much of a consolation for me. A second woman picked up. She wanted to know if I'd mistreated the instrument. No, I hadn't 'mistreated' the instrument, I said. 'But even if I did "mistreat" the instrument, I'm still entitled to a new one. Even if I'd lost it, I'd be covered. Even if I'd put it down in my own driveway and backed over it with my own car, I'd be covered. That's what *your* salesman told me.'

For this outburst, I was put on hold again. Then some more music, which is supposed to quell the wild beast. This time a personal favorite: Georg Friedrich Handel's *Water Music*. Even Handel has his limits.

Then another voice. Maybe it was just later in the morning, but this woman seemed a better fit. She wanted to know exactly what was wrong with the Sports Walkman. Then she wanted to know if I'd tried to get the rubber seal back into the groove myself.

'No, I didn't try that,' I said. 'I paid eleven dollars for insurance on a Walkman that cost fifty-seven dollars and ninety-seven cents. I expect to be covered. I was told that I'd be covered. No matter what.'

More music. Sinatra again this time. I wondered what Frank Sinatra would do in a case like this. I guessed it wouldn't be pretty.

Finally, the manager came on the line. He was in a good mood. His name was Pat. Pat wanted to know why I was so upset.

I explained at some length and in considerable detail why I was so upset. 'Now it turns out I'm not covered,' I said.

'Of course, you're covered,' Pat said. 'Come in, and we'll void the contract. Come in, and we'll give you a refund for the full amount.'

Of course, I'd run out of time. I couldn't come right in. I had a boy who needed to be picked up at a birthday party. I'd used up my allotted hour.

'I'll come in tomorrow,' I said. 'Will that be all right?'

'Sure,' Pat said.

And so the very next day I went to Tops. First I had to stand on one line and fill some papers out. Then I had to stand on another line. Then I had to wait until Pat came back from lunch.

While Pat was eating lunch, I was buying a new Sony Sports Walkman. They had the same unit on sale now for $44.97. But no, I didn't buy the insurance. When the salesman started in, I gave him such a blast, he shut right up.

Pat came back from lunch. He waved his hand. 'The contract is voided,' I was told. I suppose this indicates that there are stalwarts who will try to get a unit replaced twice on the same insurance.

I didn't mind having the contract voided. I didn't expect to have the Walkman replaced twice. I was very pleased to have had it replaced once. I got an invoice entitling me to $57.97 at Tops. I'd already bought a new Walkman, so I didn't need the credit. Besides which, it seemed too precious to use immediately. I put the document in the glove compartment of the car. I still have it. The print is faded now and can't be read at all, except in a very bright light.

Every time I've bought a computer, I've also invested in the extended warranty. I always go for the plan that entitles me to a free home visit by a licensed technician. I think of the pictures on the brochures I've given out at CompUSA and at Nobody Beats the Wiz. These feature a beautiful woman on the telephone, her face a map of thoughtful and informed consideration. In the background, or on a separate page, I see the van speeding through the night. The van is chock-full of licensed technicians.

Or that's what I'd guess, although I've never seen one. I've never had a licensed technician come to my house to honor any of these extended warranties.

I've had laptops fixed, of course, but always I needed to ship them away, and always it was the manufacturer who repaired them. Repairs have never been done for me by the extended-warranty provider. Not once.

And yes, I've asked. I've navigated endless phone menus. I've looked up serial numbers and faxed copies of my receipt. I've begged and fumed. I once told a warranty provider that I was writing a book and that if he didn't come to my house and fix the disk drive on my Performa, he'd be in the book. 'Featured.'

That rattled their branches. I went right up the chain of command. An appointment was made. A licensed technician was going to come to my house Tuesday. 'No question about it?' I asked.

'No question about it,' I was told.

Monday the phone rang. I'd been cancelled. I forget now why I was cancelled. The reasoning was too arcane for recollection.

Yes, yes, I did get a refund that one time. I got it for a Walkman. But I had to make a stink. I had to make several stinks. I was angry. I was unreasonable. It seems entirely possible that a person as angry and unreasonable as I had been might have gotten a new Walkman without having bought the insurance at all. A person that unreasonable might have gotten a new Walkman without having purchased one in the first place.

Electronics stores sell the insurance, proclaiming the spirit of the law; they honor it only to the letter of the law.

So next time, I wouldn't buy the insurance. Not unless you want to help the salesman. Don't be too angry, though, at the people who try to cram this paper down your throat. They have to do it. It's their job. And most of them have forced themselves to believe in what they do.

Dean Witter: The Happy Ending

You don't have to be
on Wall Street to
work on Wall Street.

Dean Witter — one of the country's largest investment firms — is right
here in your own area.

We're looking for ambitious, sales-oriented men and women to join our
professional team as Account Executives.

If you qualify, you'll be part of our in-depth sales training program. And,
through personal attention and constant support, you can develop your sales
ability to the fullest.

A career with an investment firm can be quite exciting. And with the
possibility of unlimited earning potential, quite rewarding. You can learn
more about it by attending a free seminar conducted by Dean Witter
managers and recruiters.
Your successful career on Wall Street isn't very far away at all. It could be just
a phone call away.

Hiring for White Plains, NY, Mt. Kisco, NY, and Rockland County, NY
Date: Wed., June 19, 1996
Time: 6:00 P.M.
Place: 11 Martine Avenue. 8Th Fl. White Plains, NY

(914) 683–3202

On the evening in question, I drove to White Plains, parked, and
walked to the office building. Two men got off the elevator I was

waiting to get on, both in suits. One said to the other, 'Took me two and a half years to get my first account.'

Upstairs, I joined a group of ten to fifteen people, all seated in ranked chairs in a room with a TV in front. When we'd settled down and filled out rudimentary forms, we were shown a video. Then a fetching woman gave us a talk. She told us we could make a lot of money. Or not. She said it would be up to us.

Dean Witter was looking to hire twenty people They'd seen more than two hundred since the hunt began, and hired eight. It was hard to make the cut. Ph.D.'s were being turned down left and right. I wasn't worried. I've rarely held a job for which Ph.D.'s haven't been turned down left and right. Ph.D.'s are notoriously unemployable.

On the other hand, she told us, the rewards were substantial. 'After five years, the average broker makes well into the six digits. You can earn more than top lawyers. You can earn more than doctors.' But there was a caveat: 'You have to be ready to set aside two years of your life for training.'

Then we were each given a brief interview. I was led to the office of a pleasant man in his late fifties or early sixties. In another life he might easily have taught the classics at Yale. He had a mop of gray hair. He smoked Salems. He had a bronze model of a steer on his desk.

He was quite frank about the fact that the work would be hard and undignified at first. I told him that I had been working recently as a computer salesman, and also in telemarketing. When I said 'telemarketing', I thought I saw his face light up.

'Were you any good?'

'Yes, I was.'

'Can I call you Ben?'

'Ben is fine.'

He said that the ideal salesman would be a cross between a writer and an actor. I nodded. I said I was sorry that I'd never learned to act, because it seemed so important. I said that acting had turned out to be as important as editing when I was at the *Reader's Digest*. I

said that even if you wanted to write books, you had to sell. 'You
have to sell your books.'

He seemed to like this. He wondered what sort of salesman
Shakespeare might have been.

I thought Shakespeare must have been a decent salesman. 'Else,
we might not now know who he was.'

We got along famously. He stood. I stood. We shook hands.
He said I'd hear again from Dean Witter within twenty-four
hours.

When I headed back towards the elevator, I passed another
prospect who was speaking earnestly to the receptionist. His face
was contorted with sincerity. He may actually have been perspiring.
'I'd like to work here,' he was explaining, 'but I don't need to make
that much money.'

So this would be it, I thought in the elevator. The end of the book:
I'd be the Shakespeare of Dean Witter. That's actually what I
thought.

I'd call Adam Bellow, who was still my editor then. I'd tell him,
'I've got my happy ending.'

The next day I waited by the phone. Nobody called. Thursday, I
was nervous as a cat before an electrical storm. Nobody called.
Friday, I called Dean Witter.

A woman picked up. I said that I was a job applicant and gave my
name. 'The man I spoke with said I'd hear within twenty-four
hours.'

'Okay, Ben,' I was told, 'hold on.'

I sat there on the other end of the phone, my heart thumping,
my palms as cold as ice.

The woman came back on the line. She said they'd call me
Monday.

'Promise?'

'I promise.'

But Monday, nobody phoned. Nor Tuesday, either. Wednesday, I called Dean Witter. When I gave my name, the woman who
had answered the phone shuffled some papers, then said she'd tried

to call me Monday, 'but the line was busy'. Could I come in Friday at 1:30 P.M. for a test in reading comprehension and math?

'You bet I could.'

The reading-comprehension part sounded good, but not the math. I asked if I could bring a calculator. The woman didn't know. I said I'd bring a calculator, then ask if I could use it on the day of the test.

She said that sounded all right.

So Friday, I drove again to White Plains. I didn't bring the printing calculator that had stood me in such good stead when I was taking the course at H & R Block. I brought my Psion organizer, which has a calculator built right in. A calculator that I had rarely used. A calculator that I had not mastered.

If bringing a calculator was cheating, then bringing a calculator I couldn't exactly work was somehow preferable. More honest. I've often confused losing with being a good sport.

I gave my name at reception. A young woman named Heather came and led me to an empty office. There were two desks pushed together. These were wooden desks with nothing on them.

I asked Heather if I could use a calculator. She wasn't sure. She left me alone with my calculator and my conscience.

At first, I was afraid somebody was going to glance through the window and see me using the calculator and disqualify me. Then I didn't care. The questions were hard. Or they were hard for me. Correction: For me the questions were impossible. I hadn't done any math since H & R Block, and before that, I'd hardly done any math at all.

My wife was a math major. When we first started dating, I used to take the pulse in my throat after running. I'd take it for fifteen seconds and multiply the result by four. It takes me a long time to multiply something by four. Once, after we'd gone for a run together, Janet noticed that I was standing stock-still with two fingers pressed against my throat and a deeply philosophical look on my face.

'What are you doing?' she asked.

I said, 'I'm taking my pulse for fifteen seconds and then multi-plying by four. Now I've lost my place. I'll have to do it again.'

'It took you that long to multiply by four?' she asked.

I nodded, losing my place again.

She thought this was hilarious.

'Why not take your pulse for six seconds,' she asked, 'and multiply by ten?'

Dean Witter had a lot of multiplying they wanted me to do. Multiplying and worse. Just for instance: If a client owned 70 shares of one stock at 35 dollars a share, and 45 shares of another stock, and his total holdings were $7,500, then how much was the second stock worth per share? I knew I should be looking for x, but I had no idea where x might be.

Outside of my office, I could hear the P.A. system encouraging the people who already had jobs to work harder pushing an IPO, or 'initial public offering.' Why wasn't IPO on the test?

When I finally moved to reading and comprehension, I was so deeply rattled that I would have had trouble with 'Run, Spot, run'. Is the dog named Run or Spot? I was experiencing the sort of despair I hadn't known since the end of my formal schooling. The reading test had excerpts from Twain's *The Prince and the Pauper*.

I'd read *The Prince and the Pauper* once. This didn't help. I have the sort of memory that only works when the fact I want to recall has inherent interest, some sort of electrical charge.

Names, for instance, I can't ever remember unless they're ridiculous.

If the name isn't interesting, then I fix on something else that is interesting. Crooked teeth, for instance. Or if he's a spitter. If I meet somebody who has his wig on backwards, I remember, *bald*, but I don't remember his name. Or if I meet somebody whose child drowned, I remember that.

Which means that if I ever run into either person again, I have nothing I can say. 'Moths got the wig?' isn't any sort of icebreaker.

Same was true with the reading-and-comprehension test. I remembered a lot, but not what I was being tested on. I had counted on acing this part of the test. This clearly wasn't going to happen. I was running out of time. I wasn't certain at all, however, that more time would have helped me find x. Heather came back and asked if I was interested in working in the New City office. I said White Plains or New City. It sure sounded like *she* thought I had the job.

Then a young woman, I think it was still Heather, although I was dizzy with defeat, came and told me my time was up. She led me to the office of the man who had become my mentor. The gray-haired Salem smoker met me at the door. 'Should we call you an overachiever today or an underachiever?' he asked.

'I think we should call me an underachiever today,' I said. 'I had a terrible time with that test.'

He had a phone call to make. I sat in his office. I remembered sitting in the offices of older men while they did their work. I used to have to do that a lot at the *Reader's Digest*. I remembered how when I had my own little department at the *Digest*, it was thrilling to have somebody wait in my office while I finished up a phone call. Or put the finishing touches on a manuscript.

I noticed the office furnishings. There was a plaque with 'Nothing Is Impossible' engraved on it.

My mentor got off the phone. We made polite conversation. He said that my results would be ready momentarily. The phone rang. 'Probably your results,' he said.

He picked up the phone. His face fell.

'I did badly,' I said.

He nodded.

'Very badly?'

He nodded again.

Then we shared a long and painful silence. He put down the receiver. He said we'd have to wait a week. He said it was possible that everybody else would also do very badly on the test. If that happened, he said, they might give me the test again.

I said that I thought I could do better, if I took the test again. 'I mean if I had a chance to prepare.' He nodded.

He said that if everybody else did badly, they'd call me. I could take the test again. 'And we'll destroy this one.'

He never called.

Halloween Town and Telemarketing: A Large Family

I DON'T WANT YOU TO THINK I NEVER FOUND WORK. FOR instance, I was hired right off as an actor for Halloween Town, which was set up in the parking lot outside of Sears.

Actors
Halloween Town located outside Jefferson Valley Mall, now hiring for Friday/Saturday/Sunday evenings in October. Must be enthusiastic. Over 18.

I got there early on the first night and waited on a stage, where two white coffins rested on sawhorses. I began to talk to a young man with a ponytail and a tattoo. He was smoking. He said acting wasn't the way to make money. He said the way to make money was to work on a long-distance moving truck. 'You get a dollar for every hundred pounds you move. Move a piano that weighs, like, eight hundred pounds, you got eight dollars just like that. You get eight dollars in ten minutes.'

He said he could make six hundred dollars a week. I asked why he'd left the job. He said he'd been fired, because his boss was gypping him on his paycheck. I didn't ask why he was the one fired, since he was also the one being gypped. The way he said it, it seemed to make sense.

We all filled out applications. Then we were told that we needed two things for the job: a sense of responsibility (call us if you're not going to show up) and a good scream. Among the applicants was a woman dressed entirely in black, with black fingernails, and lots of eye shadow. She told the organizers she had worked for them at the Haunted Hayride in Patterson, N.Y.

'When?'

'I don't know. Ninety-one.'

'I don't remember you. What did you do?'

'Sure, you do,' she said, and stepped forward to give her interlocutor a profile. 'I was a witch, a person without a head, and the automobile-accident victim. I was the dead bride.'

Then we walked through Halloween Town together, and were shown the haunts, or posts, and told how to act in them. One of us would stand behind a wall, howling and moving drawers in and out of an old dresser that had been tricked up so that the drawers could be operated from behind. One of us would pop in and out of a picture frame. We all wanted the Portosan post. You hid in the Portosan and then burst out wielding a fake chain saw. One of us would sit in an electric chair and scream whenever the strobe light flashed.

'Nobody has ever been taken out of here in an ambulance,' we were told, 'although we did have one old gentleman who peed his pants.'

This was all done with good cheer, although there were warnings: 'There's never any need to touch anybody. You'll get poked once in a while. Can't help that. But otherwise don't let them touch you. And don't you touch them.'

After the tour, I drove the former mover back to Peekskill. He said Peekskill is a bad town. He said they had a riot last year, and some kid shot up a police car. He said that if you walked around at night, somebody would try to sell you crack. I asked if he used crack. 'No. I tell them I don't want crack. I want to get drunk.'

The dress rehearsal was at 6:30 P.M. We filled out our tax forms. No matter what job, no matter where, you have to cross Uncle Sam's palm with silver. Then we went into the Beware House. The class was broken in half. First my group walked, and others frightened us inexpertly. Then we were each given posts. I was stationed behind the dresser. Standing on tiptoe, I could see through a one-way mirror. When somebody came into the room and walked in front of the dresser, I banged the drawers out. When they got past this room, I jumped out from the side and roared. My haunt was back to back with that of a tall, slender young man whose job it was to occupy a jail cell. He was supposed to hang on the wall. When people walked past, he was to scream out his death agony. We decided we'd switch jobs periodically. 'To keep it fresh.' I started out working the dresser. Once, when I scared somebody well, my partner said, 'Did you hear what happened in Patterson at the Haunted Hayride?' I hadn't heard. 'Somebody gave some big guy a great scare, and the guy turned and hit him. Knocked him out.' He smiled ruefully. 'Stories not to tell the wife,' he said. After a while we switched roles. I hung in the cell; he worked the haunted dresser. There was another cell across from ours, with a young woman hiding behind the drop cloth in the hearth. I believe her name was Rose. Rose never came out. 'She never comes out,' I told my partner. 'I know,' he said, 'I guess she's antisocial.'

The following night would be the real thing. Six dollars an hour. The poster:

Introducing Halloween Town
Featuring Beware House, the 21-room haunted mansion,
7 P.M. – 11 P.M., rain or shine.

Only at Jefferson Valley Mall, Rt. 6, Yorktown Hts., NY, outside the Mall.

Big Mazzo's Monster Band
Trail-of-Terror Maze
Museum of Horror
'Spider-Mobile' Rides
Live Stage Show & More

Every Friday, Saturday & Sunday in October & Columbus Day
Special 'Lights-On' tours for younger audiences, Oct. 14, 19, 26, 1–4 P.M.

Admission was $10.95 per adult. On the big night, I wasn't at the dresser where I'd worked so hard to perfect my technique. I was in a haunt right off the front hall. There were three of us. At first it was very slow. Since we'd all worked in retail, we traded terrible-customer stories. One young woman worked in Customer Service for a supermarket. She said people would go into the store, grab a couple of big packs of Pampers, come up to the register, and try to return them. Say they'd lost their receipts. 'So it's our word against theirs.' The really clever ones had actually bought Pampers on another occasion, and kept the receipt. 'So you have to check the date.'

She told me that her supermarket had one old widow who went to Florida every winter, and before she left, she'd empty out her cupboards and try to return all her supplies for a full refund.

'Did you accept them?'

'Most of them.'

The young woman had a lever to pull. This shut the front door behind the customers as soon as they got inside. Then somebody from another haunt popped out at them. Then I popped out. I had a door where the knob was on the side that didn't open. This added to the confusion when I sprung out and howled, 'Boo'! or 'Argh!' at the top of my lungs. I wore black gloves and a black ski mask. Young couples would come in with the female in front. I'd burst out of my doorway, make the loudest sound I could manage. The girl would scream, throw her arms up in the air, and the boy behind her would grab her breasts. I saw this happen over and over again.

I also worked at Telemarketing Concepts in Yorktown. At orientation we had to fill out a getting-to-know-you question-and-answer sheet. Then we went around the room, and each of us had to read from our sheet. Under hobbies and interests one young woman had written, 'I have a five-year-old boy'.

There was one girl in the class with bronchitis. Everybody else smoked. Everybody else but me. So we all went out for the cigarette breaks.

A number of the girls had tattoos. A pretty blonde showed me her new tattoo. It was a rose. This was on her back, and it looked as if it had been copied exactly out of a book. Maybe traced. She said her uncle drew it for her. 'He's a biker and is always tattooing himself and his wife,' she told me. 'He has a big gut and sits there drawing on his own stomach. He's running out of room.'

At the end of the day we were quizzed on what we'd been told. I got four and a half wrong on my twenty-question test. The girl whose hobby was a five-year-old boy got five wrong.

Telemarketing didn't require a urine test. At first I was surprised by this. Then I figured it out: Nothing to steal.

This was the first job ever with flexible hours. I had a computer screen with my text on it. The computer dialed the numbers for me out of a mailing list the company had purchased or rented. I called businesses in an attempt to sell low-end Pitney Bowes postage meters.

'Hello, this is Ben Cheever calling for Pitney Bowes. I need to speak with an owner or office manager. Who would that be?'

The computer recorded how many calls we'd made, and also our average length of contact with customers. Even if you couldn't sell, you got credit for keeping them on the phone. It took hundreds of phone calls to make a single sale. (A customer who specifically asked to be taken off the list was taken off the list.)

I noticed that my circumstances changed the demands of language. One of my lines was 'Do you currently own a Pitney Bowes postage meter?' As a former editor, I wanted to cut *currently*. *Currently* is an unnecessary word. I am trained and also inclined to cut unnecessary words. But *currently* was needed here. I still don't know how to explain it, but it's a much grander thing to currently own a Pitney Bowes postage meter than it is just to own one.

Most of the people I called hung right up on me. Some were rude, but the atmosphere at the shop itself was genial. You were allowed to go to the bathroom anytime you wanted. If you bought a mug at Dunkin' Donuts, you could fill it with coffee or tea and bring that to work. Supervisors listened in sometimes, to check on our delivery, but criticisms were rare and never harsh.

It was highly unusual to get a live prospect, but when you did, everybody pitched in to help you land it. I wasn't entirely familiar with the software, so I nearly lost the first sale, but the black woman at the keyboard next to mine hung up her own phone, reached over, and led me through it, keyboarding the necessary changes.

Most of the other telemarketers were women, but I had a man in the cubicle beside me one morning. I must have said, 'Hello, this is Ben Cheever calling for Pitney Bowes' two hundred times before he reached over and tapped me on the back.

'Are you related to the writer?' he asked.

'What?' I asked.

'John Cheever, the writer. I used to see him in Ossining sometimes.'

I shrugged, gestured around at the booth I was in. 'What do you think?' I asked.

He shrugged back, looked vaguely embarrassed. 'I don't know. It might be a large family.'

Section Three
Shelf Life

The idea that the poor should have leisure has always been shocking to the rich.

— Bertrand Russell

There are many ways, in the contemporary world, in which people who have never met meet, appraise, and identify one another. Accents, clothes, how much they spend, airline class in which they travel, people whom they know, universities they have attended, things more subtle and ineffable. Nothing, for Americans at least, seems more immediate than institutional affiliation, the place where they work, and in what capacity.

— Renata Adler, *Gone*

Cosi Sandwich Bar: Slow G

IN *ENEMIES OF PROMISE* CYRIL CONNOLLY NOTES THAT while alcoholism and opium addiction are common to writers, 'the harmless activities of daydreaming and conversation are more insidious. Daydreaming bears a suspicious resemblance to the working of the creative imagination. It is in fact a substitute for it and one in which all difficulties are shelved, all problems ignored, a short cut ending in a blank wall. This is even more true of conversation; a good talker can talk away the substance of twenty books in as many evenings. He will describe the central idea of the book he means to write until it revolts him'.

I don't know if I'd characterize myself as a good talker, but I am certainly a devoted one. Having started to write this book in 1995, I've talked most of my intimate friends into a stupor, and button-holed relative strangers to astound them with anecdotes about how I, Benjamin Cheever, worked as a Burns security guard, a computer salesman, and a spook in the Halloween Town outside the Jefferson Valley Mall.

The more I talked, the less I did. Getting a job is like jumping into ice water. Once dunked, I'm invigorated. The longer I stay out, though, the harder it is to go back into the water.

My third novel was published in the spring of 1999, and while the world didn't exactly stop to read it, I did have a plausible excuse to stay home. After the petit mal of publication publicity, I segued easily into the role of house husband and miniature celebrity, the world's smallest pooh-bah.

On Thursday, October 8, 1999, I was fifty-one years old. The

Great Books Society of Briarcliff Manor had recently paid me one thousand dollars to make a twenty-minute speech at their Guardian of Civilization dinner. No, I wasn't the Guardian of Civilization, but I knew him, Maurice 'Mitch' Freedman, director of the Westchester Library System.

I needed badly to get back into the water. My friend Ruth Reichl, editor of *Gourmet*, prodded me. She said I seemed happiest, most alive, when I was working. She said that if I got a job in food service in Manhattan and wrote about it, she might publish it in her magazine.

I thought this one would be easy. We were right in the heart of the Clinton boom. I wore jeans and a sweater. I have one of those watches designed to whisper, 'I cost a lot of money.' I left this at home.

On the train from Pleasantville, I found an alarming piece on the front page of *The New York Times* The headline: 'Poverty Rate Persists in City Despite Boom: Twice as High as Nation, Analysis of Data Shows'. 'Despite the strongest economy in years, nearly one out of four New York City residents had incomes below the Federal Government's poverty threshold last year . . . ,' the story said.

The article reported that 1.8 million New York City residents were below the poverty line, which was set at $16,665 a year for a household of four.

So maybe it wasn't going to be that easy to get a job.

By the time I got off the train, I had remembered how little I enjoy being humiliated. I walked up and down Forty-second Street. I saw a bright orange Help Wanted sign in the window of the combined Roy Rogers and Dunkin' Donuts store on the east side of Forty-second between Vanderbilt and Madison Avenues. No, I didn't charge right in and apply. I'd save Dunkin' Donuts until all else failed. If all else failed.

There was a new restaurant opening in Pershing Square. It was called, oddly enough, Pershing Square. A sign said that they were serving breakfast and lunch but soon they would have a full day's schedule. I walked up to the bar. One young man in a splendid uniform was teaching another guy to use the register. I waited politely until the transaction was complete, meanwhile looking nervously around to make certain no customers were in earshot.

'I want to apply for a job,' I whispered.

'Will you fill out an application?'

'Sure.'

He gave me a form and a pen and let me sit at a table. I said I had a résumé. I asked if I could use that and fill in the blanks not covered. He smiled warmly. 'We'll just staple the forms together,' he said.

Back on the street, I felt much better. To say, 'I want to apply for a job' is to risk being told, 'We don't have any' or worse yet, 'We don't have any for you!' Instead I'd ask for job applications. The meanest thing they could say would be, 'No, we don't have any job applications.' I crossed the street, walked back up Forty-second past the Dunkin' Donuts, ducked into the Starbucks, and ordered a tall skim-milk latte. 'And could I have a job application with that?' I asked, just as if it were a raisin scone I wanted.

The man in line behind me looked down at his feet. He was embarrassed. So was I. The man at the register rifled through three drawers but couldn't find any applications.

'Thanks anyway,' I said, as if it were a matter of little consequence.

The man at the register smiled. He said I should come back when the manager was there. He told me the manager's name was Scott. 'We're always looking for good people,' he said.

Now I *was* encouraged. 'We're always looking for good people.' That was me, then: good people.

So I tried the two other Starbucks in the neighborhood. They didn't have job applications, either. I tried a third Starbucks. Still no job applications.

Having circled Grand Central Terminal, I went up Forty-fifth Street and tried Alonti. They did have job applications. I was given one to fill out. I don't believe I'd ever filled out the desired-salary slot before, but this time I did. I put down nine dollars an hour. That summer there had been signs on the side of the road near our house in Pleasantville that read, Summer Jobs, $10 an Hour. It's true they had appeared on some of the same telephone poles that used to have signs that read, Thirty Pounds, Thirty Days, Thirty Dollars, but then ten dollars didn't sound outrageous. Where it said experience I wrote, 'none'. Where it asked when I was willing to start, I wrote, 'immediately'. I attached the résumé that said I had published three novels and worked for a decade at the *Reader's Digest*.

Then a slender woman with red hair appeared, and asked, 'Is there any chance you can come back at quarter to three?'

'Sure,' I said, 'certainly.'

'Come back at quarter to three, and I'll give you an interview,' she said.

I smiled, nodded, and walked back out on to Forty-fifth Street.

I looked where my watch should have been, and remembered I'd left it at home. I asked a passerby the time. He said it was 1:40 P.M.

Not bad, I thought. *Been in town for an hour and five minutes, and already I've gotten an interview, very possibly a job.*

After that, I went through other doors, probed the depths of the job-application shortage, but mostly I killed time. I went into Grand Central Terminal and took notes. I practically had a job, after all. I'd always wanted to serve breakfast, dole out fresh bagels and strong coffee as dawn pinked the canyons of Manhattan. I'd get to know the customers. 'The regular?' I'd ask when they came in. I'd cast off witticisms about the weather. 'Hot enough for you?'; 'Cold enough for you?'; 'Wet enough for you?' I'd call all the men Doctor, all the women Princess. I'd be a legend. Charles Kuralt would film my life. Or was he dead?

Back at Alonti, I asked the counterman there if it was 2:45 P.M. yet. 'Almost,' he said.

'I'm here for an interview,' I said.

'I'll check,' he said, and went off to the part of the store that couldn't be seen from the dining area. He returned immediately and said, 'She's busy. She'll be with you in a minute. Do you want anything?'

'No, thanks,' I said.

'Take something,' he said. 'A cup of coffee?'

I said that a cup of coffee would be great.

'Help yourself, then,' he said.

So I poured myself a half a cup of hazelnut coffee. I didn't want to appear to be a terrible freeloader. I sat at a long table, turning my chair so that I faced the counter.

I was nervous. I didn't have anything to read, so I walked to the display at the front door, and brought a menu back to my seat.

I read: 'Breakfast: Taco served with eggs, cheese, and potatoes with your choice of bacon or sausage, $1.75'. I looked up at the counter. Still no redhead. Back to the menu: 'Vegetarian Taco: Eggs, cheese, and potatoes, $1.75'. Out of the corner of my eye, I saw a man in a slightly rumpled yellow polo shirt come and sit at the other end of the table. He didn't have any food. He seemed to be angry. He had a little black beard on his chin. The beard was neat. Otherwise, he was not neat.

One of the rules I'd learned about the city was that when a perfect stranger stares at you, you'd better look away. So I looked politely away. 'You want to talk to me?' he said.

He sounded like Robert De Niro saying, 'You talkin' to me?' to the mirror in that scene from *Taxi Driver*. I didn't want to get in a quarrel with a stranger just when I was applying for a job, so I pretended not to hear him. 'You want to talk to me?' he said again, and he was louder this time. I stood and moved towards the counter. Now the man in the yellow polo shirt was shouting. 'You want to talk to me?' he said. Then: 'He doesn't want to talk with me.'

I didn't look at him. I was in New York City; many of the bigger mental hospitals closed years ago.

The redhead appeared behind the counter. I moved towards her eagerly. 'My interview?' I asked.

She nodded towards the man in the yellow shirt.

'Is *he* supposed to interview me?' I asked.

She nodded. 'He's the district manager,' she said.

'I didn't know that,' I said, my voice cracking. 'I was only trying to be polite.'

The redhead shrugged.

I turned to face De Niro. 'You want to talk to me?' he said again.

I said, 'Yes, I want to talk to you.'

'Okay,' he said, and went up to the counter. 'Get me that résumé,' he said, and the counterman pulled my application and résumé off of a pile of trays and passed it out.

The district manager sat down again at our table. I sat facing him. He looked at my form.

'You say you want nine dollars an hour?' he said.

I nodded.

'You say you have no experience?'

I nodded again.

'Basically, you have no experience and you want nine dollars an hour.'

I nodded again.

He gave a great shrug. 'I'd have to train you,' he said. 'That would be very expensive. The best I can offer you is a job as a dishwasher for five-fifteen an hour.'

I might have gone for it, but I'd already been a dishwasher. Plus, we didn't seem to get along brilliantly.

'That's not enough,' I said. I asked for my résumé, and he gave it to me.

Back out in the street, I headed right for the Dunkin' Donuts. First I went downstairs and used the men's room. Then I came back upstairs and waited until there was no line. I went up to the coffee counter. The woman at the register had a ring in her nose.

'I want to apply for a job,' I said quietly.

She looked dubious.

Maybe she hadn't heard me. 'I want to apply for a job,' I said again, more loudly this time.

'Cashiers,' she said. She spoke slowly and deliberately. Clearly English was a second language, or even a third. 'We need cashiers.'

'Do you need to know how to operate a cash register?' I asked. She wagged her head.

'So you could train me?' I said, my voice rising in hope.

'Girls,' she said slowly, as if I were incredibly dense, as if I were the one having trouble with the language. 'We need girls.'

The next time I saw the district manager from Alonti, I was behind the counter at the Cosi Sandwich Bar at Forty-fourth and Third. I had on my black Cosi shirt, my snowy apron, and Cosi baseball hat. Even so, I had trouble breathing. I don't know now what I thought the man with the beard would do to me. Yell? Fire me? Of course, he didn't do anything. He didn't even recognize me. Not that I blame him for that. In the following weeks, people came in from the homeless center where I sometimes volunteer. These people didn't recognize me, either.

The district manager from Alonti had on another yellow polo shirt, or maybe the same yellow polo shirt. There were three people in the Alonti party. One of them might have been the redhead. One of them was a man I'd never seen before with a Polo windbreaker. I screwed up my courage, and when they got near the counter, I asked if I could help the man in the windbreaker. He smiled at me and said they were just looking. I heard them talking to one another. They were casing the place. Checking up on the competition.

The fast-lunch competition is tough in this part of New York. Walking across Forty-third Street from Grand Central to the Cosi I worked at on Forty-fourth and Third, I pass an Au Bon Pain: The French Bakery Cafe then featuring the Hot Roast Turkey Club: 'What Pilgrims might have had for lunch'. I also passed a Ranch★ 1. 'The Best Grilled Chicken Sandwich on Earth,' their slogan says in neon lettering.

I was happy to be at Cosi. The place is clean, and they have two gimmicks. The first is the vast oven, which you see and smell immediately after stepping through the door. Two people wielding

paddles bake pizza romana, the fresh bread on which the sandwiches are made.

The second gimmick is even simpler: They're kind.

It had taken me more than a week to get behind that counter. I
hadn't actually been turned down for many jobs, or not that I knew
of. It takes time and luck to be turned down for a job. First you
need to find a place that has an application and fill that out. Then
you need to come back when there's a manager on hand and with
the inclination to look at it. I had walked in a dozen different doors
and come back to some of them several times. I had finally found an
application at the fourth Starbucks I tried. I had filled it out, and
came back once to see if they'd looked at it. They hadn't looked at
it yet. They never did look at it.

Not that Cosi had job applications, either. I had lucked into the
general manager, though. I came after the rush, and she was right
out in the front of the store, and had a minute. She said that if I
came back the next day, they might have applications.

'And if you don't,' I said boldly, 'will you interview me
anyway?'

She said she would.

I came back the next day. They still didn't have job applications,
but she agreed to look at my résumé.

In this case I had listed the jobs I'd held up until I left the *Reader's
Digest*. I hadn't put down the fifteen or so jobs I held for this book.
Too confusing? Too depressing? A little of both.

'But you haven't worked for ten years?' she said.

I said I'd been writing. I said I'd published three novels.

'Terrific,' she said, and she said it with genuine enthusiasm. No
irony. No satire. I could see right away that she wasn't one of my
people.

'This will be very different than the literary life,' she said.

I said I knew that.

She asked me why I wanted to work at Cosi.

I said I liked the food. I said I'd eaten there once. I said it looked
exciting.

'But why food service?'

'I thought it was a job I could just walk in and get,' I said.

I can't know, but I assume that when I say I think a job might be interesting, employers assume I'm in much deeper than I've let on. They respect my need to keep a wall around my despair.

The general manager at the Cosi on Third Avenue then was named Andrea, a humorous, dark-haired woman in a Cosi shirt with a collar – collars indicate management. Sandwich makers, on the other hand, wear T-shirts. But all of us wear chinos – except for the bakers, who wear white pants and shirts. Managers wear beige baseball hats; the rest of us wear black ones.

She said she'd like it if I worked from ten to two, Monday through Friday, for a twenty-hour week. I said that was perfect. She explained that I would try out first for a day. 'To see if it's something you think you want to do.' OJE, they call it. 'On-Job Evaluation'.

She said she would have tried me out that day, that minute. 'But,' she explained, 'my boss is going to be here and he's great, but he's highly strung. He'll be like, "What are you doing? Do this for me right now." '

I nodded. 'I don't like to be yelled at,' I said. She said I should come in the next day just before ten A.M. 'I'll give you a shirt and a hat, and I'll put you to work. Afterwards, we'll give you a great lunch.'

I felt that I'd come ashore on high ground. I'd been fretting about never getting a job. This woman was going to give me a tryout. And a shirt. Plus she was protecting me from her sharp-tongued boss. Leaving the store, I noticed a sign in the window saying, Managers Have Limited Access to Safe. I liked that, too. It seemed to indicate a concern for the employees.

I walked on air to Grand Central and called my wife at home from one of the pay phones. She had her doubts. 'But don't you suppose Ruth would rather you worked at Le Bernardin?' she said.

I exploded. 'I don't have a job at Le Bernardin,' I said. 'I couldn't get a job at Roy Rogers. Starbucks won't call me back.'

I told her I had an interview at Ranch★ 1 in an hour.

She said that wasn't going to help.

I said that before my interview at Ranch★ 1, I'd walk to Restaurant Row and drop off some résumés.

I headed across town. It was cold, and there was a terrible wind blowing against me from the river. This seemed the outward manifestation of my inner reluctance. I definitely wasn't going to try Orso. I'd eaten there with Janet. It was a hangout for *Times* staffers. *Eventually somebody will recognize me there,* I thought, *or they won't.* Either outcome would have been excruciating.

Fortunately, a lot of the restaurants were closed that morning. I did get in downstairs at Joe Allen's. I asked if they had job applications. The woman I spoke with didn't know. I said I wanted to apply for a job.

'As what?'

'As a waiter.'

'You'll have to come back,' she said. 'The person who handles that isn't here.'

So I asked if I could leave a résumé.

Sure, she said. 'Leave a résumé, and you won't have to come back.'

They would call me if they wanted me to come in for an interview. They haven't called yet. Nor has Starbucks. Or Pershing Square. Or the Oyster Bar.

The manager at Ranch★ 1 did offer me a job. Night grill was one of the positions she had available. She told me the work was grueling. 'I can see you're an older gentleman,' she said. I said I'd try other places first, but asked if I could come back. 'Anytime,' she said.

I showed up for my Cosi tryout that Friday at 9:30 A.M. You clock in, so theoretically, if you arrive early or leave late, you're paid for it. My name wasn't in the company databank yet. I wore a battered cotton sweater. I'd ripped out the Ralph Lauren label. I thought this would isolate me from the other workers. This was silly. Later I would see Ralph Lauren labels at

Cosi. When I started looking, I also saw them at the homeless drop-in center.

Andrea gave me a T-shirt and a hat. The shirt was new; the hat was not new. Andrea apologized for this and helped me line the inside with paper towels. I changed in the rest room. I was introduced to the head of the sandwich department. He was a young black man whose manner was both friendly and relaxed.

'What can I do? I don't know anything.'

'You can make the vinaigrette,' he said, and showed me how. I followed him around that morning, doing what he asked. I brought up ice for the line. I put the paper liners on the metal trays on which sandwiches are served. I filled up plastic cups with ice and ice water, stored them in the refrigerator case. I refilled the vinaigrette bottles and also filled custard cups with vinaigrette for people who wanted it on the side.

At the Cosi on Forty-fourth and Third, the sandwich line is below street level, so walking in is like coming down into a sunken living room. The floors are stone; many of the surfaces are stainless steel. The big circular oven is clad in black iron and set at the head of the line. The sandwich makers live and work in the aisle between two counters. The counter that separates us from the customers holds bowls and platters of sandwich fillings on ice. The one behind us is stainless-steel, and there is a refrigerator underneath for refills. During business hours, there are tubs of lettuce and sliced tomatoes on the counter above the refrigerator. The music is mostly early vocalists: Peggy Lee singing, 'You've come a long way from Saint Louie, Louie.'

Much of the food preparation is done outside the store, but the ingredients are put together, the utensils are washed, and the dough is mixed in the basement. The bread is baked and the sandwiches are assembled upstairs. There's a lot of rushing up and down the flight of stairs to the basement.

The line manager had worked at Cosi for two years. I loved his style. Everything I did, he said, was perfect. This has always been my idea of excellent management.

The sandwich business at Cosi (coffee and muffins are sold from seven in the morning) begins at eleven A.M. and gets most intense between noon and two P.M.

It was a sort of joyous hell working there the first day. I was the only white man on the line. I thought this might be a problem, but one of the bakers lanced that boil immediately. A big man with his hair in cornrows, he broke the ice by calling me homey. After he'd done that a couple of times, he called me nigger, and so I knew that we were friends.

When I got off work that day at 2:15 P.M., I was exhausted. My hands were raw from the hot bread, my throat hoarse from shouting, 'Mayo, mustard, or vinaigrette?'

I didn't serve anyone a dead rat, but even I could tell how slow I was and how badly I wrapped my sandwiches in aluminum foil when they were to go.

Riding the train home, I got a seat in front of a posted advertisement that featured a man of about my age sitting in his chair in a corner office. Out the window you can see the Manhattan skyline. On his desk there's a computer and a telephone. He has his chair tipped back, his hands clasped behind his head. He's on top of the world.

The text: 'Tomorrow he could be crawling under the carpet. THE TRUTH. DEAL WITH IT. REUTERS WWW. REUTERS.COM.'

The next day, Monday, I went to the store at Thirty-six Street and Seventh Avenue for orientation. The fresh recruits gathered down-stairs in the back off the restaurant. These were boom times, but thirteen of the fourteen applicants who'd agreed to show up for orientation at Cosi showed up. My group was mostly dark-skinned, mostly young. One of the other cadets was reading Richard Wright's *Native Son*. Another was a foreigner who had severe difficulties with the language. He appeared to have come down in the world. He was a courtly man, as old as I was, and wearing wide-wale corduroy pants from Tommy Hilfiger. I don't know if it was his accent or his bearing, but I thought that he must have been an educated man. He was applying for a job in delivery. Delivery workers start at $5.15 an hour. Sandwich makers begin at $6.25 an hour. Bakers at $6.75.

Most of the people I worked with at Cosi were a good deal younger than I was. This may be food service. It may be Manhattan. In Westchester I've held a number of jobs for seven dollars an hour with people in their fifties and even sixties.

After we'd all gathered, we were brought upstairs to a classroom.

Our teacher was named Jim, and he was carefully respectful in the handling and pronunciation of our different names. We each had to produce two pieces of identification and to fill out our IRS forms. He said we should be kind to one another. 'If I asked everybody in this room who wants to be disrespected to raise a hand, nobody would raise a hand.'

Jim told us about the origin of the business, about Jay and Shep Wainwright and the restaurant they'd found in Paris and decided to transplant to New York. He was very encouraging, although he did say that the Wainwright boys had decided to go into business because they didn't want to work for anybody else. I wondered where that put us.

The Cosi story sounded a little fanciful. The original Paris restaurant that caught the founders' attention was started by a New Zealander named Drew Harre.

According to the *Cosi Sandwich Bar Crew Member Handbook,* from which Jim ad-libbed, 'Drew is a fabulous man, experienced in many different areas. Drew's background as a computer programmer, professional wine taster, and renowned cookbook author was not enough for him. He wanted to try his hand as a restaurateur'.

Drew decided that Paris needed a sandwich bar, 'but not just any sandwich shop, a fabulous sandwich bar. With this in mind, Drew began combing the streets of Paris for "fabulous" bread – the foundation of a "fabulous" sandwich. Drew tried French baguettes, Middle Eastern pitas, Mexican sopapillas and Jewish rye. All were good. But none were "fabulous". With great despair, Drew wandered the streets of Paris trying to figure out what to do'.

You're supposed to imagine Benjamin Franklin disconsolately trailing his kite, or Lawrence of Arabia off by himself in the desert before it came to him: 'Aquaba buy the land!'

Drew Harre, it seemed, was also stricken with divine inspiration. 'Suddenly, he smelled something "fabulous" – something warm and cozy. Drew smelled pizza romana, an ancient Italian flatbread that two old Italian men were baking in a tiny bakery hidden in a small alleyway.'

I don't know why, but most every company that's bothered to train me at all has told me something about its origins. I learned about Norman Jemal of Nobody Beats the Wiz. I had to watch the movie, too. I know that Burns Security was founded in 1909 by William J. Burns, the first man to head the FBI. The car dealership I worked at had a hallway plastered with black-and-white pictures of the service station it had grown out of. Later I would hear about the Borders brothers. Nobody much believes in God anymore, but apparently there's no employee so worthless that he won't be inspired to do a better job by being fed a creation myth.

During orientation, we were each given the twenty-seven-page *Cosi Sandwich Bar Crew Member Handbook*. One of Cosi's four core values is fun. 'Life is too short to not have a good time.'

I was also given the twenty-two-page *Cosi College Sandwich Maker Manual*. After the orientation, we each got two shirts and a hat. I'd only worked a day, and already I had three shirts. It had taken me a month to get one shirt at CompUSA. I figured I was way ahead. Then we were sent home.

First, you train for a week at one store, then you go to work at another, so Tuesday I showed up at ten A.M. at the sandwich bar at Thirty-sixth Street. There was one other sandwich maker training with me.

I learned the four Cosi questions:

1. What would you like?
2. Would you like mayo, mustard, or vinaigrette with that?
3. Would you like a drink?
4. Is this for here or to go?

I learned that a piece of bread should be seven and a half inches long and four inches wide. I knew the six reasons for discarding bread:

1. Undersized
2. Cold
3. Hard
4. Burnt
5. Soggy
6. Misshapen or torn with holes

Mornings, we studied. In the afternoons we worked on the line with our trainer watching and correcting whenever time allowed. Over the course of the week, we took three written tests. I got a perfect score on the first, 90 per cent on the second, and 98 on the last. 'You definitely have to do something about this handwriting,' I was told.

I shrugged. 'I've been told that before,' I said.

The following Monday, I went back to work at the store on Third Avenue. My old friend the baker was there. Same line manager as well. Everybody talks exactly like my thirteen-year-old son: 'Wassup?' they say, instead of, 'Good morning'. 'Wasshappening, homey? This ain't the hood, my bad.'

After the line was set up and before the rush, we'd take fresh bread, slather it with spread, and cut it into bite-sized chunks. Then a worker wearing a green Cosi shirt would go out on to the street and give these away.

One of the employees with this assignment was a pregnant woman of color. At one point early in my tenure, I was told by a manager to prepare her samples for her.

She told me not to. She told me she prepared her own samples. If I prepared samples for her, she told me, 'I'm gonna throw them away.'

I told her I didn't care about her samples, but that I did care about doing what I was told.

We had a little back-and-forth, and then my friend the baker came popping around from the oven where he works and paraphrased Rodney King. 'Why can't we all just get along?' he said. This made everybody laugh.

The only other time race came up was when Andrea's boss, a white man, visited the store and complimented the single black woman then on the line. Let's call her Mary. Mary was a young woman I'd gotten to know quite well. She was also short and seemed a girl to me, although she wore blue eye shadow with sparkles in it and had a child to get home to. The manager stood on the outside of the counter, while we all massed behind it. He spoke only to Mary. 'You're the best, Mary,' he told her. 'You *are* the best.' After the manager left, several of her colleagues turned to Mary and pointed. 'Mary, you're white,' they said. 'Now you're white.'

Mary and I and the line manager were the first ones there in the morning, so we set up the line together.

'How old are you?' Mary asked me.

'Old,' I said, 'very old.'

'How old is very old?'

'Fifty-one.'

'You should be retired. Don't you want to retire?'

I shrugged.

'What makes you think you can keep up with us young folks?'

I said I'd have to see.

'What did you do before this?'

'I wrote books.'

'Why are you doing this now?'

'For a change. And because people seem more interested in buying sandwiches than they are in buying my books.'

Then she relented and tried to teach me the job. I'm afraid she found me a very slow learner.

Downstairs I was picking up something heavy when my friend the baker shocked me by saying, 'Careful there. Don't want to croak you, Pops.' Pops? What could he have been thinking?

After we set up the line in the mornings, we had a weigh-in. The fillings are in metal bowls with ice-cream scoops or tongs or simple spreaders. The line supervisor has everybody take an estimated serving of all key ingredients. Most ingredients, tandoori chicken, for instance, or Buffalo chicken, are supposed to be doled out in four-ounce dollops. You give five ounces of portobello mushrooms and six ounces of tuna. The spreads, such as chili – black bean and sundried tomato, are supposed to be served in two-ounce smears.

The Cosi 1, which cost $5.95, had one key ingredient; mayo, mustard, or vinaigrette; a piece of romaine lettuce; and three slices of tomato.

The Cosi 2 had two ingredients and cost $6.95. What's confusing is that spreads, such as spinach-artichoke, are considered ingredients, while lettuce, tomato, mustard, mayo, and vinaigrette are not.

So a person could have roast beef and Swiss with caramelized onions and run up a bill of $7.95 while having a sandwich no bigger than that of a customer who had roast beef, mayo, mustard, lettuce, tomato, and vinaigrette and paid $5.95.

There was a monthly special that entitled the customer to two ingredients for the price of one. When I started work the special was Caesar chicken with grated Parmesan. Later it became Santa Fe chicken with chili – black bean spread.

The largest meal for the least money was the soup and half a sandwich, because it wasn't actually half a sandwich, but three quarters of a sandwich with two ingredients, plus a small soup or salad. This cost $6.95.

Everybody wanted to make the best sandwich possible. The rule seems to apply to all businesses. I've worked with dramatically different people. Some were bitter, some proud. But they all wanted to make the best sandwich.

Most of the customers were jolly and enthusiastic, but not all. We were behind the counter, and that made us slightly less than human. I remember an impressive young man, in a suit and wearing suspenders, for whom I was making a sandwich. I dropped a nugget of his Buffalo chicken into the mayo. He was horrified. Of course I threw the meat away, but this didn't win his forgiveness. I could see he was thinking, *Why do they let these people into the country?*

During the rush, we all made mistakes. It was impossible not to. The pace was furious. On a good day our store would sell six hundred sandwiches on the line and send out another hundred from catering, which was down in the basement. (Everybody remembers the day Goldman Sachs had a take-out order of more than two hundred sandwiches.)

The pad of Cosi notes, which is worn at the side in a holster complete with marker, holds fifty slips. On more than one occasion, I used up more than one Cosi pad in a day. I was shown how to fold up the corner of each slip. Otherwise, the vinyl gloves, oily with condiments, make it difficult to tear one slip off at a time.

There was a large bowl in front of the oven with small pieces of the fresh bread. Bait. Often people would come in and take a piece, and then have a sandwich. Others came in, took a piece of bread, then looked as if they'd just remembered what a hurry they were in and rushed out without buying anything.

During one lull, a man came in and found several of us slumped back against the wall. 'Where do you work?' he asked, and pointed at the man next to me.

'Here.'

'Well, then could you please wait on me?'

But this unpleasantness was dramatically out of place.

I've been told that men are predators, and if so, we must have hunted in packs, because that's how we eat. When one person came in alone, he or she would often eye the offerings like a single wolf looking at a healthy stag and then retreat without ordering.

For this reason, when the business fell off, it really fell off. We got tired of asking people what they wanted and having them flee the store.

But when it rains it pours. It's lunchtime, and the line stretches out to the sidewalk. Suddenly, there are five people standing coyly near the mouth of the oven, consulting with one another and trying to decide what they want or even if they want to eat at Cosi at all. Meanwhile, another twenty people in a terrible hurry have stacked up behind them.

We all begin to bay. 'Can I help the next person who is ready to order? Please step down if you're ready to order. Can I help the next hungry customer?'

I like a challenge. That's what I tell myself, heart racing, sweat pooling in the fingers of my vinyl gloves. 'If you're ready to order, please step down!' I yell.

The sound system is playing 'My Blue Heaven'. I grab a piece of bread that is so hot it burns my hand. While running a large serrated bread knife through it to open the pocket, I begin to shout in the direction of the customers. But I'm also concentrating on the knife. It's possible to cut the bread incorrectly. I have done so. Then you have to throw the piece away, and the bakers hate you.

'Can I help the next person, please?'

I catch the eye of a middle-aged woman with short blond hair and thick glasses. I wave my bread at her and she comes out of the line of deliberators and up to the counter.

'Can I help you, miss?'

A woman is always miss, a man is always sir. The older a woman is, the louder you 'miss' her; the younger a man is, the more definite the 'sir'.

She points at the tray of tomato, basil, and mozzarella.

'Would you like that?'

She nods.

'Is that all you want?'

She nods again.

Another two sandwich makers have come between me and the

oven. I'm not moving fast enough. One of them is angry. 'Don't baby-sit the bread.'

I move down.

I give her three slices of TBM.

'For here or to go?'

'For here,' she says.

I'm turning to the back counter to wrap her sandwich, when I hear her asking a question. 'What kind of cheese do you have?' I turn back to face her.

'Swiss, cheddar, and Brie.'

She points to the red chicken.

'That's tandoori chicken. You want that?'

She nods.

Now I'm supposed to put back one of the portions of tomato, basil, and mozzarella. If you're having the TBM in a Cosi 1, you get three portions. If you're having a second main ingredient, you get two. I don't put the portion back. I give her a large scoop of tandoori chicken.

'Mayo, mustard, or vinaigrette?' I ask.

'Mustard.'

'Honey-mustard or Dijon?'

'What's that?' she asks, and points.

'Spinach-artichoke spread.'

'Give me some of that.' By now the two other sandwich makers have passed me. I need to poke between them to get at the spread.

Does she want lettuce?

During the rush, it's not uncommon to have nine people racing around in an aisle about four and a half feet wide by twenty feet long. We're all hollering and banging into one another. If the word *pandemonium* hadn't been thought up yet, this would have been a good time to do it.

She does want lettuce.

I turn to the stainless-steel counter behind the line and get her a piece of romaine lettuce.

Vinaigrette on that?

'No.'

I ask her to go down to the end of the counter. 'I'll bring you your sandwich.'

I can't remember now if she wanted the sandwich to go, in which case I need to wrap it in two pieces of aluminum foil. I put the sandwich in its paper envelope. I move down to the last station on the line. Each station has a cutting board, paper envelopes, aluminum foil, a knife, and a bottle of vinaigrette. 'For here or to go?' I ask.

'For here,' she says.

I put the sandwich on a metal tray, tear off a Cosi slip, and mark it.

This is a memory test. We discussed mustard, but that doesn't matter. She had TBM, tandoori chicken, and spinach-artichoke spread. I need to remember all of those, mark each one off, select Cosi 3 at the top of the page, and put the note on the tray with the sandwich. 'Would you care for a drink, miss?'

During the rush, I often have to pause to remember what's in the sandwich I'm writing up. Sometimes, and this is shameful to admit, I have to pry the bread open to remind myself.

The confusion is heightened by the fact that everybody else is shouting ingredients. Did you just shout tomato, basil, and mozzarella, or was that somebody else?

Often, I turn back to the crowd and can't remember whose sandwich I've made. You have a bad nanosecond, but most of the time they remember you.

I'm slow, but even for me, the entire process of making a sandwich takes less than a minute, and I might have to keep working like this for two hours. Modern physics has taught us that time is relative. I'm not a physicist, so I couldn't say if time stands still or races during the rush, but it's different. That much I know. *Un coup de feu* is what Orwell called it when he was working as a *plongeur* at Restaurant X in Paris.

Fortunately the food is all good at Cosi, so you can't go terribly wrong there. The Cosi sandwich was voted the number-one sandwich by *Zagat's* for two years running.

'I watched in astonishment as he built my sandwich, stuffing the fillings in until the bread could hold no more,' wrote Ruth Reichl in *The New York Times*. 'It was a hefty meal for $7.95. The bread was fabulous, crusty, and slightly burnt in places.'

The customers are generally in good spirits. Maybe it's the novelty, the smell of fresh bread.

Whatever your character flaws, they come up in your work, whatever your work. I'm terrified of displeasing anyone. I wanted to get a smile from each customer. I ask too many questions: Would you like vinaigrette on the lettuce? Can I cut your sandwich in half?

I know from my experience years ago at the *Reader's Digest* that if you're a manager and you want to criticize somebody, you should touch them at the same moment. This seems to ground the criticism.

Halfway through my first day on Forty-fourth Street and Third Avenue, the manager of the sandwich line put a hand on my waist and one on my shoulder. 'Would you do me a big favor?' he asked.

'Sure,' I said.

'Would you please *not* cut everybody's sandwich in half? If they ask you to cut it in half, then do that. But don't offer to cut everybody's sandwich in half. You're slowing the line.'

He was right. I knew he was right.

The expertness with which I was handled seemed to fit neatly with the entire philosophy of the place. We served good food. We ate the food we served. (Each worker was entitled to a free sandwich and two drinks for every day he worked.) Food that should be thrown away was thrown away.

This is not the case at every restaurant. Years ago, I worked at a diner that has since gone under, and we used to wash the dressing off the salad and serve it again. Seltzer was put in the pastry displays overnight so that the 'today's baked goods' stayed damp enough to maintain the illusion. The ingredients at Cosi were genuinely fresh.

The second day I was faster, but still not very fast.

Most of my coworkers had nicknames, or actual names that sounded like nicknames. One guy, for instance, was called

Supremo. I was called Ben, Benny, Big Ben, Pops, or Gramps. One tall young man known as Loverboy himself, used to call me Papadopolis, or Papa Doc. 'Papa Doc's on point,' he'd say when I wiped down the counter during the rush. One day when we were only moderately busy, I heard somebody say, 'Slow G.'

'Who's that?' I asked.

'Just an expression we use,' I was told.

'What does it mean?' I asked.

'Slow Grandpa,' I was told.

'Is that me?' I asked.

There was a terrible silence.

At the end of the day at the end of the first week, the sandwich manager waved to me on the way out the door. 'You're not Slow G anymore,' he said.

So I thought I was over the hump. But then the next Monday the line manager, my mentor and protector, was gone. Fired. Yes, I asked why. Nobody would say. 'He did something very, very stupid,' Andrea told me. She wouldn't say what. Then my baker friend, the stocky guy with the Rodney King quote, was moved to another store. The new manager was pleasant enough, but I felt abandoned. My two champions were gone. One of the men I'd trained with was being transferred out. I told him I'd miss him. He said he was glad to go. 'What they say behind your back around here . . . ,' he said, and looked at me meaningfully. I wondered if people had been saying things behind his back. I certainly hadn't heard anything. Then I wondered if people had been saying things behind my back. I decided I wouldn't think about it. I'd work harder.

It wasn't until the Tuesday of my third week on the job that I made a sandwich you might have taken a picture of. Up until then I'd always thought, *God, I hope nobody opens the bread and sees what a mess I've made*. But finally, on Day Twelve, I felt I'd hit my stride.

The rush is a grueling workout. Ordinarily, I run five miles a day. Working at Cosi rendered this unnecessary. After work, I hobbled over to Grand Central, swilled down a Diet Coke, and tried to remember which end was up. There's also a vulnerability associated with this sort of exertion. I enjoy running the New York Marathon, because when I come down off the Fifty-ninth Street Bridge at sixteen miles, and the crowd cheers, I'm stupid enough to think it's me they're cheering.

Working together feverishly between the counters, we all touched one another a lot, and I enjoyed that. My coworkers weren't always friendly, but they were always present, always direct. There was a good deal of affectionate horsing around. There were squabbles, but there seemed to be very little hypocrisy. I was part of a team here. I felt loyal, included. I knew that I was slow, but I figured that as long as I took my bread right away from the oven, at least I wasn't getting in anybody else's way. I was working as quickly as I knew how. I made a good-looking sandwich.

I didn't know how deluded I was about my adequacy until my third week on the job. It was late in the rush. We were all shouting and scrambling over one another. I was heading back to the oven when another sandwich maker – a woman I didn't recognize – grabbed my arm in two hands. 'You've got to go out and get your customers,' she shouted. 'You're slowing the line.'

I smiled, broke free, and went back to work. I knew that I was supposed to call my customers down. Furthermore, I *was* calling my customers down.

Ten minutes later, I had a piece of bread and a partial order. I was heading away from the oven when this same woman I didn't know grabbed my arm again. She shook me angrily. 'You're *got* to go out and get your customers,' she shouted. 'You're not calling your customers down.' I tried to keep on moving; she forced me to stop.

Now I figured I was in the right. I had my bread. I had an order. She was getting between me and my customer. 'Listen, I'm not blocking the line. I've been taking my bread back here,' I said, showing how quickly I moved from the bread board.

She stood there, glaring at me and holding my arm. 'I'm not trying to ride you. I'm trying to give you some advice.'

I was in a panic now. What would the customer think? I'd forgotten my order. And besides this, I was moving as fast as I knew how. I tried to shake free. She wouldn't let me.

'Leave me alone!' I shouted.

'I'm not trying to bust your hump,' she said, still holding me.

'Then leave me the fuck alone,' I said, and shook out of her grasp. Everybody else on the line had stopped talking. They were all listening.

We both went back to work. I found my customer. Got the order repeated. Made the sandwich. Of course I was even slower than I had been. I could barely hear the orders over the roar of blood in my ears.

When I checked out at the end of that day, I saw the woman standing alone. I went up to her. 'No hard feelings,' I said. 'No hard feelings,' she said. 'I don't mind advice,' I said. 'Just not during the rush. I can't think during the rush.'

'I was trying to tell you to call your customers to you,' she said.

'I know that,' I said.

Then she looked as if she were sorry to go on. 'It's just that everybody else was saying you are so slow,' she said.

I walked out of the store. 'Everybody else was saying you are so slow.' That was the line that stuck. I went over to Grand Central, stopping at a deli to buy a Diet Coke. I went down into the basement at the terminal and used the men's room. Then I took the escalator back up to the main concourse. I couldn't have said for sure if the escalator was on or not. That's how tired I was. Tired and disheartened. Everything blurred. Like a tongue searching for a sore tooth, my mind kept coming back to that line, 'Everybody else was saying you're so slow.' Everybody?

The woman who had yelled at me wasn't around the next day until the rush, but as soon as it began, she appeared and I felt her there, watching me and disapproving. I tried never to pause at the bread board. I tried always to grab my loaf and move right down the line, cutting the bread at another station.

At one point the line got long, and Andrea showed up. I

wondered if she was there to protect me. She smiled. I smiled back.

As soon as I got a piece of bread, I'd begin to wave it in the air, and call out for the next customer at the top of my lungs. Usually there's so much other noise that you can't even hear yourself, but once there was a lull in which mine was the only voice. I sounded overeager, nervous, bugling my eagerness to please: 'Can I help the next customer, please!' Nobody else was saying anything right then. I heard myself. So did everybody else, and at least one person snickered.

During the next slowdown, the line manager asked me to wipe down more trays and put paper on them. I was doing this at the back of the counter, when Andrea's boss showed up. Andrea's boss was the white guy who told Mary she was the best. He didn't like the way I was wiping the trays. 'That's not properly clean,' he said. I nodded and started wiping more carefully. Then the dread woman came around the corner. 'You shouldn't be here,' she said angrily. 'We have a line.'

Was it possible to do two things wrong in the same instant? I was wrong not to wipe the trays properly. I was wrong to wipe the trays at all.

I didn't say, 'How am I supposed to see the line from here?'

I didn't say, 'But I was told to do this.'

I didn't say anything.

'Not now,' she said, gesturing angrily at the work I was doing. 'We have a line.'

I looked up at Andrea's boss. The boss of the bosses. The white guy.

He wagged his head. No help there. 'She's a manager,' he said. 'You have to do what she says.'

It wasn't until that moment that I realized that my enemy was wearing a beige hat. She also had a shirt on with a collar. So that was why she felt she had to manhandle me. She was a manager. I scuttled back to my place on the line.

Maybe she was an anomaly. Or maybe Cosi was getting too big now to care so much about fun. Or maybe I was too slow to put up with. Now that I had a manager on me, I figured she probably wouldn't let go. I've had these jobs. They don't let go.

The company is new. Run by young people. Jay Wainwright was twenty-nine at the time I worked at his store; Shep was just twenty-seven. The first Cosi Sandwich Bar opened at Fifty-second Street in New York in February of 1996. In the fall of 1999, there were thirteen of them in New York, eighteen nationwide. Cosi has merged with Xando. There's talk that they'll bring the company public. I know they'll keep the ovens. The bread is good. It's fabulous. I hope they remember the second gimmick, too, though. Because the second gimmick is the most vital. It's kindness.

People did get fired. Others poured in to fill the vacancies. This despite the fact that *The New York Times* kept running stories about how difficult it was to get decent labor at a reasonable price.

In the meantime, I'd been applying for a job at Borders. Seven dollars an hour, they promised. Looked like I might get it.

On page 25 of the *Cosi Sandwich Bar Crew Member Handbook,* under the heading 'Separation of Employment', it reads:

Notice:
Crew members wishing to terminate their employment relation-ships with Cosi are urged to notify us at least two weeks in advance of their intended termination. Such notice should be given in writing to your general manager.

And in the very next paragraph:

All employment relationships with Cosi are on an "at-will basis." Although we hope that our relationship with employees will be long-term and mutually rewarding, Cosi reserves the right to terminate the employment relationship at any time.

So they could fire you on a dime, but you had to give them two weeks.

I wanted the job at Borders. I still liked the job at Cosi. I thought

I'd work two jobs. People do. Many of my colleagues at Cosi had two jobs. My first day at Borders was to be a Monday. So on my first day at Borders, I went to Cosi from ten A.M. until two P.M. and then to Borders from three P.M. until ten P.M. I was exhausted. Dizzy with fatigue. Markedly depressed.

Tuesday I asked to have the day off at Cosi so that I could attend a school conference for my thirteen-year-old son. Andrea was understanding about this.

I planned to quit on Wednesday. I always make a big deal in my own mind about quitting. I can never sleep the night before leaving a job. I play and replay the drama, which often goes off with a whimper and very little bang. This time I was wondering how angry Andrea would be. *But if I'm so slow,* I thought, *then why ever should she care?*

One of the great lessons I've learned from this project is that I'm never anything like as important as I suppose myself to be.

Wednesday morning, I actually hung around in the lower level of Grand Central, trying to figure out what to say to Andrea. I even wrote out a couple of little speeches, which I thought might ease the transition. I wanted to tell her as soon as I got to work. It might be easier, I thought, to wait until the last minute. Then if she got angry, I could just trot out of the door.

But what if she was dramatically understaffed the next day? I should give her twenty-four hours to prepare. She'd always been sweet to me.

I finally settled on a little speech with three parts, which I even drafted in my notebook.

'I have three things to talk about,' I said when I found Andrea alone in the office.

She nodded.

Then I tried to sound offhand. 'First, I've got a job at Borders. They're going to pay me seven dollars an hour. So I want to quit.'

Andrea's face fell. 'Why didn't you give me two weeks' notice?' she asked. So I said, 'I didn't know until Monday night.' Which was almost true. So she said, 'It's now, what, Wednesday?' So I said,

'Well, I was frightened.' At which point she softened. 'I don't bite too bad,' she said.

'It's not that I was unhappy here,' I said. 'It's just that this bookstore job is something I think I can do well.'

She nodded. 'And what were the other two subjects?'

So I told her how I'd failed to check out on Monday, which meant the computer wouldn't have my accurate hours. She nodded again. Then I said that I had been to the teacher's conference for my older boy.

'He's doing great?' she asked.

'No,' I said.

'Well, he's not failing,' she said.

'No,' I said, 'but he's goofing around.'

'It's so hard to explain to them that it matters,' she said.

'Yeah,' I said, 'it's hard.' I backed out of the office, went upstairs to work.

Then at 2:10 P.M., after I'd punched out for the last time, I went downstairs again and knocked on Andrea's door. She was in there, halfway through her complimentary Cosi sandwich. We shook hands.

'So I have to know,' I said. 'Has anybody ever been slower?'

There was a pause as she chewed her sandwich. She swallowed. 'Plenty of people are slower,' she said. 'A million people are slower. Nobody else is so kind.'

When we talk about others, we talk about ourselves. When Andrea said I was kind, she was also telling me that she was kind. Kindness mattered to her.

Softheartedness is often associated with softheadedness, but I don't think the two need to be connected. It's smart to be kind. I'm talking bottom line.

I've seen a lot of people lose their jobs since I started working on this book. Some did plummet, but most were caught in a network of friends and acquaintances. Adam Bellow was a friend and without him, I might not have sold this book.

Affection has always been central to my life. During much of my life, I've gone to work to see my friends. Admiration for my father is what drew me to writing.

I thought I might write a teary passage here about the value of friendship. I could have quoted the epitaph, the closing lines of Gray's 'Elegy Written in a Country Churchyard':

> *Large was his bounty, and his soul sincere*
> *Heav'n did a recompense as largely send:*
> *He gave to Mis'ry all he had, a tear,*
> *He gain'd from Heav'n ('twas all the wish'd) a friend.*

In preparation for writing this I even reread Emerson. His work on friendship is exhaustive. And convincing. I drafted this section many times in my head. It sounded saccharine. I was missing the sour to go along with the sweet. It's not just love that makes the world go round. There's a practical side to the network that keeps many of us afloat. Besides which, the people I knew were often not saved by friends. Hiring a friend can be a sticky business.

Then Malcolm Gladwell lit the light for me.

In his book *The Tipping Point,* Gladwell quotes Mark Granovetter's 1974 study, *Getting a Job.* Gladwell reports that in a study of several hundred professional and technical workers, Granovetter found that 56 per cent of those he talked to found their jobs through personal connections. 'This is not surprising; the best way to get in the door is through a personal contact,' notes Gladwell.

But, curiously, Granovetter found that of those personal connections, the majority were 'weak ties'. People didn't get their jobs from friends, but from friends of friends.

That sounds right to me. It's best not to have to beg your friends for work. You won't like doing it. They won't enjoy it, either. But if they speak highly of you, then somebody they know might throw out the life ring.

Which brings us to Dale Carnegie: Why not pretend to be everybody's friend? It doesn't work. Make as many friends as you can, keep as many as you can actually enjoy, but don't stretch it. Which brings us back to my teacher at Nobody Beats the Wiz: 'If you stink, you don't sell.' If you lie all the time, it's going to spoil your digestive system. Your breath will stink.

Borders Books and Music: 'The way the other writer did.'

'BOOKS,' PEOPLE WOULD SAY WHENEVER I WAS STUCK between jobs and complaining about the general unemployability of an English major. 'You could work at a bookstore.'

Truth was, I didn't particularly want to work at a bookstore. Reading books, the right books, I enjoy that. Buying books is fun, too. But selling books. Where's the sex in that?

Besides which, the great joy in this project has been the discovery of a delicious anonymity. At a bookstore the name Cheever might ring a bell. Not my bell, either.

I did try, though. Just, for instance, take the Borders in White Plains. I'd given a reading there in 1993 when my second novel came out. The man in charge was very enthusiastic about my father. I told him I admired my father, too. Then he got on the P.A. and said that the author John Cheever would appear momentarily, to read and sign books.

Even with this announcement, which should – at the very least – have attracted the Elisabeth Kübler-Ross crowd, all I got was a half a dozen very sleepy people, most of whom seemed to have taught me in elementary school.

You can see why I wouldn't want to work *there*. Finally, though, during a particularly long jobless spell, when I was in that store to pick up a book, I did fill out an application. Then I lingered in the café. I fully expected them to come after me over the P.A. 'Is Benjamin Cheever in the building?' Then I'd walk up shame-faced to the front desk. The manager would be there. 'We're sorry for you,' he'd say, referring to the fact that a published writer such as myself had come to this, 'but ecstatic for ourselves.' Nobody came over the P.A.

For several days afterwards, I expected a call.

'I can't believe we almost let this one slip through our fingers,' I'd be told. No call came. Nor did any letter. What could Borders Books and Music be thinking? Was the economy so sour that E. L. Doctorow was already working in the stockroom? Was the woman with glasses at the register actually Cynthia Ozick?

Having gotten over my initial fright, I filled out the occasional bookstore application, but I never got a call back until the fall of 1999. I applied at Borders again, but this time I tried the store on Park Avenue at Fifty-seventh Street. I didn't think I should try for a position with Barnes & Noble, because I had recently served as one of three judges for their first-novel contest, and I was afraid this might set off an alarm in their database.

My work at Cosi helped. I'm always braver about applying for new jobs when I already have one. When unemployed, or rather when employed full-time as a novelist, I begin to think of my personal cranium as somehow central to the universe. This makes it extremely difficult to put myself at risk, since any damage done to the sacred self might have national, perhaps international, consequences. Left to my own devices, I grow self-importance as a pond grows scum. If you've been making sandwiches week-days from ten A.M. to two P.M., it's easier to move about in the world.

I asked the security guard at the front desk at the Park Avenue Borders for an application. A jolly sort, he gave me the form and suggested that I go up to the Borders Cafe and fill it out.

I said I was in a hurry.

'How long's it going to take?' he asked. 'Unless you're a rocket scientist.'

So I went up to the café, answered the questions that weren't already dealt with in my résumé, and brought the form and my résumé back to the guard. 'See,' he said, 'that didn't take so long.'

'The rocket–scientist stuff is in here,' I said, and showed him the résumé.

I'm not a rocket scientist, but the document in question did show that I'd been an editor at the *Reader's Digest* from 1976 until 1988 and had 'published three novels and contributed to several books of nonfiction'.

Among my references I listed Kathy Robbins (literary agent) and my sister, Susan Cheever (writer). *A noisy hint,* I thought.

Two days later I got a call. I was pleased. Whenever I apply for a job, no matter how undesirable, I want it. The woman didn't ask if I was related to John Cheever. An interview was set up. This was to be in the afternoon, when I'd finished my shift at Cosi.

When I got to the bookstore, I went right to my friend at the front desk, and a manager was paged. When he arrived, his manner was friendly and informal. We went together up to the third floor and through one of two doors with the sign that read, Employees Only. There was a large piece of posterboard attached to the back of the door which said, Have You Swiped In/Out Today???? Directly inside, there was a bathroom, an employee lunchroom with refrigerator and microwave, a wall of lockers, the time clock, and then a hallway with offices on one side. At the end, the hall opened into one large office with several desks pushed against the wall, lots of telephones, and a number of computers.

The manager of all the managers was in the large office during my first visit. It is my tendency, when in the presence of superiors, to always fawn and pull my forelock, but this was clearly not appropriate at Borders. I knew, by the way that the junior officers sat and lounged around the head man, that this guy held his authority lightly.

Tom and Louis Borders opened the first store in Ann Arbor, Michigan, in 1971, and the informality seems to have stayed in the corporate culture, despite the fact that the brothers sold the company to Kmart Corporation in 1992. Three years later, Borders bought its stock back from Kmart and joined forces with Waldenbooks, according to information provided over the Web by

Borders. The same source states that the independent company is now 'the world's second largest retailer of books, music, video, and other informational, educational, and entertainment products, with more than 300 stores in the United States'.

While waiting to do my paperwork, I was told that the store no longer posted the *New York Times* Best Seller List, because the *Times* had begun to charge for the right to do so. Borders now ran a list of the most popular books called Borders' Best instead.

The manager of the Park Avenue store had just finished reading *American Psycho*. He said he hadn't liked the book but that when he starts to read a book, he always finishes it. He wouldn't say if it was a good book or a bad book, but only that he hadn't enjoyed it much.

'Books are like perfume,' he said. Which I took to mean that there is no accounting for taste. I wanted to get into an argument right then and there but thought it would be more prudent to at least wait until I was hired.

When the manager in charge of vetting me arrived, we stepped into a side office, and he asked me why I wanted to work at Borders. I said I liked books. 'But why Borders?' he asked. So I said that I particularly liked recorded books and that Borders – particularly Borders Park Avenue – had a terrific selection. I picked up my knapsack. 'I have a Walkman in here with a cassette in it of Peter Matthiessen on writing, which I was listening to when I took the subway here today. I bought it right here in this store.'

When he asked if there was any particular department I'd like to work in, I said I'd love to work with recorded books. I'm embarrassed to acknowledge this on the page, but I seem to remember saying, 'I could sell some recorded books for you.'

A couple of former *Reader's Digest* people I'd known now work at Borders, and I'd heard that the screening process was extensive. I had three separate interviews. There was no urine test.

The people who talked to me were all apologetic about the low salary and explained this was just because I was temporary, seasonal help. Employees were entitled to 30 to 40 per cent off on Borders products. I didn't tell them I'd been working to exhaustion at Cosi for $6.15 an hour. And not measuring up.

If you're going to ask me now how anybody can live on seven dollars an hour, then I'd have to tell you I have no idea. You might be interested to learn, though, that there are 28 million people in this country who work now for less than eight dollars an hour. I don't know how any of them live, but I would have to guess that for the vast majority of the people who worked on my level at Borders, Park Avenue, there's a one-word answer: family. Many of the staff seemed to be students, or in that curious economic and social limbo that surrounds higher learning in this country.

I don't know if all my coworkers actually were big readers, but reading and an intimate association with books were clearly considered desirable. When reporting for work, the security guard at the door notes any books or cassettes and puts a sticker on each. When you leave in the evening, the stickers are removed, the list checked. I was reading a bound galley of Ben Yagoda's *About Town: The New Yorker and the World It Made* while working at Borders, and when one of my colleagues saw this, she said, 'And where do *you* get *your* bound galleys?'

So I was once more part of the world in which bound galleys are status symbols. The nut had fallen close to the tree.

During the vetting process, I was given an I.D. number and asked to sign a document provided by Pinkerton. I was then left alone in the office and told to dial an 800 number. A voice on the other end – recorded or digital, I'm not certain – told me to press 1 for *yes* and 3 for *no*.

There followed a series of questions, most of which seemed intent on exposing the felon within. Is fifty dollars a lot to steal from your employer? Is ten dollars a lot? Is one dollar a lot?

Would I guess that about 10 per cent of people are dishonest? About 20 per cent?

I was asked if I'd ever told a lie. This was a tough one, because I wanted to appear to be the goody two-shoes that I am, but I didn't want to appear insane, or profoundly dishonest, so I said that yes, I had told a lie. Me and George Washington.

After the test I was given a brief tour. Everybody smiled and said hello. 'I'm not going to remember your name,' I kept saying. 'We won't remember yours, either,' they said back.

After the last interview, I was told that they would call me. They didn't call me, but when I called them, they said I was hired.

At the Cosi Sandwich Bar, we were required to wear chinos and the black Cosi shirt and – if you were a sandwich maker – the black Cosi baseball cap.

At Borders you could wear whatever you pleased, although I seem to recall that there was a ruling against T-shirts with obscene messages. One of my fellow employees had a pierced nose, one a pierced eyebrow.

One of the higher-level managers wore a tie, but this was markedly unusual. The quickest way to distinguish between employees and customers at Borders, Park Avenue, is to remember that the customers are more apt to be neatly dressed and groomed. Also, a Borders employee will wear a beaded or fabric necklace with a plastic envelope on the end in which a tag has been inserted that reads: Borders.

I also noticed that almost everybody who worked at Borders had something negative to say about Barnes & Noble. When I was taught to dress the shelves – pull the books or audiocassettes out so that their edges are flush with the edge of the shelf – the manager I was with said, 'It's a nice look. Not like at Barnes & Noble.'

When I remarked to another manager that everybody seemed well-read, he said, 'Before they hire you, they like to ask you what are the last three books you read. It's part of the test. Not like at Barnes & Noble. You can go in there, and nobody knows the new Oprah.'

The harshness of these judgements seemed way out of line with the good-natured passivity otherwise on display. But then Horatio Nelson had a great heart and was so beloved that after England's critical victory at Trafalgar in 1805, grizzled seamen wept to hear the news of his death. And yet Nelson always said, 'You must hate a Frenchman as you do the devil.'

Having come directly from the sandwich shop, I also noticed immediately that nobody at Borders would touch me or look me in the eye.

When somebody at Cosi looked at you, you got looked right through. I had the distinct impression that everybody at the sandwich bar knew what sort of underpants I wore, and also the last four digits of my Social Security number. At Borders, they'd look away.

I wonder if this has something to do with bookishness, too much time spent in the presence of an omniscient narrator. Or is it about class? Are richer people naturally more diffident?

Many of the people at Cosi held two or three jobs, so on my first day I put in my ten A.M. to two P.M. shift at Cosi before working at Borders from three P.M. until 10:20 P.M. By the time I caught the eleven P.M. train out of Grand Central, I was literally reeling with exhaustion. I don't know how anybody keeps up this sort of schedule, although many do. I sat next to a laborer also taking a train from Manhattan. He fell so fast asleep that his friends couldn't wake him up for his stop at White Plains. I woke him up and got him off at North White Plains. He kept saying that he'd already missed his station. He didn't know North White Plains. North White Plains is near White Plains, I kept saying. 'Brewster will be worse! Brewster will be worse!' I said, pushing him off the train.

When I first began at Borders, I wasn't supposed to try to handle customers. I spent hours learning the software used to search for books. I was also given a second and more thorough tour of the building.

When I was released from training, I was placed in Recorded Books, the very section I'd requested. Still, the job was dull. This despite the fact that I adore recorded books. Outside of Robin Whitten, the editor of *AudioFile,* a magazine of audiobook reviews and information to which I sometimes contribute reviews, I've probably listened to more recorded books than any other sighted person alive.

Since audiobooks are not widely reviewed, since they are often more expensive than even their hardback cousins, and since you can't simply flip them open and listen to a page, I had expected to provided a vital service. I had imagined myself charming Park Avenue heiresses with my extensive knowledge of the quality of narration and also abridgements.

Once, I did get a young man who wanted to talk. He told me his interests; I tried to match them; and we were both well pleased. Most customers wanted me to look up a specific title. After that, they wanted to be left alone, please!

When somebody stumbled into the recorded-books section looking bewildered, I'd come zooming at them out of the fluorescent lighting, seize the opportunity.

'Can I help you?'

'Great that you like audiobooks.'

'Oh, I see. Does your grandmother like fiction, then?'

My enthusiasm seemed strangely out of place, and actually alarmed many of the customers. Often the exchange would become so awkward that I'd have to walk away. 'I'll leave you alone, then. Please ask, though, if you have any more questions.'

The moment I turned the corner, the unhappy customer would unload most of the books I'd recommended and flee the area.

We had an information desk, with a podium, phone, and computer terminal. This was not just for Recorded Books, but also for the video, gardening, sports, health, and magazine sections, our entire floor. We were supposed to take turns there at the computer monitor. Sometimes the person on duty would wander off to perform some other, more essential chore. Even on a busy day, you could stand there for twenty minutes without being asked a single question. The question, when it did come, was apt to be 'Are the rest rooms on this floor?' They were.

Questions were often unrelated to the sale of books. For instance, I recall one young man who was interested in Mt. Everest.

We showed him the mountain-climbing books. Then he said no, what he actually wanted was the circumference of Everest at sea level. We said it might be in one of our books but that nobody on the floor knew for sure. 'We haven't read every book here.' I suggested he go to the basement and look in the reference section.

'I was there,' he said. 'They sent me here. Can't you just look it up for me on the Web?'

In Cooking, I found a woman who wanted a picture of a peach. We looked together through the cookbooks. I showed her the gardening section. She wasn't finding what she wanted.

I suggested she go to the basement and look in Photography. She was exasperated. 'Don't you have . . . ?'

'A peach section?' I asked.

She nodded.

'No, we don't.'

New recordings came in, and I shared the responsibility of putting them out where they belonged and in alphabetical order. Each book and each recorded book has a tag on it with the price, and also the section in which it should be shelved. The decisions as to which category for which book seem to be made at head-quarters, and are usually correct, but not always.

A collection of Shirley Jackson short stories was stamped as essays, and shelved with the essays. Isabel Allende's novel *The House of Spirits* had been miscategorized as poetry. I lost a sale when a woman came in asking for it, and I looked in Fiction.

Customers like to come to Borders, Park Avenue, get an armload of books and magazines, pick up a cappuccino at the café, and have a good read. Sometimes they take notes. One woman actually set up a little office for herself, complete with laptop and cell phone. Another woman used to come in regularly, pick up a book, sprawl on the sofa, and fall fast, fast asleep. She'd lie there with her mouth wide-open, snoozing away for hours at a time.

I never saw anyone disturb her. I thought this an admirable policy. Reading makes me sleepy, too.

I even saw a man I knew from a writing program for the

homeless I'd been attending. He sat at a table and fell into a doze.
He didn't seem to recognize me. Nor did I introduce myself.

The function of the large chain bookstore as a sort of public
meeting place seems entirely positive. People were clearly so
thrilled to be able to settle down with coffee and a fresh book
that it was difficult to resent them.

The café staff would collect the books – not from the limp hands
of sleeping shoppers but from tables that had been abandoned; it
was our job to reshelve them.

Each book is a puzzle. Very gratifying if you find exactly the spot
and can get your reshelve in right beside another copy of the same
book. A little plunking sound in the mind.

Yes, I was so bored, this passed for fun. Although finding out
exactly where a magazine went was even more difficult – much
more difficult – than finding out where a book went.

There is, for instance, a magazine titled *Jane*. One month it had a
naked woman on the cover – no frontal nudity, she had her
shoulders hunched, but neither were there any clothes that I could
discern. The tease read, 'Pamela Anderson Lee. Naked in so many
ways.'

I assumed it belonged in Men's Interest, or Erotica. Nope. *Jane* is
a fashion magazine.

The erotica section created its own reshelving problems. Pla-
toons of teen boys came in, grabbed copies of *Penthouse* or *Later* – a
magazine that actually featured a free beer-bottle opener during my
stint at Borders – and carried them off to Hobbies and Collectibles,
or the decorating section.

Sometimes a couple would come and peer together at the dirty
pictures. This I didn't understand. I thought pornography was
something to enjoy alone. One evening, I saw a man and woman
both looking at the cover of a magazine called *Perfect 10: The
Connoisseur's Magazine*. This was illustrated with a picture of a
blonde with one hand under each breast, as if she were holding
them out for inspection. Like a couple of oranges, or doves. 'All
natural,' the magazine boasted.

I could easily imagine why a guy might want to look at this picture, but why would he want to share it with his wife or girlfriend? Was the model somebody they knew? Was the wife considering plastic surgery?

Putting away books and magazines was a large part of the job, and I didn't resent it, except when somebody came back to buy a book and was horrified to find the dust jacket rumpled or coffee stained: 'Somebody has been reading this!'

I suspect that the importance of the book's condition is directly related to the fact that many of today's offerings are meant to be bought but not necessarily read. Since they may never be opened, these books need to look good at the moment of purchase.

Billions of dollars have been spent on Madison Avenue over the last decades, trying to confuse the point of purchase with the point of orgasm, and at least for me it's worked. I rarely make a useless purchase without feeling as if I've done something carnal and a little embarrassing. I'd just as soon not share the moment.

This feeling must be heightened for people buying clearly useless books, or those playing to their most obvious and pathetic delusions. Reading is about fantasy, and our dream life is not always something we want to share.

You want to win the Nobel Prize? Fine. You want to screw the Dallas Cowboys cheerleaders? OK. You want win a Nobel Prize for screwing the Dallas Cowboys cheerleaders? Maybe. Do you want to share this fantasy with colleagues? with your wife?

I've heard lots of complaints from fellow book lovers about how the staff at chains can't answer your questions, and certainly these complaints are justified. Everybody wants a store clerk who will sit around like a potted palm until asked about Chesterton's *Heretics,* whereupon he will immediately present you with a two–dollar copy of the book in question, plus a brief life of the author.

There are other bookstore purchases you'd just as lief not have anybody know about.

Ossining had a grand old independent bookstore, since deceased, called Books & Things. That's where I bought all my books. A fine place to go, too, if you were filling in your Yeats collection, or asking for something else by Pascal. Not so fine a place if you're buying *Sugar Busters!: Cut Sugar to Trim Fat,* or Paul Zane Pilzer's *God Wants You to Be Rich.*

I once made the mistake of ordering a cassette of *Black Elk Speaks* from the independent bookstore in Pleasantville. Afterwards, the proprietor brought it up when I came back. 'I didn't know you were into Black Elk,' she said.

I'd listened to the cassette once and was shamed to be associated with it, but the connection was made and too difficult to unmake. Here's an excerpt:

> Once we were happy in our own country and we were seldom hungry, for then the two-leggeds and the four-leggeds lived together like relatives, and there was plenty for them and for us. But the Wasichus came, and they made little islands for us and other little islands for the four-leggeds, and always these islands are becoming smaller, for around them surges the gnawing flood of the Wasichus; and it is dirty with lies and greed.

Sounds just like something I might have written about the coming of the chain bookstores. And certainly we Wasichus have been hell on the ecology. It's too late, though. We can't be stopped. Nor, I suppose, can Borders or Barnes & Noble.

Besides which, I happen to be a Wasichu, a white person, a round-eyed long nose. I'm fascinated by the cultures of Native Americans, and there's no question that our culture could be enriched by theirs. I also happen to know that their lives were not Edenic. It must have been magnificent to see nature unspoiled, a hillside without a Mobil station or a ranch house to shatter the symmetry. It was probably a lot less fun to have your son die of strep throat.

But back to books. Today's stores are designed to sell today's books. These books are much more like mayflies than old friends. The attempt by titles to lure you in is hysterical, sometimes even threatening.

Just glance in the specialty-foods section, and you come up with titles like *Bowl Food, A Good Day for Soup, A Celebration of Soup,* and finally two copies of *Saved by Soup.*

Or take fitness. *Fitness Is Religion: Keep the Faith* is the title of a book by Ray Kybaratas, who trained Madonna and took the title from Madonna's habit of saying, 'When's church?' when she meant 'When are we going to work out?'

The Fitness Instinct: The Revolutionary New Approach to Healthy Exercise That Is Fun, Natural, and No-Sweat is written by Peg Jordan, R.N., who, judging from the cover photo, is not in outstanding shape herself. 'Most of what you've been taught about exercise is wrong!' she says in the cover copy.

Taking a page from Nurse Jordan, Edward J. Jackowski's title is *Hold It! You're Exercising Wrong!* Dare you not to buy that one.

The taste for novelty leaves one with the distinct impression that our culture is falling away from greatness. Just, for instance, the audio-religion section, which featured one copy of the New Testament read by Gregory Peck, four copies of *Zen and the Art of Motorcycle Maintenance* by Robert M. Pirsig, and nine copies of *Ethics for the New Millennium* by His Holiness the Dalai Lama.

For this reader, the grab for hope looks more desperate, and less likely to produce results. These fruits are meant to be harvested by anonymous readers and in solitude.

As for my own anonymity, it didn't last. I outed myself. During my interviews, I kept hinting that I was a writer. Nobody lifted an eyebrow. Ultimately, I said, 'My father was a famous writer.'

'Oh,' said the man on the other side of the desk, 'I was going to ask.' Then during my final tour, I was accosted by a handsome young man in the basement who asked if I was Ben Cheever. I said I was. He told me John Cheever was his favorite writer and said he particularly liked the story 'Brimmer'.

'Isn't he a TV writer?' I asked.

'Nope,' said my colleague-to-be. Brimmer is the guy on the boat who gets all the women.

After this encounter, word of my pedigree spread throughout

the building. When I got back up to the lunchroom, several people were at the table. One young woman said she had looked me up and found out that I was a published writer with books in the store. I shrugged, and pawed the ground with my feet. I puffed up. I've warned you about how quickly I puff up. Then another woman chimed in. 'Just don't spend all your time checking your Borders ranking,' she said, 'the way the other writer did.'

Acme – The Fastest-growing Company in the Country: 'We eliminate the middle man.'

EXCERPT FROM *BARNUM'S OWN STORY: THE AUTOBIOGRAPHY of P. T. Barnum*. (This is a recent manifestation of a work first brought out in 1855. Barnum used to republish the book regularly, and sell it at the circus.)

Every morning at sunrise my eyes were running over the columns of "Wants" in the New York *Sun,* hoping to hit upon something that would suit me. Many is the wild-goose chase which I had in pursuit of a situation so beautifully and temptingly set forth among those "Wants." Fortunes equalling that of Croesus, and as plenty as blackberries, were dangling from many an advertisement which mysteriously invited the reader to apply at Room No. 16 in the fifth story of a house in some retired and uninviting locality; but when I wended my way up flights of dark, rickety, greasy stairs, and through sombre, narrow passages, I would find that my fortune depended firstly upon my advancing a certain sum of money, from three dollars to five hundred as the case might be; and secondly, upon my success in peddling a newly discovered patent life-pill, an ingenious mouse-trap, or something of the sort.

I remember that, on one occasion, an advertisement was headed "IMMENSE SPECULATION on a small capital! – $10,000 easily made in one year! Apply to Professor –, at Scudder's American Museum." I had long fancied that I could succeed if I could only get hold of a public exhibition, and I hastened with all dispatch to call on the kind Professor who held forth such flattering promises at the Museum. Being ushered upon the stage of the lecture-room in the third story, I was grieved to find a dozen applicants already ahead of me. I instantly sought out the Professor, and calling him aside, took a few moments to recover myself, for I was nearly out of breath from running so fast up stairs, and then I asked him whether he had yet disposed of his speculation. "Not positively, but several customers are ready to close with me immediately," was the Professor's reply. "I beg of you to give me a chance; you will find me just the man you want," I replied with great earnestness.

"Well, as you are so anxious, and seem to be a young man of energy, I will give you the first chance," replied the kind Professor. I felt exceedingly grateful, and asked him the nature of his enterprise. "I am the proprietor of the great Hydro-oxygen Microscope," said he. "It is the most extraordinary instrument now extant. Its public exhibition through the country would in a very short period secure to its owner an independence. My health is feeble, and I will sell for only two thousand dollars; one thousand cash – the balance in sixty and ninety days, on good security." My golden visions vanished and I abruptly informed the Professor that I declined becoming a purchaser of his instrument.

Although Barnum famously did go into the museum business, he weathered this particular crisis by opening a boardinghouse and buying part interest in a grocery store.

It's extraordinary how little has changed. Here's a 'Want' I found and responded to.

Environmental/Health Sales

If you want to love your career, help clean up environment, and live fanstasticlife (sic) style call us. International company. Expanding locally. Then a phone number.

'Acme Corporation,' I was told over the phone, 'is the fastest-growing company in the country. We have over four hundred offices. We started out with sales of fifty million four years ago and now we're up to two hundred million dollars.'

The man on the phone gave me an appointment for ten A.M. the next day. I took down an address in Tarrytown, New York, minutes from my house.

The following morning, after driving the children to school, I put on a tie and jacket and showed up at 9:50 A.M. at the address I had been given. This was a large glass office building right off the old Albany Post Road. Naturally, I couldn't remember what floor to go to; so after I'd parked, I went to the building registry. But there was no listing for the Acme Corporation.

I found a man in the lobby washing windows. I asked him if he knew where the Acme Corporation was. I had brought the classified advertisement. Now I checked this, but the advertisement didn't have the name of the company. 'I think it's called Acme,' I said. The window washer put his squeegee in a bucket and pulled a sheaf of Post-its out of his pocket, which had the names of the building's tenants written on it. He couldn't find Acme, either.

'It's the fastest-growing company in the country,' I said.

The window washer wagged his head sadly.

'There *is* a company called Eastern,' he said. I took directions for Eastern, but the people at Eastern weren't hiring. Heading back to the elevator, I came upon a man with a friendly, open face; I asked him if he'd heard of Acme. He said he thought so. 'But don't they have a different name now?'

I shrugged.

'Are they Riverside?' he asked.

I didn't know. I took directions for Riverside, found the sign, rang the bell. An eager young man in a suit met me at the door. I told him I was Ben Cheever. He said he knew. He'd been waiting. He was pleased to see me.

This man was a good deal younger than I, and with a good deal more energy than I had, and even less hair. He led me into a waiting room. The walls were decorated with the framed covers of magazines, all of which carried stories about the Acme Corporation. One of the magazines had a picture of a mother with a child. The child was wearing a T-shirt that read, Replacing Ignorance with Enlightenment. The room was sparsely but luxuriously furnished. There was a black leather sofa, a black leather armchair, and a coffee table. Plus a rubber-tree plant. There were no rugs. Against one wall stood a glass case with two onyx rhinoceroses inside. Symbolic of what? I wondered. Virility? Myopia?

I sat on the sofa. My man sat on the edge of the armchair. He told me that I had stumbled onto a terrific opportunity. 'We're the fastest-growing company in the country,' he said. He needed to know if I was the right sort of person. Was I willing to work hard? Did I want to be successful? I could get in on the ground floor.

I said I thought I worked hard. 'Moderately hard,' I said. 'What would I have to do?' I asked.

'We sell environmental products,' he said.

'But which environmental products do you sell?' I asked.

'All kinds.'

'Which products exactly?'

'We're not product-specific,' he told me.

'Could I see a catalogue?' I asked.

'Oh, don't worry,' he said. 'I'll show you what we sell. But not yet.' Then he took me into a second room. This had a conference table and four chairs. There was a white plastic easel attached to one wall. He picked up a green Magic Marker and began to draw on the easel. 'Every business has producers,' he said, and he made a rectangle with the Magic Marker and wrote 'producers' inside of it. 'There may or may not be transportation,' he said, drawing another box and writing 'transportation' on its side. 'Then there are the middle men,' he said, and drew a rectangle and wrote 'middle man' on its side. 'Finally we have the sales force,' he said, drawing a series of small rectangles and wrote 'sales' on these. He stepped back, looked at his work. 'Does that look familiar?'

'Not really,' I said.

'But does it make sense?' he asked.

'I suppose,' I said.

'Watch this,' he said. Then he stepped up to the board and drew an *X* over the rectangle labeled 'middle man'. 'We eliminate the middle man,' he explained.

Did that make sense to me now?

I thought it made some sense.

I still wanted to know what they sold, though. 'Since success has to be connected to the excellence of your products.'

'Oh, I'm going to show you what we sell,' he said, 'but first I want to make sure that you're clear on the structure of the business.'

'You eliminated the middle man,' I said.

'Right!' he said.

Then he and I walked into a third room. This was large, largely empty, and had two distinct areas. At the far side there was a sort of altar set up with objects on it. Nearer to where we had come in stood a table stacked with literature. We went first to the literature. He picked up a paperback copy of *Think and Grow Rich,* by Napoleon Hill. Had I read *Think and Grow Rich?*

I said that I hadn't actually read *Think and Grow Rich,* but I'd certainly heard of it. I'd read a biography of Napoleon Hill. 'Did you know that he had a pistol when he was a boy? He was getting in trouble with his pistol. His mother took his pistol away and gave him a typewriter, and he never got into trouble again. Or not that sort of trouble.'

My man hadn't heard about Napoleon Hill's pistol. Nor did he seem interested. It was clear that he had a patter and he wished I wouldn't keep interrupting.

Had I heard of Andrew Carnegie?

I had.

'Napoleon Hill,' he said, 'interviewed Andrew Carnegie.'

'Yeah,' I said, 'I know that.'

Carnegie was 'the first billionaire in this country'.

I nodded.

Did I know Carnegie's story?

'I know that he gave away most of his fortune,' I said. 'Paid for libraries. I know that he started out as a bobbin boy.'

This got another scowl.

'Andrew Carnegie started out with nothing,' I was told. 'Andrew Carnegie came to this country, and he was broke. Had no job. Couldn't even speak the language.'

I was dazzled there for a moment, but then I said, 'Wait a minute. Carnegie was from Scotland. He spoke the language.'

This caused an embarrassing pause, but my man recovered quickly. 'No,' he said, 'not like you or I.'

'I suppose,' I said.

Then I heard that after Andrew Carnegie had made his fortune, America's first billionaire became concerned about others less prosperous than he. 'Carnegie found that even in this great, free nation, ninety-seven per cent of the people can't retire. They have to rely on the government or their family in their old age.'

I nodded. 'And what does this have to do with me?'

'We make sure that that doesn't happen to you.'

'How do I avoid it?'

'By selling our products.'

'As a sales rep?'

The young man in the suit nodded. 'As a sales rep or as a supervisor or as a manager. Or even as a director. Depending upon the volume of sales.'

'How is it determined where I start?'

'It all depends on how much money you have to invest.'

'But that sounds like a pyramid,' I said.

At this point my guide waxed indignant. 'Of course it's not a pyramid,' he said. 'Pyramids are illegal.'

'Who would I sell to?'

'The people you already know,' he told me, 'family and friends.'

'Seems I'd run out of friends quickly.'

'No,' he said, 'you would not.'

'How do you know that?' I asked.

'Let me ask you this,' he said. 'When did Christianity start?'

'I don't know. Well, actually I do know. About two thousand years ago. Is that right?'

'Right. And let me ask you this: How many Catholics are there?'

'A lot.'

'But is everybody in the entire world a Catholic?'

'No.'

'See,' he said with considerable satisfaction, 'there's no such thing as saturation. They've been in business for two thousand years and not even *they* have saturated the market.

'Now,' he said, 'I'm going to show you what you've been waiting for.' He led me across the room to the product area. Here the merchandise was displayed very much as religious objects might be set out in a grotto. Each item had a little pedestal. There was a lightbulb on one stand.

'A lightbulb?' I asked.

'Long-lasting,' he explained.

On another pedestal there was a water filter. A third held a gallon of bottled water.

Another stand held a spritzer of Banaca and a plastic cigarette lighter. He took the lighter, lit it, and then spritzed the Banaca into the flame. This caused the breath cleanser to flare up like a blow torch.

'Alcohol,' he explained. 'What's alcohol doing in a breath freshener?'

I didn't know. He took out his own breath freshener, spritzed it, and held the lighter up into the stream. No fire.

'Better,' he said.

'Better,' I agreed.

There was another water filter cut in half. The filter cost a lot, maybe sixty dollars. The bottled-water industry was in the billions of dollars annually, I was told. Acme sold filters that would save consumers hundreds of dollars a month. There was also a filter that could be installed in a shower. Did I know how much chlorine public drinking water had in it?

I didn't. Well, when I took a shower, that chlorine went right into my body.

There were other household cleaning agents. All environmentally friendly. All nontoxic. Did I know how many children were poisoned each year by cleaning fluid? I did not know.

'Fifty thousand children a year are poisoned with household cleaning products,' he told me. 'Ten thousand of them die.'

I left without writing a check. There were follow-up phone calls, but I managed to shrug them off. I was torn, though. The water filters seemed a strong idea. Then I went into a kitchen-gadget store and saw that they were selling filters directly. These cost a good deal less than the filters offered by Acme. And this was with the middleman right there on the premises.

I did fall for the ad that said I could be 'a movie reviewer'.

Hollywood motion-picture research firm needs 100 people to watch and rate movies at local theaters. Fantastic money.

It turned out that they first needed a check for $32.40. After they cashed this, they sent me a packet from which I learned that I had to buy my own tickets, Xerox the review form I was sent, and pay for my own postage. The reviews, if accepted, would be worth eleven dollars a piece. 'Fantastic money', indeed.

I also followed up on the advertisement that said I could 'Make MONEY READING BOOKS! $30,000/yr.' When I called up, I was told that all publishers relied on outside readers to test manuscripts before they went through the trouble and expense of getting them to stores. 'They don't just publish books because they want to,' the man I spoke with explained.

I noted that Philip Roth's latest novel, *American Pastoral,* had just won the National Book Award for Fiction, and asked if any of their people had picked it. 'I don't know about that book,' I was told, 'but you won't be reading John Grisham or Danielle Steel because they know those people are big. Those people are so big, their books will be a success even if they *are* bombs.'

I paid forty-nine dollars and got a paperback titled *Earn Money Reading Books*. With this came a partial and outdated list of publishers and writing schools.

Under a subsection titled 'Working with Writers,' I read, 'As I have said elsewhere, the big problem with writers lies in finding a writer with any money.'

'TV Viewers Needed,' read another headline.

'Track & rate programming and commercials in your area. Good money. Flexible hours.' They wanted money, too, and sent me a kit. I was supposed to watch TV and note the advertisements. Then I needed to contact the corporations paying for the advertisements and promise to track the appearance of their spots in order to make certain they were getting their money's worth. Supposedly they would reward me for this effort. It may be that there was money to be made this way, but it would have taken a good deal of time, effort, and a pair of brass balls in order to find out.

There were legitimate ways to make a little bit of money through offerings in the classifieds. I invested nothing and was paid seventy-five dollars to discuss my phone service as part of a focus group in White Plains, New York.

Before the session began, we sat around in a room together eating free sandwiches and talking about other focus-group experiences. One large man had been paid thirty-five dollars to eat potato chips. 'They were awful. I kept waiting for them to bring in the potato chips we were supposed to like. We weren't supposed to discuss the chips with each other, but I knew what everybody thought. It made me wonder about the O.J. jurors.'

We were all intensely envious of the woman who had been paid one hundred dollars to test-drive a Lexus. 'It's probably because I have the big Mercedes,' she explained.

Those of us picked were ushered into a room with a large mirror in one wall. We had a moderator with us. Behind the mirror sat phone-company executives who fed her questions and observed our responses.

The trouble with people, of course, is that they lie. We were all supposed to be entrepreneurial executives. I can't prove it, but I suspect that most of us had inflated our importance. One of the women in the group was supposed to have a cookie-manufacturing firm. She brought us cookies, but I was not convinced that she hadn't baked them at home. One of the men had had his own local-cable health show, but this had been cancelled. While being canvassed by phone, I had been asked if I was the chief breadwinner in the family. I said I was not. There was a pause, and then the woman recruiting me said, 'If they ask if you are the chief breadwinner, say you are.'

The former health-show moderator had spent thousands of dollars producing a video designed to get him a new job as a health-show moderator. When he heard I was a writer, he asked if I would look at his script.

I said that I thought if he cared about his script, he'd better write it himself. We left the building together, and when we got down to the ground floor, he made a final plea, suggesting he might pay me to work on his script.

I said again he should write it himself. 'You don't understand,' he said. 'I don't like to write. I'd rather do manual labor.' He swept his arm around to indicate the room we were in. 'I'd rather clean up this room than write. That would be easier for me. Emptying the wastebaskets. Mopping the floor.'

'Easier for me, too,' I said.

Another time I was paid fifty dollars to taste salad dressings. We each had a computer terminal and a tray with plastic cups of salad dressing. We were given saltines and water to clear the palette. It seemed that they were trying to figure out which dressings we liked and also how much those were worth – whether or not we thought a particular dressing was a premium. Most of the questions allowed us to rate our experience from one to ten. For instance, we were asked to rate the creaminess of one salad dressing from one to ten.

The loudest, and funniest, man in the group was a post-office employee who came in his tattered uniform, which strained at every seam. He said that he often participated in feeding focus groups. He liked the diversion and the free food. 'Now I don't have to make dinner.'

I was interested to see him there, since I'd recently been to a workshop designed to sell me a three-hundred-dollar course that promised to up my chances of passing the test necessary to get a job at the post office. The presentation had, of course, gone on for some length about how rich post-office employees were. We were told that your average postal worker is a millionaire. I was surprised to meet this millionaire who spent evenings stuffing himself with free salad dressing and saltines.

America Works, on the other hand, is a legitimate and entirely laudable corporation designed to take women off the welfare rolls. The company finds the women jobs, trains them, backs them up, and makes a profit off a bounty paid by a thankful Department of Social Services. I know cofounders Lee Boman and Peter Cove and went one morning to an orientation for new prospects in Manhattan. Peter Cove asked the assembled women if, before they'd gone on welfare, any of them had enrolled in a program that had promised to train them for a lucrative job. There must have been fifty people in the room, and a third of them raised their hands. When asked how many of these had taken loans to enroll in training programs, more than half of that third raised their hands again.

So they'd ended up on welfare anyway, but with debts.

I'm reminded of this quote from Primo Levi:

In history and in life one sometimes seems to glimpse a ferocious law, which states: "To he that has, will be given; to he that has not, will be taken away."

Even though local newspapers and radio stations are eager to uncover injustice and protect readers and listeners, they are loath to expose these scams. First, it's an old story and seems uninteresting. But also, if the reporter names names in such an article, there is a good chance that the group running the scam will sue the newspaper. When I was working at the *Rockland Journal-News,* I wrote a story about a pyramid scam, and it was spiked. I met with the company's lawyer, who told me that while my story might be accurate, it would almost certainly inspire a lawsuit, which the newspaper would have to spend money defending against.

And so billions of dollars a year are harvested from those least able to afford it.

Which is not to say that all sales jobs are dead ends. George Grune started out at the *Reader's Digest* as an advertising salesman. He wound up as CEO and chairman of the board.

In 1984, when Grune took over, the *Digest* employed roughly five thousand people in the United States. Fewer than two thousand work there now. Despite the bloodlettings, the enterprise did not grow profitable. The business seems to have kept shrinking to match the reduced workforce.

Those fired felt keenly betrayed, since the *Reader's Digest* had not been just a workplace. Instead it had been a magazine, an organization whose primary asset was its moral vision.

'We plan to maintain the Digest as a private company,' George Grune told the *Times* in 1986. Four years later he took the company public. The stock went up and down. The workforce went down and down again. By taking the company public, the officers generated a great deal of cash, much of which they seem to have kept for themselves.

I had known Grune to be a pleasant man. A former football player and Marine, he told us that in high school he had wanted to be a poet. He wore glasses, and I noticed that in the presence of cameras, he often took them off.

When I started to work on this book, I wrote a letter to George Grune. No answer. So I printed the letter out again and sent four copies off. Still no answer. Several months later I tried again with the same letter. Here it is:

Dear George Grune,

I sent you this letter in November. I'm trying again. Many things are lost in the mail.

You probably don't remember me, but I was an editor at The Reader's Digest for a little more than 11 years. Editor-in-Chief, Ken Gilmore, actually gave me the Mark Cross pen and pencil set for length of service.

Shortly after I quit the magazine to write, I contributed a piece to The Nation in which I criticized you and the other officers of the company for cutting back on some of the generous policies for which the Digest had long been justly famous. [Grune had discontinued the free turkey, ordinarily distributed to all employees at Thanksgiving. He'd also stopped the subsidized bus service and increased the workday by half an hour. In the meantime, the CEO himself was growing immensely rich. His discernible package at that moment totalled $13 million.]

Although I never heard anything but praise of my article from friends who still worked in Pleasantville, I have long felt uneasy about not trying harder to bring in your side of the story. I did contact the public relations department and quoted from their responses, which were not, I think, convincing. Bruce Trachtenberg, for instance, said he was happy that the company stopped giving out free turkeys before Thanksgiving, since he, Bruce, was a vegetarian.

When I was at the Digest I once sent you a memo objecting to a column you had written for the house magazine. You called me into your office and heard me out. I was flattered to be granted a personal audience. I was also under some compulsion to explain myself to the man who was the boss of my boss. I understand that you are under no such compulsion. But I did think I should at least try to return the favor you had done me.

The people who know you well seem to like you a good deal.

Is there something obvious I'm not getting here? Why fire
people from a profitable corporation? Didn't these people have
a contract of understanding with their employer? "Stay here, stay
loyal, work hard and you'll always have a job." That's how it
would have read. I have no complaint. I didn't stay, nor did I
remain loyal, but others who did stay and remained faithful to the
company were fired.

I'm working now on a book about the problems long-term
employees face when trying to start up a career again at or near
the beginning. The book is about both the trauma and adventure
of starting over, and not primarily about the lay-off process, but
still I'd like to know your side of it.

The way the story reads now in the press, the corporate
downsizers appear to be a crew of selfish and hard-hearted pirates
in suits. I'm too old to believe easily in a picture so simple and so
simply romantic.

I would be flattered by any response.

Sincerely,

Benjamin H. Cheever

This time I did get an answer. From, of all people, Bruce S.
Trachtenberg, then the director of communication. I wonder if
he's still a vegetarian.

Dear Ben:

The first time you wrote to George Grune asking to interview
him about your new book, he passed the note on to me saying
he's not interested. I guess he wanted me to know in case you
called and he wasn't in. After so long a silence, I figured you gave
up on him. Since you've written a second time I thought you
should know that he's still not interested.

Regards,

Bruce Trachtenberg

So I guess I'll never know how it feels to fire thousands of people and pay yourself millions of dollars.

I've seen Grune once since the exchange of letters. This was at a memorial service. I was still in a pew and saw him coming up the aisle. I took a deep breath and walked out and joined him. I said hello. He gave me a warm smile, said hello back, and put his arm around my shoulder. He actually grabbed affectionately at my ass.

I didn't get it. I still don't get it.

George V. Grune is now the chairman of the DeWitt Wallace – Reader's Digest Fund.

Section Four
Big Game

Nobody dast blame this man. You don't understand:
Willy was a salesman. And for a salesman, there is no
rock bottom to the life. He don't put a bolt to a nut, he
don't tell you the law or give you medicine. He's a man
way out there in the blue, riding on a smile and a
shoeshine.

Arthur Miller, *Death of a Salesman*

The Auto Mall: Wanting to Sell Toyotas

THE POSITION I ENJOYED MOST, AND RECALL WITH keenest nostalgia, was that of car salesman. When I see now – as I often do – the stickers that identify a vehicle – we liked to call them vehicles – as having been sold by my old dealership, it pleases me. *Somebody had fun!* That's what I think. *Somebody drew blood.*

Yes, I'm aware of the opprobrium which attaches to the profession. When I was in training, another cadet named Robert Garcia used to spend the late break with me at a Dunkin' Donuts. I recall a particular gray afternoon in January of 1997, the second day of class. We were sitting together at the counter, sharing a companionable silence. 'You don't suppose I've hit the bottom of the barrel?' Garcia asked me. 'Selling cars?'

I told him, 'No, of course not. It depends on what sort of salesman you turn out to be.'

Garcia said he was going to buy a camera. When one of his customers took delivery, he'd get the new owner out there in front of the vehicle – we liked to call them vehicles – with a helium balloon attached to the antenna. If possible, Garcia would insert himself into the happy diorama. Then he'd send a copy of this photo out to his satisfied customer, begin to build a reputation.

I liked Robert, and that day our alliance seemed particularly promising. When the teacher, Joe P., had warned us never to assume that the man in the family was buying the car, Garcia had chimed in with the maxim 'Assume nothing. Assume makes an *ass* of *u* and *me*.' Joe put it on the blackboard. If Garcia was the teacher's pet, I was the teacher's pet's best friend.

This was vital, since Joe P. would decide which showroom I worked in. The dealership sold Pontiac, Buick, Oldsmobile, Cadillac, Toyota, and Nissan. I wanted to sell Toyotas.

Robert also wanted to sell Toyotas. I'd heard him telling Joe as much.

I knew Robert ran disco parties and had been an advertising-space salesman. He knew I wrote novels and had been a magazine editor.

We'd spoken about how lucky we were to have wives who tolerated the ups and downs of our careers. 'Mostly downs,' I said, and we both laughed.

Fact is, I was excited. The classified advertisement promised earnings of '$75,000 + No Experience Necessary! 1 Week Free Training! Eight-Week Training Salary!!!! We Pay While You Learn!!!'.

But it wasn't just the money. It had turned out – shame, shame – that I loved to sell. Closing, the moment at which a deal is consummated, is one of the great legal thrills still left to man. Women are better at it, of course. (According to Joe P., five hundred people in the United States earned more than one hundred thousand dollars in 1995 selling cars and 75 per cent of them were women.)

As a consumer I'd never noticed the close. I was always wondering if my life really would be transformed by an electric breadmaker, or if this was the right model. The salesman – if he's good – is acting bored, but all the time he's sucking me in with patter: 'My neighbor bought one fifteen years ago, finally gave it to his son when the boy went off to medical school. This unit has the same chip they use in the space shuttle.'

As a salesman I understood for the first time what was going on behind the counter. It was as if I'd been driving in cars for fifty years without ever having popped a hood.

Plus – selling is fun. In life there are moments of intense intimacy, which, for some reason, are not openly acknowledged.

Lighting another person's cigarette, for instance, is one such point of contact.

In her book *For the Time Being,* Annie Dillard mentions that she will sometimes smoke with a stranger. 'Possibly when our brains fire their dying charges we will remember and see, to our dismay, not any best-loved face but instead some solitary figure, a stranger whose image the mind retains,' she writes.

Closing is another intimate moment. The higher the price tag, the more carnal the experience.

I had enjoyed selling computers, and if moving something that cost two thousand dollars made my heart race and my pupils dilate, what would it be like to sell a twenty-thousand-dollar car?

It looked as if I were going to find out soon, though, for now Joe P. was keeping us in the classroom up behind the service bays at Wegman Auto. He had a system: 'If you lack experience or conviction regarding the lucrative automotive-selling profession, learn the automotive success system!!!!' That's what the advertisement had said.

I'd seen the classified in the help-wanted section of the *Pennysaver* on November 10, 1996, and laid down a blanket of phone calls. I'd gotten my first appointment with Joe late that month. I was told to go to the GM showroom. This was in the afternoon. The front of the dealership's main building, a large, low-slung structure just off a central artery in upstate New York, is divided into showrooms for GM and Nissan. The service bays are behind these. Toyota is in a smaller building across the road. Parking for customers is right in front of the glass showrooms. Many of the new cars are displayed in this lot, which has three tall metal flagpoles painted white. Standing outside on a windy day, you can hear the ropes rattling. Each pole has a large American flag. One also flies the black banner raised to honor prisoners of war and those missing in action.

I took a slot reserved for customers. As soon as I hit the floor, a big sad man ambled to my side and asked which car I wanted to test-drive. I told him I was applying for a job. I needed to see Joe P.

My new friend paged Joe: 'Would Joe P. please come to the GM showroom? Would Joe P. please come to the GM showroom?' Then we talked. I asked how long he'd worked at the dealership. About a year, he said. He lived across the Tappan Zee Bridge in Rockland County.

'They don't have car lots over there?'

'Not like this one,' he said, but with a lack of enthusiasm that seemed almost comic when contrasted with his words. 'We have six different makes of car, plus this dealership has a great reputation,' he told me in a listless monotone. 'Wegman Auto didn't just open the day before yesterday. We've been in business for sixty-seven years. The service department operates until midnight. There are thirty-two service bays. You can drive in at ten P.M. and have an oil change.' There was a little upbeat on the word *change,* but he still sounded as if he might burst into tears at any moment.

He made a late-night oil change sound like the rough equivalent to riding in a white stretch limousine with an iced bowl of caviar between your knees.

When Joe P. arrived, he was with another man. They were walking in my direction, hugging each other and laughing. Joe was tall and dark, the other man was shorter and had reddish blond hair in a brush cut. Both were in suits. Both had faces that had been scarred with acne or a childhood pox. Joe was beaming. The other man had a wolfish grin. When I stepped out in front of them and introduced myself, the two men gave me the sort of look a cat might give a mouse if the cat wasn't particularly hungry.

Joe shook my hand, gave me an application to fill out, and he and the other man vanished. I filled out the form, attached a résumé, and left.

I didn't wait for Joe to call me back: I phoned him. I kept calling him. Finally he set up a second appointment. This was for nine A.M. on Thursday, December 5, 1996. I arrived a little before nine A.M. Joe appeared at 9:15, beaming. He had a desk in the back of the GM showroom. I was given a chair in front of it. I noticed three large brown envelopes on the desk. All three of them had

'Declined' written across the front in red grease pencil. One of them had 'Bankrupt' written below 'Declined'.

I was wearing my best Polo suit, my most earnest smile, and I sat forward in my chair to explain. I told Joe how much I had enjoyed selling computers at CompUSA and Nobody Beats the Wiz. 'I was brought up to disdain sales, but I like the work. It's fun. It's like fishing.' I told him how eager I was to try cars. 'I see this as the big-game hunt of retail sales.'

Joe didn't commit. 'I wouldn't want you to just park yourself here for a while until something better comes along. You have to look at this as a career,' Joe told me.

I said I wanted that, too. 'Start you out at forty thousand dollars,' Joe said. 'I see you made eighty thousand at the *Reader's Digest*. We'll try to get you back up there.'

Now I'd already had a dozen jobs and I'd been making between five and eight dollars an hour. That's less than seventeen thousand a year – assuming a forty-hour week and no vacation. I had become convinced that until I was willing to wrench shamelessly at every personal connection and somehow locate the same sort of intricate editorial chores I'd performed at the *Reader's Digest,* I was never going to earn much more than minimum wage. Now I wondered if an end run was possible. Might I earn a decent salary without knowing anybody? Without even having to read? Just do it on heart alone?

I've always been susceptible to the psychology of self-improvement. In high school I read Emerson, *Walden,* and *The Three Pillars of Zen.* Waiting outside in the car while my girlfriend shopped at Saks, I would count the in-breaths, trying to see color in the air. In college I read Hermann Hesse, and Aldous Huxley's *The Doors of Perception.* At the *Reader's Digest,* I edited countless articles designed to make readers more positive, successful, and contented. While there, I also took up jogging.

At the time of my second interview at Wegman, I was working at Franklin Quest in the Westchester, a mall in White Plains, New

York. We sold binders similar to the Filofax or the Day Runner, and a system for using them. I was a time-management specialist. We also sold encouragement, including, for instance, a framed poster which had a picture of a basketball hoop and the legend 'You'll always miss 100% of the shots you don't take'.

I was earning approximately $7.20 an hour and having *no fun*. The store was pleasantly furnished in dark wood cabinets and rich green carpeting, like the library in a B movie. The decor was meant, I suppose, to be relaxing, but I never relaxed while I was there. The manager was an intelligent young woman, but highly motivated and very tightly wound. When I went there for my interview, I was wearing a suit and a mock turtleneck sweater. She told me that a shirt and tie were required. She said that mine was a 'very nice sweater', but that if she made an exception for me. . . . So I wore a tie and jacket, except on dress-down Fridays, when I and everybody else wore Franklin Quest T-shirts with the slogan 'What Really Matters?' emblazoned across the back.

At Franklin Quest there was a yellow Post-it on the toilet seat reminding the men to put it back down after urinating. 'Please restore seat to down position,' it read. The daily closing involved an arduous bookkeeping procedure, which often kept us in the mall for an hour after the last customer had gone home. One night we had to run through the entire set of computations twice before the books balanced, and then the manager found a penny on the floor. I groaned noisily, and maybe that's why she didn't start again at the beginning. Instead she took the penny and put a Post-it on it. 'Penny unaccounted for,' it read.

I'd gotten up at five A.M. in order to work on my notes. By ten P.M. I was drunk with fatigue. If I'd seen the penny before she had, I would cheerfully have swallowed it.

That wasn't the worst night, either. The worst night was inventory. We were in the store until 2:30 A.M. We had to count everything. The chore took longer because one of the time-management specialists didn't make it in. He'd been to some sort of business convention. On the way home his car broke down. He phoned twice, but never showed.

The next day he took me aside. 'Can I trust you to keep a secret?' he asked. I said he could. 'I'm not going to stay here my whole life,' he said, waving a hand to take in the showroom. I nodded. 'There's no real future here,' he said.

I shrugged.

'I was at a convention,' he said. 'A business opportunity. I can get in on the ground floor. We eliminate the middle man. It's the fastest-growing company in America,' he said. 'Acme Corporation.'

Now I was wagging my head. 'I think I've heard of them.'

He lightened considerably and nodded.

'You've heard of them?'

'I don't think they're a good idea,' I said.

His face fell. I tried to explain why, but he didn't want to hear me. In any case, we couldn't argue openly.

Despite having missed inventory, this particular young man was a hard worker, and gung-ho. He studied the rules of time management with great care. 'I want to be a product of the product,' he said once at a staff meeting. In some ways his susceptibility to Acme had to do with our work together at Franklin Quest.

It's hard to state precisely what's missing from the Franklin Quest philosophy. When I took the free seminar to which I was entitled as an employee, I came home all fired up and explained it to my wife. 'It's a little dorky,' she said. That sounded about right. But then a close friend said she'd never seen any kind of real change without a phase of extreme dorkiness. That sounded right as well.

I was a believer and agonized deliciously over what sort of Franklin Planner I would buy and use. I finally settled on the Classic. I chose a binder made out of recycled materials and bordered with simulated leather. For the pages, I picked the manly Monticello 'A Classic in Time.' I also used my employee discount to outfit family and friends. If time is money, then is money time?

Even with my discount, I came close to using all the money I earned. In this I was not alone. At one point I got a glimpse of the house account of another employee and found that he'd spent more than five hundred dollars in a three-month period. 'Saint Peter don't you call me, 'cause I can't go./I owe my soul to the company store.'

I suppose that what can go wrong with the time specialist's outlook is the loss of a sense of irony or humor.

We had a large binder, kept in the main desk, in which we were expected to sign our names daily. There were messages from our manager, quotations, and also notes like this: 'Eat the cake in the fridge. I want to share it. Love, always. R.'

One day the manager stapled a torn-out display ad to the page:

Our Policy
Rule 1. The customer is always right.
Rule 2. If the customer is ever wrong, reread Rule 1.

The prophet quoted was Stew Leonard, the famous operator of the supermarkets that carry his name. Now Stew Leonard is a very successful businessman. He was also jailed in October 1993 after pleading guilty to using a computer program to skim $17.1 million off the books of his Norwalk store. He served forty-four months of a fifty-two-month sentence for tax evasion.

I don't want to throw out the bathwater with the baby here. The bagels at Stew Leonard's may be good and also cheap. I do think, however, that his life is trying to teach us a lesson: Businessmen who say the customer is always right lie to the customer.

I've always had difficulty distinguishing that which is simply silly and in bad taste from that which is truly pernicious.

The very first time I was given a chance to write anything for the *Reader's Digest* (I wrote almost daily for the newspaper) it was an author's note for a reprint of a work by Dale Carnegie.

I rushed into the corporate library, located *Book Review Digest* for 1937, and found many positive encouraging reviews. The one that woke me up, though, was a review of *How to Win Friends and*

Influence People and written by *New Yorker* stalwart James Thurber for the *Springfield Republican*:

> Mr. Carnegie loudly protests that one can be sincere and at the same time versed in the tricks of influencing people. Unfortunately, the disingenuities in his set of rules and in his case histories stand out like ghosts at a banquet.

I'd read *Macbeth*. I knew what that meant.

It was Gunther Grass, though, who wrote that innocence grows back, and so years later I still found the Franklin Quest ideology encouraging.

I liked the quotations that were everywhere: 'Dost thou love life? Then do not squander Time, for that's the Stuff life is made of.' So wrote Ben Franklin. Benjamin Franklin didn't carry a Franklin Planner, but the planners we were selling were named after him. I was a believer, but I was also dying to get out of there.

During my second visit to Wegman Auto, I saw that Joe P. had a Franklin Planner opened on his desk. 'I'd be lost without it,' he said. I told him I worked at Franklin Quest in White Plains. He asked if he could call me at the job. He said he needed to order refills. When he called, though, he didn't place an order. I suspect he was checking to make certain I actually held the job.

'You don't just sell binders?' he asked when he had me on the phone. I didn't understand what he was getting at. I said that we sold refills and quote cards and inspirational posters. We had a line of 'Successories'. One poster featured a cheetah racing at full speed. 'Attack every problem with enthusiasm . . . as if your life depended upon it,' the legend read. Our catalogue carried a durable PCV-molded vinyl floor mat that read:

> We can't spell *s ccess* without
> U.

So I knew something about psychology, but Joe was way ahead
of me. As I'd mumbled on about our merchandise, he broke in to
make his point.

'But you sell yourself?' he said.

I said, yeah, I supposed that I sold myself.

'When you come here, you'll be selling Ben Cheever first,' he
told me over the phone, 'then the dealership, and only then the
sheet metal. The cars are incidental. Can you sell Ben Cheever?'

This was a good question, I thought. Whether or not I ever sold
cars, this was a good question.

After our little talk, Joe said he'd get back to me, but he went to
Vegas first. I made several panicked calls to his voice mail. Finally, in
mid-December, I learned that I'd made the cut.

I gave notice at Franklin Quest. The manager was sore as a
hornet. I could have pointed out the poster we sold which had a
picture of a tiger peering through foliage. The legend: 'In Today's
World There Are Two Kinds of Companies . . . the Quick and the
Dead!'

January 7 was the first day of training. We had all been told to park
at the Caldor lot, which was across a side road, but we were to use
spaces far away from that store, so as not to interfere with
commerce. We walked out of the Caldor lot, crossed the road
and the Wegman lot. We came in the GM doors, through to the
back of that showroom, and down a hall which had a glass display
case with framed certificates for community service and a picture of
the service station from which the dealership had sprung. This hall
opened on to a windowless lounge with a coffeemaker, tables,
chairs, and a TV high up in one corner. Across from this lounge was
a window into the business offices. Beyond the lounge was a
hallway. You turned left for the rest rooms, or went straight
through a metal door to the service bays.

In order to reach the classroom, we walked through this fire-
proof door, past several vending machines, and out into the service
area, with its high ceiling and smell of motor oil. This vast, echoing

chamber was more than two storeys high and seemed as long as a football field.

One day as we were walking through Service, Garcia heard the echo of my cowboy boots on the cement floor, turned, looked at my feet, and said, without malice, 'Benny, I didn't know you wore lifts.'

The service area was colder than the rest of the building and also politically more conservative. The Snap-On Tools box had a sticker that read, 'I make my living with Snap-On Tools. Please don't ask to borrow them.' There were also two Nintendo stickers and one that read, 'I'm NRA and I vote!'

Back behind the second bay, on the right, a door opened on to stairs leading up to a large room with a long rectangular table. This had a TV with an ancient VCR at one end and a blackboard at the other. The walls were lined with shelves that held manuals. Even with the door closed, we could smell motor oil and hear the whine of pneumatic wrenches.

Class was supposed to start at two P.M. that first day. Most of us were in chairs by 2:05 P.M. We were all casually dressed. I had on chinos and the sweater I hadn't been permitted to wear at Franklin Quest. I asked one of the other cadets what the week of free training meant. 'That means we don't get paid for the first week,' I was told.

According to the other students, this was not a bad deal. After the first week, we *would* be paid. Some dealerships charged prospective employees a couple hundred dollars for training.

I said I hoped the generosity didn't mean that Wegman Auto was desperate.

Nobody seemed to think so. One of the other cadets said he'd followed a red Lotus into the parking lot. 'So somebody here is making good money.'

At about two-fifteen a veteran salesman named George Santos came up and told us Joe P. was on his way. 'Joe is great,' he told us. 'The method that he's going to teach you, it always works.'

Joe appeared at 2:30 P.M. and gave the group a generous smile.

You'd think we were the ones who were late, and that he was forgiving us.

Because he was the authority figure, I naturally assumed that Joe was older than I was, but I was forty-eight at the time, and he was probably in his late thirties or early forties. He was dressed down for the occasion, wearing a blue denim shirt with the top button fastened, a light cardigan sweater, and pleated chinos. His face was slightly pocked, his thinning dark hair combed straight up and back. Joe was not a particularly handsome man, but he radiated warmth. He seemed always to be having the time of his life. And thinking of letting you in on it.

We went around the table and introduced ourselves, said what we'd done and why we wanted to sell cars. There were fourteen cadets, ranging in age from those in their early twenties to a vain retired painting contractor who claimed to be fifty-five. There was a woman named Loretta who identified herself as a professional singer. However, she had heard about the opening at Wegman when she was working at Caldor and had sold popcorn to a couple of veteran salesmen. She was pretty and ebullient. You could see immediately why the veterans wanted to have Loretta around. There were two auto mechanics. One had black curly hair. The other had straight sandy hair. He had a limp, and carried an aluminum cane. There was a young man who had been laid off by Avon. He had worked on mainframes, but said that the machines had gotten so efficient that most of the mainframe staff had been let go. He seemed not to have been scarred by the experience.

The painting contractor sat directly across from me, and we took an immediate dislike to each other. His name, I later had too many opportunities to learn, was Victor Amato. He had a moustache and wore his shirt open so that you could see his chest if you wanted to. Amato had a gold chain and a thick gold I.D. bracelet. He had both a pager and a cell phone. 'This is all new to me,' he said. 'All my life I've worked for myself. I bought twenty-seven new cars. I never knew how much play they had. That's part of why I'm here, to find that out. I still don't know how much any of those people made off me.'

Our only former car salesman had sold Toyotas in New Rochelle. 'Liked the job,' he told us, 'but I didn't like the place.'

Joe bit the bullet immediately. He told us that his own parents had been upset when he took his first job in an auto store. 'I don't think any mom or dad wants their son or daughter to grow up and sell cars,' he said.

He said he loved it now. He said we'd love it, too. He said we'd be our own bosses. He said there was no limit to how far we could go, how much we could earn. No limit.

He told us that Wegman Auto employed 250 people and sold five thousand cars a year. I don't remember where, but I'd heard somebody in the business office boasting that Wegman sold four thousand cars a year.

We were each given a handout of car-sales statistics. We were also each given a forty-seven-page, stapled-together 'bible'. This is the document out of which we would work, Joe told us.

Under the heading 'Selling Profession,' it begins, 'The art of selling is one of the oldest vocations. We know that Stone Age men traveled great distances to trade for goods they could not find where they hunted and gathered food. There is reason to believe barter is older than war, and we are all descendants of peaceful traders (salespeople), who exercised crude forms of salesmanship, rather than from violent marauders, who lived on plunder.'

Joe told us that 20 per cent of the people who walk into a showroom will buy a car right then. Twenty per cent is the industry average, according to Joe. The Wegman average was 30 per cent, he said. 'So that's three out of ten people.' Our sheet of '15 eye-opening statistics' also stated that 85 per cent of prospects had decided to buy a car before they ever left home.

He's pumping us up, I thought. I'd been trained now for other jobs, and they always pump you up.

Morale is crucial. 'Morale is to all other factors as four is to one.'

That's what Napoleon said. Hope is the one benefit that costs an employer nothing.

Anybody who appears in the showroom is a prospect, Joe told us. 'It's not like a mall. People don't come to car dealerships because they want to kill time. OK. They don't like us. They'd rather be home watching the game.'

Of all the things we had to learn, Joe told us, we had to learn first to be cheerful. People are naturally negative, Joe told us. 'You can't be. You have got to be cheerful. It doesn't matter if you like people.' Then, beaming, he said, 'I hate people. What about you?'

We also had to be confident. People are confident in confident people, he told us. Confident, but cheerful first.

'There's a switch in there,' he said. 'You need to be able to find that switch and turn it. There are no natural-born salesmen. It's all training.' He asked if any of us had seen the video clip of President Reagan being shot. Some of us had. 'Everybody hit the deck, but there was one man standing tall,' Joe told us. 'That was a Secret Service agent. When a gun goes off, it's human instinct to hit the deck. But that man didn't. He was supposed to take the bullet. That's the triumph of training over instinct.'

At this point Joe was paged. Would Joe P. come to the GM showroom? Would Joe P. come to the GM showroom?

There was an audio system piped throughout the building. Local radio stations were played, including the advertisements placed by Rushneck Pontiac in Tarrytown and other competing dealerships. The music was interrupted when somebody came on to page one or all of us. For instance, 'Vinnie T. has a birthday today. Would everybody please wish Vinnie T. a happy birthday. Vinnie, are you out there?'

On this, our first day in class, they began to page Joe P. at a little before five P.M. Joe called in and found that a man was downstairs waiting to see him. Joe said he'd be right down. He spoke to us for another fifteen minutes. The phone rang again. Again, Joe said he'd be right down. Joe released us at 5:40, and we lined up to have a private word. We all had the same question: 'I was wondering, could I work in Toyota?' The man downstairs was still waiting. I can't know what Joe's Franklin Planner did for him exactly, but it certainly didn't make him punctual.

But back to my lust to sell Toyotas. I had friends who drove Toyotas. I didn't have friends who drove American cars. Economics trump taste, though, because Victor Amato drove a Ford Windstar and he also wanted to sell Toyotas.

When I got home and told my wife that I hoped I could work in the Toyota division, she said it was a bad idea, because John Updike had written the book *Rabbit Is Rich*, about a man who managed a Toyota dealership.

I told her I knew that. I told her I had read the book. 'You don't understand,' I said, 'I want to sell cars.'

Driving to class on the second day, I saw the red Lotus I'd heard so much about the day before. There was smoke pouring out of the rear of the car. I followed the Lotus into the Caldor lot and parked near it. The door opened and Ralph, the former automobile mechanic with curly hair, got out of the driver's seat, walked around, and opened the trunk. Apparently the trunk had gotten so hot that the handle of a screwdriver had ignited and was billowing clouds of pungent gray smoke. I watched while Ralph put the fire out with a rag.

'Must be a fun car to drive,' I said when the emergency was over.

Ralph didn't say anything.

'Attract girls?' I asked.

'Not really,' he said. 'It's a guy magnet.'

I didn't mention that his car had come up the day before as proof that there was big money to be made in auto sales, whereas he'd clearly bought the car when he was a mechanic. Or before that. He didn't mention this, either.

Upstairs in the classroom, we'd lost one prospect and picked up a man whom I had known when he'd worked in Data Processing at the *Reader's Digest*. I recognized him immediately because he wore a great many gold chains. Let's call him John. John and I exchanged greetings. John told us all that he wanted to come to work for Wegman because he'd bought all his cars from that dealership. I believe he'd bought fourteen cars.

While we were waiting for Joe to come, we talked. The other mechanic from our class – the one with the sandy hair, the cane, and the limp – pulled up his trouser leg to show us a bump, about the size of an orange, just above his ankle. He said he'd been working under the hood of a Pontiac Trans Am and somehow the car had popped into gear, driven forward, and smashed his leg. He said his disability payments weren't enough to live on. He didn't feel that he could be a mechanic anymore, but he could sell cars, although he didn't want to sell Pontiacs.

I asked if it hurt when he broke his leg. He said not at first, but that he'd had to wait hours for the doctor to arrive to set it, and that it hurt terribly while he was waiting. For some reason he still wasn't clear on, they couldn't give him a strong painkiller. The doctor had gotten caught in traffic.

Joe arrived late again, but cheerful as ever. He told us about dealing with the customer's FACC. This stood for 'Fear, Anxiety, Cynicism, and Confusion'.

Joe talked us through page four of the bible, regarding 'the Dichotomy within the Prospect'. This 'dichotomy' was between the prospect's 'conscience mind' and his 'subconscience mind'. The gifted salesman found a link between the two. I waited a little while and then asked if Joe didn't mean the prospect's 'conscious mind and his subconscious mind'. I had hoped to get a laugh, but nobody noticed, nor was Joe openly thankful to me for the correction.

Getting right back to business, Joe said it was a commonplace for customers to think they were making their purchasing decision based on price alone. He said this was an error. He said that the first and most important factor in any sale was the sales consultant. 'You,' he said, and pointed around the table. The second was the dealership. The third was the car. He told us price was the least-important consideration and therefore should be left for last. 'Never discuss the price until you've sold the car.'

Since customers were bound to try to ask about price before we wanted them to, we were told to memorize four 'bypasses' that were laid out in the bible:

1. I can appreciate your concern for price. It is certainly an important consideration. However, I've never had anyone take ownership and feel they had paid too much. That reminds me: Did you want another . . . or . . . ?

2. I can appreciate your concern for price. It is certainly an important consideration. However, I have difficulty just keeping up with our 300-vehicle inventory, never mind the best price on each of them. Aside from price, did you prefer the . . . or . . . ?

3. I can certainly appreciate your concern for price. I feel just as you do when I sit in your chair. Fortunately, as the largest auto mall in the five counties, we always give the greatest value. That reminds me: Were you going to take . . . or . . . ?

4. It's not unreasonable to expect my best offer on this specific model. After all, it is your hard-earned money. Unfortunately, there are factors such as inventory age, which will impact a vehicle minimally or significantly. If I guess too low and cannot deliver, you will become very irate. If I guess too high, you may just lose interest. For the sake of all parties it is best that we pick the perfect vehicle first and then discuss price in great detail. Therefore, were . . . or . . . ????

When somebody in the class said that memorized material sounds canned, Joe said, 'It's only canned until you internalize it.'

Joe said that we must learn these bypasses but we should also feel free to ad-lib. He told us, 'You might just say, "We have more than three hundred vehicles on this lot. Each has a different price. I'd have to be Al Wegman to be able to remember them all."' Al Wegman was the owner of the dealership. He was a large, genial man, who wore dress shirts and suspenders. He often had a golf club in his hands. He didn't seem at all like the sort of prodigy who could easily hold the prices of three hundred cars in his mind.

When I got to the floor, a couple of men who had been to high school with Wegman came in to test-drive a car. Wegman came into my cubicle and spoke with them. He told them he had a new driver in his golf-club collection; I believe it was called a killer bee. He said that it had added greatly to the distance of his drives. He said that if they bought a car, he'd see that they got a good price, and also put his old driver in the trunk. He told me to treat these men well. 'They have something you can't buy,' he said.

'What's that?' I asked.

'Loyalty,' he said.

I wanted to say, 'You don't pay enough for loyalty', but I shut my mouth. Besides which, I didn't know the half of it.

When I got his old buddies out in the car, they told me, 'We knew Alvin Wegman when he stuttered.'

But I'm getting ahead of myself. During training, we're taught to say, 'Welcome to Wegman Auto. I'm John Doe, and you are?' (I've changed the names of the dealership and of the people involved.) We read in the bible that 'we incorporate the word "welcome" during our greeting. Sales psychologists have concluded after extensive analysis that the word "welcome" reduces some of the fear and anxiety experienced by consumers, resulting in dramatic reductions in heart rate observed in members of the control group. Moreover, it enhances the ambiance with additional warmth'.

Next you were supposed to ask if they were first-time Wegman customers, both to discover the facts and also to establish a phantom army of previous Wegman customers – all apparently well-satisfied.

Then Joe wanted us to say, 'And who's the lucky person buying a new car today?'

He warned us never to assume that it's the man buying the car. He said he's seen women stride right out of a showroom when they had intended to buy a car but the sales consultant had mistakenly focussed on the husband, boyfriend, or father.

A salesman is a leader, we learned. You sell the customer a car, or he sells you on the idea that he can't afford a car. Either way a sale takes place.

Because of computer connections, we learned, it was now possible to spot a car, to sell it and take the trade, and do it all within a couple of hours of the time Mr. Customer first stepped on the lot. We should always try to spot-sell, we were told. 'Every day is the Super Bowl,' Joe told us.

We were taught to always present the prospect with at least two alternatives, both of which would lead to an immediate sale: for instance, 'Do you want to buy a car today in red or in green?'; 'Would you like to lease the car you're picking out today, or would you rather finance it?'

Joe said we'd probably all heard that invention is 10 per cent inspiration and 90 per cent perspiration. 'Well, in our business there's not a lot of sweat. It's ten per cent perspiration, ten per cent product knowledge, and eighty per cent inspiration.

'Sales is the highest-paid hard work, and the lowest-paid easy work. You'll find this business is very simple. It's so simple that it's hard. Salesmen are leaders. It's great to be a salesman,' he said, 'because you get to create reality.'

After class that evening, I went to a nearby mall and bought the four-cassette audio version of *Zig Ziglar's Secrets of Closing the Sale.*

When I told Joe about my audiobook purchase and he approved, I was heartened by the program. Ziglar is highly entertaining, but perhaps most important, he maintains that integrity is essential to a success in sales. 'You can't make a good deal with a bad guy,' he said.

He said that the impression held by many people of salesmen is false and misleading. This started because the original Yankee peddlers were hard men, he said. 'And then Arthur Miller wrote that abominable monstrosity called *Death of a Salesman.*'

With all the success salesmen have had in this country, Ziglar says, they have failed to sell their own profession.

'I can say to you that if my son were to ever come to me and ask me what career I think would offer him the most security, I would tell him, "Son, I believe the profession of selling is the most secure of all the professions." If he would say to me, "Well, Dad, isn't that a commission job?" I would say, "Yes, son, selling is a commission job, as is everything else a commission job. Whether you're a dentist, a doctor, a secretary or the manager of a plant, you are on commission for the very simple reason that if you don't perform effectively, you're soon going to lose your job or your customers or your business." My friend, you're on a commission whether you're on a salary or not. And you can even go to the top. You can get the biggest job in the whole world, you can get to be the president of the United States, and if you don't produce, they'll flat get you.'

In class we were alerted to the most common pitfalls of car sales. If the always-cheerful salesman's first mandate was to avoid mentioning price, then his second most vital concern was to avoid the TRADE-IN AMBUSH.

Forty per cent of the people who buy a car will have a trade-in, Joe told us. The difficulty with a trade-in is that the dealer is talking wholesale and the customer is thinking retail. The customer identifies with the car he's disposing of. (Notice the use of the word *dispose*.) The salesman's countermove is to play down the value of the car being traded in and also to take some of the money off the list of the new car and add it to the apparent value of the trade-in.

You need to establish immediately if there is a trade-in. Then you want to go out and look at the car with the owner. This is the 'silent appraisal'. You walk around the customer's car with a sheet of paper. You don't say anything, because if you say anything, Mr. Customer might contradict you, or even get mad. You just look critical and make little noises of disappointment.

There are people who come in 'upside down'. A car owner who is upside down still has a loan outstanding on the car he's trading in, and owes more on the loan than the car is worth. I once had a couple who seemed interested in buying a new car, but when I had their trade-in assessed and they figured out that they still owed two thousand dollars on a car for which we were planning to pay them one thousand, they were both suddenly furious with me, sprang out of the chairs in my cubicle, and stormed out of the showroom.

Handling the trade-in is always difficult, but it's manageable if you know from the get-go that there is going to be a car to trade in. If they ambush you, you're cooked. You've given them the best price you can afford on the new car, then they produce the trade-in. 'It's like you're standing with your pants down around your ankles,' Joe said. At this point it's altogether possible that no matter how good a deal you've given the customer on the new car, he's going to be so offended by the offer you make on the trade that he'll walk.

'And how did you get here today, Mr. X?' we were supposed to ask over and over. 'Will you be disposing of that car today?' (Notice again the use of the word *dispose*.)

If the car had undercoating or rustproofing or acid rain – proofing, we were advised to give these improvements an inflated value. The notion was that this would encourage the new car buyer to pay for the same or similar options again. 'Spend more, get more.'

I came into class late one day and found my fellow students listening spellbound while the young man who had managed a shoe store told how he'd had an operation on his throat with local anesthesia. 'I saw everything,' he said.

Four of the incoming cadets had some sort of surgical procedure between the first day of class and the first day selling. Most of us had had surgery at least once in our lives. I wondered if there was a connection to be made between financial and biological vulnerability.

This admission of frailty contrasted with the gung-ho attitude we were shooting for. We were meant to be tough. It was felt, of course, that Joe must have an iron fist inside his velvet glove. I never saw it. He did tell us that he met his wife at a roller-skating rink. He liked the way she looked, skated in her direction, pretended to lose control, and knocked her down.

Since he was the teacher, we were all intensely curious about Joe, but he wouldn't talk about himself, except to make a point or get a laugh. 'I was an only child. I played a lot with myself,' he said, whenever we became too serious. Victor Amato, on the other hand, would talk about himself endlessly and with the least-conceivable excuse. We learned that a good paint job used to last forty years, but now that they'd taken the lead out of the paint, a good paint job lasted seven years. We learned that Victor had done a lot of work for IBM until IBM didn't have so much money. He said he saw them firing people who had expected to work at IBM for life, saw research scientists being carried out of the Watson Research Center in Yorktown Heights in tears. 'Geniuses crying.'

One of his favorite phrases was 'hard as Chinese arithmetic', and he told us more than one joke in which somebody's 'dick was as hard as Chinese arithmetic'.

Vic had started out in the city when the painting business was still his father's. They used to mix their own paints. He worked so much with lead paints that when he was a young man, a ball of lead formed in his stomach, 'this big'. He cupped his hands together, as if they held a golf ball.

I asked if it had been surgically removed.

'No,' he said, 'I just drank a lot of milk.

'You can't kill me,' he used to say. 'I've been shot at twice. I've been knifed.' I bet when Victor was knifed, he squealed like a pig.

There were people in the class I liked very much, but Victor Amato wasn't one of them. He was always telling us how much money he'd earned in his painting business. He was on his third wife. He made this sound like an accomplishment.

Joe P. told us that the Internet was changing the business. For instance, nobody could 'chop a clock' anymore. There was a service called VinGuard, he said, and when anybody brought a car in to be serviced, the service station would type in the car's vehicle identification number and also its mileage. So if you got a car in with fifty thousand miles, and you found that it had had fifty thousand miles on it two years ago, you knew the clock had been chopped.

When he asked if anybody was interested in computers, I raised my hand. He said he would use me then, maybe to set up a Web site. I told him I liked the idea, but nothing ever came of it.

All through the course, Joe kept hinting at 'the Mother of All Closes', but when I read ahead to it in the bible, it was actually fairly simple, bald – and in most cases it seemed to me that it would be unworkable as well. When Joe finally presented it, of course, he made it sound terrific. Here it is, the Mother of All Closes: If you've finally got your customer up against the wall and asked him a question and he's failed to reply, he's speechless, you are supposed to say, 'Mr. Customer, when I was a little fellow my mamma taught me silence was golden and meant consent. My mamma wasn't wrong, was she? Mr. Customer, would you like to pick up your car this afternoon, or do you prefer this evening?'

The manufacturer's suggested retail price (MSRP) was what we aimed for, but we could come down 5 per cent in a heartbeat. The more expensive the car was, the more room we had to bargain. With our sales manager's approval, we could dip down to very nearly the price we were told the car had cost the dealer. The front-line salesmen were not ordinarily told what this price was.

But this was not what we were supposed to concentrate on, Joe told us again and again. Our work was to keep cheerful, keep hopeful, and keep right on working towards that close.

The example I liked best was the one with the customer who admired a twenty-five-thousand-dollar car but said right off that she couldn't afford it. What you said was 'All right. You like that car, right?'

If Ms. Customer said yes, she did like that car, but wouldn't dream of spending that much money, you went back a step.

'I know you can't afford to pay twenty-five thousand dollars for your personal vehicle. Let's leave that issue aside for a moment. What I need to know now is whether or not you like this exact car.'

If Ms. Customer said she did like the car, you'd ask again if she was absolutely sure.

Sure, she was sure, but it was too expensive.

'I understand that it's too expensive,' you'd say, 'but what if you didn't have to pay this much? If we can arrive at a mutually agreeable price, would you buy this vehicle from me today?'

The customer is exasperated. 'I don't have twenty-five thousand.'

'But if you won the lottery, you'd buy that car from me today?'

'I didn't win the lottery.'

'Fine, I understand. Here's a question for you, though. What would you be willing to pay?'

'I'd pay fifteen thousand dollars.'

'Let me make sure I've got this straight. If I could get you that vehicle right there. If I could get you that twenty-five-thousand-dollar car for fifteen thousand, you'd buy it from me today?'

'Yes, I would.'

'Are you absolutely certain?'

'Yes.'

'That exact vehicle. There's not another vehicle here on the lot you'd like better?'

'No, there's not.'

'Is there anything you'd change on this vehicle? Do you want a pinstripe, for instance?'

'A pinstripe might be nice. A yellow pinstripe.'

'You're right. It's good to customize your personal vehicle. Don't want it looking like everything else that ran off the factory floor.'

'I'd like a pinstripe, then, if that doesn't cost a fortune.'

'Not a fortune,' you say, and wink.

'Okay, let's go for the pinstripe.'

'All right. Then this is the perfect vehicle for you? This with a pinstripe?'

'Yes.'

'Well, I'm going to do the best I can for you. You wait here, and I'll go in and see my manager.'

So then you go in and see your manager. Try to take as much time as you can. You want your prospect out there imagining herself in the new car. You want her picturing herself using the new CD player, if it has a CD player. You want her imagining how the new antilock brakes might save her life. You want her thinking about the new long-lasting paint job and how the plugs don't need to be changed for one hundred thousand miles. You want her picturing the envious looks on the faces of her friends.

When you come back out of the manager's office, you have the world's biggest smile on your face. You're standing up straight. It's training over instinct. You're breathing deeply. 'Have I got great news for you. You can have that vehicle. The vehicle you want, the exact vehicle you want, that vehicle is available. You can have it today, with a yellow pinstripe, for 22,999 dollars.'

Joe told us repeatedly that it was not our mission to rob anybody. We wanted to give each customer the best value possible. We wanted to make them all customers for life. Always better to make a sale than not to make a sale.

In making this point, Joe neglected to connect it with our pay plan, which entitled us to a percentage of the markup. We worked on commission, so if we sold a lot of cars at dealer cost, we made nothing on those sales, and therefore had no income. None. You might as well go to work for the Red Cross.

When we moved down into the showrooms, Joe told us, we should put up pictures of ourselves and our families. Even pets. 'We want them to know you're human, too,' he explained.

Robert Garcia had a picture of himself with Muhammad Ali. He and his wife had been on a bicycle trip and met the champ at a service station. Robert knew immediately that he wanted a picture of himself just about to take one on the chin from the champ, and Ali had cheerfully complied. This was the picture he planned to frame and put out on his desk. 'As an icebreaker.'

Joe asked us if there was anything we thought might be done to improve the dealership. We all sort of looked away.

'No, I'm serious,' Joe told us. 'I need to know what you want. Anything you want?'

A couple of the men leered.

'Anything but that,' said Joe.

'Like what?' I asked.

Joe shrugged. 'Better office furniture, a cappuccino machine.'

We all were nodding now. A cappuccino machine seemed a splendid idea. There was a station in the lounge with free coffee and tea, but cappuccino or espresso, that would move us all up a rung.

'Yeah,' said Garcia, 'a cappuccino machine would be great.' Turning to face an imaginary prospect, he said, 'And while we finalize the details on your new vehicle, Mr. Customer, would you care for an espresso?'

Joe was nodding, too. He said he'd look into it.

After our final class, Garcia produced a bottle of Chablis and some plastic cups. We traded stories about applying for jobs. Loretta remembered having had a great interview and then, she said, 'the employer asked me if I had any questions about them, so I slipped back into my chair, and I cut a fart.'

'So did you get the job?' I asked.

'Yeah, I got the job. They must have said, we want the girl who farts.'

I still didn't know where I was going to be working. I'd been trying to get Joe alone for days. I knew that Robert Garcia was going to Nissan. Loretta had some special job as a lease advisor. They planned to capitalize on her ebullience.

Several of the cadets, including my friend from the *RD* and both the mechanics, would be selling preowned cars. In the past, used cars had been sold on the side, but now a separate preowned department was just opening. Part of the new regime.

I kept tracking Joe down and asking him where I was going to be posted. He kept saying it hadn't yet been worked out. Which I didn't mind hearing. I figured Joe might be holding off on the announcement because the news that I was going to Toyota would create a firestorm of envy. Nobody else had been posted to Toyota, except the shoe-store manager, the one who'd had his throat cut while he looked on.

I asked him how he got the plum. He said he told Joe a lot about Toyotas. I asked him how he knew so much about Toyotas. He said he'd sent away to Toyota for a CD.

After our final class, I finally caught Joe P. alone in the hallway. Cornered, he turned and gave me one of his great smiles. The man was like a potbellied stove. He radiated that much heat.

'So where am I going to be?' I asked.

He nodded, as if he were about to do me an unexpected favor. 'We tried younger people in GM,' he said, 'but you know, GM customers like a more mature face.'

'So I'm going to be in GM? I'm not going to be in Toyota? Or even Nissan?'

'Yup.'

'When I am diagnosed with cancer,' I told him, 'I want you to bring the news. You'll make it seem like my lucky break.'

Joe smiled again.

'And who else is going to GM?' I asked.

'Victor Amato,' he told me.

The Auto Mall: 'Benny, here, done phenomenal!'

'MANAGEMENT ALREADY TOLD ME I GOT A GREAT FUCKING personality for selling cars,' Victor told me when we came downstairs together into the big GM showroom. He'd heard a story about a friend of his who once threw a customer up against the wall and said, 'You're not leaving here until you buy a fucking car.' This was Victor's model. I was taking the opposite approach. I was going to be the New Age salesman, the sensitive salesman. I had a bowl of clementines for my desk, plus a windup toy seal in tin to amuse the children while I charmed their parents into ruinous debt.

I had brushed my cowboy boots and wore a Polo suit. Victor had on a suit, too, and French cuffs on his shirt. And a tie tack. We were pumped.

Outside of the radio playing over the intercom, it was dreadfully quiet, though, which is no good when you're in Indian territory. Or in sales. I had a sinking feeling. I remembered the joke about the play Zig Ziglar so detests: It's not that Willy Loman had a flawed character. It's just that New England has always been a rotten sales district.

We set up our cubicles. I had a Magic 8 Ball as an icebreaker, a framed picture with both of my sons in a fake wanted poster. Victor had In and Out trays. Victor had a calculator with a huge readout. I brought in a smaller model, but it printed. We each went separately to the mall and had nameplates engraved. We waited. We sat in our cubicles and read brochures and waited. Almost nobody came through the glass door.

Garcia, Amato, and I would take a demo out to lunch. We'd look under the hood, figure out how to pop the trunk. Once we took a Nissan Maxima. Once we took a Buick Le Sabre. Victor knew the neighborhood. 'I painted that house,' he'd say. 'I fucked the woman who lived in that house. I painted that house.' Victor and I agreed that the Pontiac Grand Prix was a better car than the Nissan Maxima. Garcia, the Nissan salesman, wasn't so sure.

I bought myself a desk-blotter calendar, and at the top I wrote, 'A man sits as many risks as he runs.' Henry David Thoreau wrote that. Also, 'To ask permission is to seek denial.' Sun Microsystems chairman Scott McNealy said that.

When I set up my files, I found a manila folder left by the last sales consultant who'd occupied my cubicle.

The man's name was Frank, and he'd taken his notes on lined yellow paper. He'd recorded the specs of the cars and also the mechanics of the close. It was all upbeat and impersonal, except for one page where he'd written in longhand, 'If you can't manipulate, dictate. Question: How do we know when we are being managed, and how do we know when we are being manipulated?'

The sensation seemed not unlike that of uncovering Robert Falcon Scott's papers with his frozen body near the South Pole: 'Had we lived, I should have had a tale to tell of the hardihood, endurance, and courage of my companions which would have stirred the heart of every Englishman. These rough notes and our dead bodies must tell the tale. . . .'

I asked if anyone knew where Frank had gone. Nobody did.

The man I'd met my first day, the man who told me about how you could have an oil change at ten P.M., he was gone. He wasn't named Frank, though.

Our general sales manager at GM was the redhead I'd seen hugging Joe P. the first time I came to the car store. I'll call him Jeffrey Stern. Once in a while, he'd come into my cubicle for clementines and to ask the Magic 8 Ball, 'Will I hit the lottery?'

Jeffrey tried to make up for the lack of business by having us work the phones. The Wegman computer coughed up the names and numbers of people who had had cars serviced in any one of our thirty-two bays. We were given printouts.

'Hello, this is Ben Cheever calling from Wegman Cadillac. I wanted to tell you about the terrific deal we have on the Cadillac Catera. It's a thirty-six-thousand-dollar car, and you can have it for $999 down and $399 a month. Would you like to come in for a test-drive today, or can I pencil you in for later in the week?'

Mostly I got answering machines, or prospects who said, 'No, thank you,' or prospects who said, 'Would you *please* leave me alone?'

If the person had had a Buick serviced, I would say, 'This is Ben Cheever calling from Wegman Buick, and I wanted to invite you in to see the new Buick Century.' To one customer who was shown on the printout to have had a Riviera serviced, I said, 'Why don't you come in and see the new Riviera?' There was a bewildered pause, and then the householder said, 'You know, I actually own a Riviera. What a coincidence.'

Cold calling isn't any fun, but I worked at it, sometimes making more than twenty calls in a day. Trying always to sound cheerful, confident, the bearer of good tidings. I noticed that the older salesmen simply refused this indignity. Given their lists, they'd grumble, retire to their cubicles, and glower out at the room. All the time, they were keeping their eyes on the door.

In clement weather, the veterans wouldn't even wait for a customer to come inside. Danny Johnson was often out front, smoking and scanning the lot. A big man, he was a retired building inspector for the city of New York, and the joke was that he'd been trained not to see. He favored a white cardigan sweater with large pockets on the sides. 'For inserting bribes,' he used to say. He didn't pace around the showroom so much as tack, like a sailboat, covering the area in diagonals.

He said he was going to take me under his wing. 'I'm gonna take

Benny here under my wing,' he said. This mostly involved calling out to me whenever I came into sight, 'Hey, Benny,' he'd say, 'what's happening?'

'Don't know,' I'd say. 'I just got here.'

Apparently he'd also been trained not to hear. 'Benny,' he'd say again, 'what's happening?'

The pay plan rewarded high performance by increasing the percentage of profit the salesperson was entitled to, so Danny suggested I give all my sales to him. We could split the total and both earn more. He said he would do this for my own good.

I told him this reminded me of how during the war in Vietnam, people said that we were killing the Vietnamese for *their* own good.

He thought this was rich. 'Killing the Vietnamese for their own good,' he'd say, and chuckle.

Danny didn't go with any of this 'Welcome to Wegman Auto'. He'd just arrive right off the prospect's shoulder, like a second airplane flying in a tight formation. Danny was a heavy smoker, and you could hear him breathe, so they knew right away that he was there.

He rarely gave Mr. Customer an excuse to tell him to get lost, because Danny almost never asked a question. He started right in the middle of the conversation. 'Red's a popular color,' he might say, 'easy to keep clean.' Or else, 'We've got a great lease program on this one'. Or 'It's a much roomier car inside than it appears to be'. If they didn't say anything, he wouldn't say anything, either, but all the time they could hear him back there breathing noisily.

He was famous for once having left a couple at his desk right at the close. They had agreed on a car, but were refusing to meet his price. Danny stood up and walked out of the show-room. Nobody knew where he had gone. The customers were baffled and hurt. They got up and looked for him. They asked around.

After an hour, Danny reappeared. Immediately they accepted his deal.

'Where did you go?' I asked him.
'To lunch,' he told me.

Bentley Rusk didn't wear a crown, but we all knew he was the king of the salesmen. He'd run his own dealership for twenty years. He had a beard, and a son, who worked in 'F and I' (Finance and Insurance), whose name was Bentley Rusk Jr. Bentley had a cubicle way over near the wall farthest away from Nissan. He read the New York *Daily News* and sometimes the *New York Post*. None of the rest of us were allowed to read anything but the brochures. Reading was thought to be insulting to potential customers.

He came up to me my first day. 'Chivas Regal,' he said. 'We're going to call you Chivas Regal. Or else Achieva. Benny Achieva.' (Oldsmobile had had a car called the Achieva, although it had been discontinued. I believe we had two left on the lot.)

When I'd been downstairs for a couple of days and I was driving him up to Prep (a second lot with a warehouse for preparing the cars for delivery), he asked, 'What did you learn up there?'

'Customers for life,' I said, 'bypasses the Mother of All Closes.'

'You spent two weeks,' he said disdainfully. 'I could have taught you everything you needed to know in one afternoon. It's simple. Be cheerful. Be thankful.' And then he said something that I still consider profound: 'Always ask a customer to give you a hand. I don't care if your shoes hurt or your wife beats you, when a customer comes in the door, you're pleased to see him.' Then he echoed one of Joe's best lines: 'We sell life.'

Once when I was making cold calls, he took my list just to show me how it was done.

'Hello, this Bentley Rusk. I'm up here at Wegman Cadillac. I wondered if you could do me a favor. Could you just come in some day this week and take a look at one of these new Cadillac Cateras?' He got a much higher rate of response than I did. His spiel was better, but it was mostly in his tone of voice.

Bentley and Danny and a man named Mark Y got most of the 'ups'. Mark Y had been fired by IBM. 'I moved way up north to be near my job,' he told us one morning, 'then they fired me.' We laughed. He laughed, too.

Prospects were called ups, because of the 'up sheet'. This is a legal-sized form with three carbons. There was space at the top for your name and Mr. or Ms. Customer's name and the car or cars under consideration. The body of the form was for evaluating the horse they rode in on.

At the opening of the sale, we were supposed to ask the prospects what they like about the car they have and what they don't like. This helped determine what to show them. It also protected against the dreaded TRADE-IN AMBUSH.

I rarely got my own up, and when I did, I never got very far down on the sheet. The first priority was just to keep them around, keep them in the store. Flypaper, that's what we were. Human flypaper.

Our first goal in the showroom was to lure the customer back into the cubicle. Here you tried to get names and phone numbers. Then the test-drive was crucial. According to Joe, one of the great failings of many sales consultants was in not offering a test-drive. Customers are shy about asking, because they fear it indicates a commitment, but 99 per cent of them want to drive a car before they buy it.

Of course the sales consultant was all for commitment. The drive might whet the buyer's appetite. At the very least, it kept the customers on the lot and occupied. Before we were allowed to let a customer drive a car, we had to make a Xerox of his or her driver's license. Even if they gave a mock address or a nonworking phone number, you had something to go on.

Once you had an up, the customer was yours. Nobody else was supposed to sell that person a car. You kept one copy of the sheet, and the others were distributed, with one going to the manager's desk where the crucial data was typed into a computer. Every morning I was given a printout of all my ups, and every day I was expected to make follow-up calls.

Jeffrey Stern, the general sales manager (GSM), was very hot on follow-up phone calls. He and Joe P. had come over from Toyota. Word was that Joe P. had promised Al Wegman that he could make the same sort of success out of GM and Nissan as he had out of Toyota.

Stern insisted that we call every active customer every day. 'He's in Florida,' I explained once. 'He's going to come back, and his answering machine is going to be chock-full of messages from me. If his mother phones, she won't be able to leave a message.'

'I don't care. Call him.'

'I'm just going to annoy him.'

'When he tells you never to call him again, when he tells you to get lost, then you've done your job.'

I had a couple of friends come in, and I'd fill out up sheets for them. This meant I had to call my friends every day and stay on the phone for as long as possible.

I don't think the older salesmen called their ups at all. The GSM knew who he could push around (me and Victor) and who he couldn't push around (most everybody else).

Under the veterans there was a layer of salesmen who were relatively new, but not absolutely green. Rick Kaiser had the cubicle next to mine. Rick was a retired New York City cop. He'd been on the floor for a couple of months.

Rick often wore his Glock to work. I could see the bump under his suit jacket when he leaned forward. To report this gives exactly the wrong impression. Rick was a most gentle, almost womanly man. He had the best equipment: a bookshelf, plants, a bowl of candy, and sometimes a jar of pretzels. He had a label maker and Scotch-Tape dispenser, both of which he loaned out to the rest of us.

On my other side was a woman, the only woman on the GM floor. She must have had a strong stomach because the atmosphere was high-male.

I believe I was the only man on the floor who couldn't belch and fart at will. Foul language was a commonplace, as were foul jokes.

'What did Raggedy Ann say when she sat on Pinocchio's nose?'

'I don't know.'

'Lie to me! Lie to me!'

Claudia Le Blanc had been pushed out of a middle-management job at a large corporation after a buyback and worked six days a week, trying to keep up the payments on her house.

She drove a cranky old car that had lights pointing out at grotesque angles. One of her grievances was that salespeople didn't get demos. The GSMs got cars, as did all higher-level management.

Claudia was attractive but not a stunner, and while her age and single status might not have been remarked upon in Toyota or even Nissan, the general feeling on the GM floor was that she was too ripe to be unmarried.

When she had a customer, she talked quickly and incessantly. Sometimes she talked that way when she was alone. From across the showroom, it looked as if she were having a violent argument with herself.

'When you're having one of those disagreements with yourself,' Danny asked her, 'do you win?'

'No,' Claudia told him, and smiled, 'I always lose.'

Out in the middle of the floor was a cubicle occupied by a former armored-car driver who had back trouble. He'd come in at the same time Rick had, and they were buddies.

'You have a pistol license?' I asked. 'You couldn't get a better job than this?' He thought not. He said driving the armored car hadn't been terribly dangerous, but it had been hard on the back. 'If anybody ever signals that you've got a flat tire,' he said, 'don't believe them.'

Under the GSM there were two assistant managers, each of whom handled four salespeople. The more popular of the two assistant managers was a large, relaxed guy named John W. 'There you go,' he would say, as if any outcome were somehow satisfactory. Everybody wanted to be on his team. I wasn't on his team. My assistant manager looked exactly like a Mafia don's second bodyguard. Not the good-looking one. Gary wore little black lace-up shoes and billowing double-breasted jackets. His thinning black hair was combed straight up and back. His face was that of Nathan Lane in *Guys and Dolls,* only the spots didn't have to be painted on.

When Gary got a prospect on the phone, he'd throw his whole body into the conversation, lean into it: 'Yous are going to get a good value here.'

Thoreau says a man's face is his masterpiece, and Gary had the countenance of a man who had just murdered a chorus girl, chopped her up, and put the pieces into the trunk of a car. But he was a sweet man, although a little defeated. One night we suggested he ask the Magic 8 Ball if his wife was going to let him fuck her when he got home. 'Don't bother,' he said. 'Don't waste it.'

Once Gary went for a weeklong family vacation to Florida. When he came back, he told me he'd rented a convertible. The only convertibles we had on the lot were Pontiac Sunfires. I asked him if he'd rented a Sunfire – the economy car with all the high-end options built right in – and he got a look of inexpressible sorrow on his face. 'I just couldn't spend a week in one of those things,' he told me.

Gary was in his late twenties when I worked for him. I never met his wife, but a son came into the showroom once. He was taller than Gary. Taller than I am. When Janet asked why I was anxious to please and even fearful of somebody so young, I said, 'He's my manager. Besides which, he seems older than I am. He's one of those people whose children seem older than I am.'

Looking back now, it's difficult to explain what was so wonderful about being out there on the floor at Wegman. This career seemed somehow more genuine than anything else in my life. Saki wrote that 'the stage, with all its efforts, can never be as artificial as life.'

Despite Claudia, our one female sales consultant, the setting was unequivocally masculine. In today's world I'd pass easily as a male chauvinist, but not even I will deny that a room with ten men in it will have a collective I.Q. well below room temperature. Two men may be smarter than one, but twelve men working together can be outwitted by a clever bar of soap.

Franklin Quest had been a largely female environment. The attention to detail was punishing. I was often made to feel stupid. At Wegman Auto I felt like a Rhodes Scholar.

I remember one morning when four of us had a ten-minute debate as to whether it was snowing. What had Jeffrey heard on the radio the night before? What had Rick heard on the radio this morning? Bentley recalled that it had snowed on this day last year. The showroom was encased in glass, but nobody thought to look outside. Nor did anybody mention that Victor still had his coat on and the shoulders were dusted with flakes of snow.

We were always losing keys, license plates, scratching the new cars. Just before I arrived, one of the staff had been run over. He was all right. He didn't even have a limp, but he had been run over.

We were trained liars, of course. But this was completely out in the open. I'd worked a decade at the *Reader's Digest,* and you had to lie there, too, but it was more painful, because you couldn't admit that you were lying, not even to yourself. The difference between deception at global headquarters in Pleasantville and deception at Wegman reminds me of what Mr. Dryden says to Lawrence of Arabia in the David Lean movie: 'If we've told lies, you've told half lies, and a man who tells lies – like me – merely hides the truth, but a man who tells half lies has forgotten where he put it.'

There were often explosions of laughter. Somehow, for reasons that escaped the naked eye, it had been decided that Rick Kaiser's nose was far too long. 'You ought to hire that thing out as a vacuum cleaner, Rick.' Har, har, har. 'You should incorporate that nose, call it The Nose Knows, and take a deduction.' Har, har, har. 'When you drive, where do you put it? On the dashboard? Between your legs?' Har, har, har. After a round of Rick's Nose jokes, I once picked up my Magic 8 Ball and said, 'Oh, Eight Ball, tell me, is Rick Kaiser's dick half as long as his nose is?' At this point,

Rick, himself, leaned over the partition. 'What does it say?' he asked. Then I pulled back. 'Jesus, Rick,' I said, playing to the audience, 'you need to ask the Magic Eight Ball how long your dick is?' This got a big har, har, har. I was the Oscar Wilde of the GM showroom.

There was a lot of good-natured badinage. 'You don't think the dead can come back to life,' Rick used to like to say, 'you should see Ben Cheever at quitting time.'

We weren't supposed to eat on the floor, and I remember coming in from the lot one day and seeing both Rick and Victor eating. Each of them had a sandwich, and they were being furtive about it.

'Looks like feeding time in the monkey house,' I said.

'Yeah,' said Victor, 'only one of the monkeys got out.'

Over in Nissan, Robert was selling cars almost every day, and once in a great while one of our veterans would move a Buick, but business was so slow that I wasn't emotionally engaged in the competition.

Then one afternoon I noticed that Victor's posture had altered. He was walking around on the balls of his feet, the tails of his suit jacket fluttering behind him. Then he came into my cubicle, dropped into a chair.

'Did you sell a car?' he asked.

'No,' I said, and I could feel my spirits plummeting, 'did *you*?'

He had.

I was furious. I was in despair. I called my friend Rafe Yglesias. He and I have a running argument. My father maintained that writing was not a competitive sport, and I've always taken this position. 'Good prose moves the ball down the field for all of us,' I like to say. Rafe isn't as truculent as Hemingway. 'I started out very quiet and I beat Mr. Turgenev,' Hemingway told Lillian Ross in a *New Yorker* profile. 'Then I trained hard and I beat Mr. de Maupassant. I've fought two draws with Mr. Stendhal, and I think I had an edge in the last one. But nobody's going to get me in any ring with Mr. Tolstoy unless I'm crazy or keep getting better.'

Rafe's not that bellicose, but he does think writers are competitive.

When I heard Victor had sold a car, I called Rafe. 'I still don't know about writing, but automotive sales is definitely a competitive sport,' I told him. 'I can't believe this asshole sold a car before I did.'

Although I'd grown to like Victor, this was with a sizeable dollop of condescension. He told me repeatedly that he had cheated his way through high school, never went to college, rarely read the newspaper if it didn't have an article with his name in it.

Reading all these the brochures for the cars we were selling was good for him, he said. 'Because I never read anything. All this practice is going to make me a better reader.'

This was the man who'd beaten me in a fair contest. I was despondent. I suppose everybody knew it. Which may be why Rick gave me an up the following evening. It was after dark when the young couple came in, and I guess Danny must have been in the bathroom, or off duty, because they passed through the front door unclaimed.

'You take them,' Rick whispered to me. 'Pop the cherry.'

I couldn't believe my luck. He was handsome. She was pretty and very pregnant. They were both employed and driving a 1985 Oldsmobile Cutlass with 155,000 miles on it. Perhaps most important, they were already sold on a 1996 teal Pontiac Bonneville with a spoiler that was sitting right out on the showroom floor.

They'd come in a couple of months ago, but said they'd been frightened away by a salesman who was too aggressive. I loved them for that. We sat in my cubicle. I listened; they talked. She was due in a month. She'd been pregnant seven times since they'd gotten married and they'd lost all the babies, mostly to miscarriages; but I think one or two had been born and then died. This child had already been carried almost to term. Even if she miscarried now, they thought the baby would survive.

They seemed entirely ingenuous. No trade-in ambush. Nor did they have to be convinced of the superiority of American cars. The Cutlass still ran like a clock.

I looked the Bonneville up on the computer, and it was marked sold. I asked around. Mark, the fleet salesman, had moved the car. I left the Wonderfuls and found Mark. He said, 'I was told to get rid of the car. I'm just moving metal. If you can get a deal, then take a second deposit.'

He wouldn't tell me for sure that he could free the car up, but it sounded as if he could. Meanwhile, the Wonderfuls were putty in my hands. I wrote down their home phone number. I got his office number. He told me the good times to call.

'Of course you want a new car to bring the baby home from the hospital in,' I said.

The Wonderfuls both smiled at me and nodded. I wanted to give them the car. Why not? Mark was only moving metal.

When you first get customers into your cubicle, you sit behind the desk, and they sit in the visitor chairs. Then you go to your assistant sales manager with the specifics of the deal, and he works it up on the lease-and-loan computer. He writes down for you the terms of the lease or loan and what the monthly payments will be. The first couple of times this is done, you come back to the cubicle with two columns of figures. One is what it will cost them to carry the car as a lease; the other is what it will cost to finance the car. This gives the prospects two choices, either of which ends in a sale.

The difficulty here was that the car was a 1996. The Wonderfuls could finance it with a sixty-month-loan, paying $387 a month. Or they could lease a 1997 for $333 a month, although we didn't have the color Mrs. Wonderful wanted on the lot. The sticker price on the 1997 was almost $23,000, while the price on the 1996 was $19,999. Gary explained that we couldn't lease a 1996 because, if the lease runs for any period of time, the residual (the price for which you can buy the car at the end of your lease period) ends up being too low. The Wonderfuls thought $387 was a lot to pay. We had a problem.

A new salesman near a close will bring his assistant manager back to the cubicle. The assistant manager sits behind the desk, and the original salesman stands out with the customers, as if he's one of them, as if he's on their side. It's a basic flanking move, and it can work. It is the first salesman's emotional connection with the customers that drives the close.

The trouble here was Gary's face. Remember, he looked like he'd just murdered a chorus girl. Gary came and sat in my chair. I sat with the Wonderfuls. When Gary went back to the lease-and-loan computer, Mr. Wonderful took my arm in both hands. 'Can we trust this man?' he asked.

'Absolutely' is what I should have said. 'Gary was best man at my wedding. He baby-sits my little girl. She loves old Uncle Gary.' Never mind that I don't have a daughter; that's what I should have said.

But I was green and cherishing the implication that I had a superior character. So I said, 'If you want that car, just push. I'll be here, but hold on like a bulldog. Push. Push for the car you want. Then push for the price you want.'

Gary called me over to his desk. 'What about their credit?' he asked. I was mortified. 'I don't know, but I imagine it's great,' I said. 'Two young people. No children. Both employed.'

'Let's do a five-liner,' said Gary.

'Isn't that insulting?' I said. 'An invasion of privacy?'

'Just ask them,' said Gary. So I brought the Wonderfuls a form for the five-liner, so named because the prospective customer fills out five lines. They filled it out. I gave the form to Gary, who gave it to Finance and Insurance (F and I).

The Wonderfuls and I talked some more about what a splendid car the Bonneville is. I showed them the Magic 8 Ball. We asked if they would buy a car tonight. 'Signs Point to Yes.' We didn't dare ask about the baby. Mr. Wonderful ate a clementine.

Then Gary called me back to the main desk. 'Credit's no good,' he told me, 'bankrupt.'

So I went back to the Wonderfuls, and, yes, it turned out they had had some trouble with their bills, but this was all behind them. Unfortunately, this did mean we couldn't get them money cheap. Everything had to be run through the computer again.

Finally, we agreed in principle on the price, and they actually signed a buy order, my first. They gave us a two-hundred-dollar check. When a deal is closing, the buyers move on without the salesman into one of the F and I offices, which ran along the wall between GM and Nissan. In F and I, the customers pick options, the paperwork is completed, insurance is set up, and the actual deal is made with the bank.

At this point I was thankful to the men and women in F and I, because they did the paperwork, and I don't like paperwork. This left me free to be a sales artist. Later on, I'd learn not to be so thankful.

While the Wonderfuls were cloistered with the F and I man, I heard the GSM tell Gary that it was a 'twelve-buck deal'. My heart dropped. This meant I'd get 20 per cent of twelve dollars, or $2.40. On the other hand, they were the Wonderfuls, and she was big with child.

Still, there was something that sounded wrong about this. So I asked Rick what a twelve-buck deal meant. 'One thousand two hundred dollars,' he told me. Then I felt torn again. Wasn't this a little high?

Walking out to my car that night, I told the ex-armored-car driver how shocked I was to learn that these people had bad credit. 'It would have saved a lot of time, if they had told me about the bankruptcy at the beginning,' I said to him.

He chuckled. 'Buyers are liars,' he said.

The deal never went through. We couldn't get them the financing they wanted. Weeks later I heard that they had bought a Pontiac somewhere else. How? I haven't a clue. I also heard that they had a healthy child.

So I was failing. And yet I was still enjoying myself immensely. Friends remember how changed I was by the job. I seemed a couple of inches taller, my voice was deeper, richer, more confident. I often touched people when we were talking. Called strangers 'buddy'.

We shouldn't look down on this too confidently, though. Car salesmen are obnoxious, but change the style, and they're a lot like the people we know. The basic rules are the same on the Upper East Side as they are on a car lot. I've met women at dinner parties who are far more intoxicating than I ever was as a Pontiac salesman. She reads her name card, the face goes pale beneath the tan. Just a nanosecond of regret; she won't be seated next to Michael Bloomberg after all. She's got me, and we're both below the salt. One deep breath and then she turns to me with the full, the dazzling smile. 'Benjamin Cheever! What luck! I get to sit next to Benjamin Cheever all evening.' She's making lemonade out of lemons. Car salesmen do the same.

Shortly after the sale that snagged on bad credit, a man of about my age came in to look at a new Bonneville. I was out at the door when he appeared. As I've mentioned, I didn't smoke, but I had learned to like standing out there, get my bait in the water. 'Welcome to Wegman Auto,' I said, smiling broadly.

He wanted to know what a Pontiac Bonneville cost. 'J.D. Power ranked the Bonneville the most appealing premium midsized car,' I said. 'It's a popular vehicle.' This was safe: Everybody wanted a popular vehicle. We had a Bonneville on the floor. I said he could look at the sticker, but that wasn't going to give him an accurate impression. 'Every car has a different price. First we've got to figure out exactly what you want.'

I led him back to my cubicle and got his statistics. I was very excited, but I don't think he knew it. One of the essential skills is to hide your enthusiasm. Act concerned. Act caring. Don't act as if it's payday.

We went for a test-drive. 'The Pontiac's a driver's car,' I said. I mentioned the daytime-running lights: 'You know in some Scandinavian countries the lights go on when you switch on the engine. The Bonneville has daytime-running lights. Statistics show that this significantly reduces accidents.'

Mirror the customer, Joe P. had told us. This is natural behavior. Somebody yawns, you yawn. Somebody scratches his ear, . . . But if you can scale it up, you can help move a customer towards the close of the sale. So if he's a liberal, then you're a liberal, too. 'Yes, I was part of the antiwar movement during the late sixties. Everybody in my generation was. You know, I heard recently that Nixon might have used tactical nuclear weapons on North Vietnam, if he hadn't been so afraid of what we were doing in the streets?'

If he was a military man, on the other hand, I might take a different tack. 'I've never been under fire. The people who have been under fire are all heroes. Or that's how I see it.'

Now it happens that I wouldn't be lying in either case. I was part of the antiwar movement. I am awed by people who have been under fire. But if each customer had had to extrapolate the rest of my character from what I'd offered, they would have constructed two entirely different people.

The Bonneville prospect told me that he worked as a salesman himself. I told him I liked being a salesman. I told him I thought salesmen had got a bad rap.

'Listen,' Joe had told us. I left long pauses in my speech, hoping the prospect would fill them. He was reticent, but not shy. There were long stretches of silence while he drove the car. I didn't fill the quiet with sound. He told me about the business he was in and that they were always looking for young, personable employees. He gave me a meaningful look.

I said I'd be interested. 'But let's do this first.'

Back in the showroom, we built his ideal car on software installed in the office computer. He wanted a bench seat and also traction control. I'd select *bench seat*. Then I'd select *traction control*, and *bench seat* would be deleted. After three tries, I asked around and found that this was because Pontiac didn't have a Bonneville with a bench seat in front that also had traction control.

Mr. Customer couldn't believe it. 'What do those two things have to do with one another?'

I didn't know. My man was disappointed, but this wasn't a deal breaker. I called Gary over to join us. The prospect surrendered his credit card, which I ran around to the business office. He signed his buy order. Gary always got magnanimous when a deal was closed. He'd make a speech – the mudguard, floor-mat speech – all about an option he was including gratis. 'So yous can really enjoy the vehicle.' He added a pinstripe this time. A pinstripe cost fifty dollars.

The car we sold wasn't on the lot, but there was a dealer in Vermont who would make a swap. It looked like a lock. I felt really good again for the first time since Victor popped the cherry.

I phoned my mother from the showroom. 'I believe I did it,' I said. 'I sold a car. A Bonneville.'

'A monocle?' she asked.

Not that I relaxed. I called my man every day. He went to Chicago. I called him in Chicago. We got to know each other quite well. When the car came down from Vermont, I was dismayed to learn that the hired driver had been drinking and spilling coffee with milk in it and had been eating cheddar-cheese popcorn.

Before delivery (which is what we called the handover) cars were sent to a warehouse up the road where they were cleaned and tuned and options were installed. I drove the hunter-green Bonneville with the bench seat but no traction control up to Prep.

When the car came back the first time, the popcorn had been vacuumed, but I found to my horror that when I moved the seat I heard the seat-moving engine through the stereo speakers. I brought the car back up to Prep, and they fixed this.

When the man finally came in and picked up his car, I was all over him. I meant to stretch the close out, make him a customer for life. Get his friends and neighbors to come in. I noticed he was a little cool. I was terrified he was going to back out of the deal, or make a scene. He took the car, though. Before he drove off, I gave him a card with my home phone number written on the back.

One of our obligations was to call our deliveries several times after they'd taken the car, make certain that they were happy, and tell them that if they sent us another prospect, they'd get a free oil change.

After my man took his Bonneville, I could never get him on the phone. He'd always been hard to reach, but now he was impossible to reach.

I can't know this, but I think now that he was afraid I was going to annoy him about a job for a personable young man. I sold eight cars. Three of the people I sold cars to intimated that after the deal was consummated, they'd be offering me a job. Not one of them did.

Buyers are liars.

One pleasant couple who had been talking about hiring me for their antiques business had to come in again when the 'check engine' light went on, and stayed on, in the Oldsmobile 88 I had sold them. I went into the service bay and discussed the problem with the mechanics. They thought a part might need replacement, but they thought it might also be a fluke. The mechanics got the light to go off; my customers drove the car home, and the light went on again. When they brought the car in the second time, they were both visibly annoyed with me. I saw them waiting in the lounge and went and sat with them. Customers for life, right? But they were having none of it. 'You made your money,' she said, practically trembling with indignation.

And yes, we'd planned for a gross profit of $1,151. There was a thousand-dollar cut in price being offered by Oldsmobile, which we disguised from the buyers and to which $151 had been added. Trouble here was that when they went into F and I, they took the GMAC 3 per cent financing. You can't get the special financing and also the one thousand dollars, so our gross profit had fallen to $151, of which I was going to earn 20 per cent, or a shade more than thirty dollars. 'You got a good price on that car,' I told her. She didn't believe me.

I was selling cars. Not nearly as many cars as Robert Garcia was selling in Nissan, and nothing like the numbers they pushed across the street in Toyota.

I was reminded of this one rainy morning when I ran into a couple of Toyota salesmen in the lunchroom. This room, which also had the fax, was slightly set back between Nissan and GM. There were a couple of tables, some chairs, a microwave, and a refrigerator. We were supposed to eat in the lunchroom so that the smell of our food wouldn't put the customers off their cars. The showroom secretary had put up a sign that read, 'Your mother does not live here! Therefore, clean your own mess!'

We had to go through the lunchroom to get to the pegboard that had the car keys on it. In the same closet that held the pegboard, there were balloons and also a tank of helium gas. When we made a delivery to a family, we were supposed to give the children balloons. The two Toyota men were out in the middle of the lunchroom with ten or fifteen helium balloons between them. They were attaching ribbons to the balloons. 'Somebody having a birthday party?' I asked.

'Nope,' said one of the Toyota men with a touch of condescension in his voice. 'We're making them customers for life,' said the other one.

'I wish you'd make them customers for GM,' I said.

Then the first one spoke again. 'How the fuck do you guys make a living?' he said.

'We don't,' I said.

'Why do you work here then?' he asked.

'Well, when I was in training, I thought I might go to Toyota.'

When I started on this book, I had expected to run into a lot of former CEOs and Harvard graduates recovering from having been fired. Mostly, this wasn't the case. There was, however, one spectacularly preppie young man in Nissan. One day I found that we were alone in the lunchroom. 'Are you Ivy League?' I asked him.

'Why do you ask that?'

'I don't know. You just look Ivy.'

'I graduated Tufts,' he said. 'Does that count?'

He'd had a degree in economics, which he'd never used, going to work instead with a photographer. Then he'd lost that job. The Tufts graduate seemed pleasant to me, although the general rap was that he was a snob, and not aggressive enough.

I probably wasn't aggressive enough, either, but I sure liked trying. This was the first job I'd had in which I was allowed to act up. If somebody pissed you off, it wasn't just all right to hit back: You were actually expected to hit back. For instance, when I ordered my business cards (we had to pay for our own), I didn't have exact change and the printer's representative was annoyed. 'This guy's not too smart, is he?' he told Rick, and he said it completely without humor.

'He's new,' Rick said, unwilling to pile on.

Now in my other life, an insult of this sort has to be smiled through, but not at Wegman Auto. I reached over, put a firm hand on the man's shoulder, and said, 'That's right, I didn't give you the exact change. You got a problem with that, asshole?' Which made me feel much better. It was good for my heart. I bet it was also good for my digestion.

A particularly difficult customer came in once to look at one of the Pontiac Grand Prix. He'd work me for a while, then go next door and work a salesman over there about the Nissan Maxima, which was a comparable car, although more expensive.

This went on for a couple of evenings, then he didn't come in. So I made a follow-up call. 'Cheever,' he crowed, 'you lost. I bought the Maxima. You weren't aggressive enough!' He actually said that, and he was enjoying himself.

So I went next door to Nissan, found the guy who'd sold him the Maxima. 'He's an asshole,' I said. 'I hope you didn't give him a good deal.'

'Don't worry,' my colleague said. 'You know what he's paying?'

'What's he paying?'

'Eleven per cent.'

This was about twice what he should have had to pay.

'Eleven per cent,' I said, and smiled.

'Yup. Eleven per cent over thirty-six months. He's probably never going to own that car. He's an asshole.'

It was frontier justice, and I liked it. Car salespeople had a freedom of movement unprecedented in my professional life. With prospects, of course, we were nice as pie. Which wasn't always a successful tactic.

One sunny afternoon shortly after I sold the 'monocle', a White Plains fireman came in. He was a handsome, sturdy, straightforward type. Lots of muscle. Lots of bristle, too. I led him back into my cubicle. He didn't want a clementine. He thought the Magic 8 Ball was a toy. When I asked for his name and number, he refused to give it.

'I need to take that information down,' I said. 'It's my job.'

He said that was all right, if I promised never to call him.

So I promised never to call him.

Then he gave me his number.

He told me he wasn't going to buy a car. All he wanted to know was if we had GMAC financing at 3 per cent.

I said, yes, we did, but not on every car. Everything depended on which car he was buying. What sort of car was he interested in? We needed to find out the exact right car for him, I said. But he wasn't interested in a car at all.

He might want to buy a car for his wife, he said. So we went through the showroom. He didn't like anything in the showroom. Then we went through the lot. He didn't like anything on the lot, either.

He was leading me. This is bad on the dance floor, and also bad in car sales. I kept trying to take control by showing him some great new gadget – the fold-back rearview mirrors, for instance. But he thought the fold-back mirrors were silly. He also intimated that car manufacturers were foolish, corrupt people. I kept making little objections, which he'd brush aside. It was like fighting a man with a much lower center of gravity.

In an attempt to hold his interest, I started babbling about myself.

You never do that. You listen. Biographical information is doled out sparingly and only when it leads to the sale.

I told him I'd been a newspaper reporter, a magazine editor. I told him I'd written a couple of novels. He listened, but without any particular interest.

If I couldn't get him to like a car, maybe I could find one so cheap, he couldn't resist. I brought him out to the other lot at the Prep warehouse to show him the 1996s. He said he might possibly be interested in a Cutlass. I found the key on the pegboard for a 1996 Cutlass. We had to walk through the snow to get to the car. I'd been talking about a test-drive, but the Cutlass was back behind several other cars. By the time we got there, he'd lost interest.

I'd had to climb over a snowdrift to get to the car, and my cowboy boots weren't designed for snow. 'We've come this far,' I said, 'might as well sit in it.' I opened the car door. The radio had been pulled.

Sometimes up at Prep, an unsold car will be cannibalized.

He stepped around behind me and saw the dashboard with wires dangling out of it. 'Now that doesn't look very appetizing, does it?' he said.

I nodded, trying with both hands to hold on to my smile.

'What makes me think it's easier to write novels than to sell cars?' he said. 'It's not,' I said. I drove him back to the GM showroom. We spent another half hour talking. Finally he left.

I copied his phone number and name into my Franklin Planner, took his up sheet home that night, and put it in the trash. If I'd handed it in, then the GSM would have yelled at me for not calling the fireman. Then the fireman would have yelled at me for calling the fireman. This way I could call him once. If I felt lucky.

All the sales associates came back to the classroom for the special meeting before the big Presidents' Day weekend. We even got the people from Toyota. The Toyota salesmen were a breed apart, the RAF of Wegman Auto. Ordinarily we didn't see them. All five of the Toyota salespeople who appeared at the general meeting were wearing leather coats or leather jackets. They sat together.

According to the display ad in the *Pennysaver,* the big draw for the weekend was that 'Every Customer Receives a Fabulous 7-Day/6-Night FREE VACATION in Sunny Orlando, Florida'.

The manager and assistant manager had stacks of little, brightly colored documents that we were supposed to dispense. At first, there was considerable debate as to the definition of the word *customer.* The sales consultants felt that a customer was anybody who walked in the door. The managers seemed to think a customer was somebody who bought a car.

The heat went out of the debate when somebody read the small type at the bottom of the page, which said, 'All free trips do not include meals or transportation or other incidental charges.'

In other words, we were giving away sample time-shares. A time-share is the right to spend a week or two weeks a year in a vacation spot. It's like buying an apartment, but you're buying the right to stay in it for two weeks out of the year. It's not at all unusual to give the first time-share away, in order to draw prospects. Telemarketers had tried to give me time-shares in the past. And I didn't have to buy a car to get one. Nor did I want a time-share. Wegman Auto was giving away the right to buy your own airline tickets, fly to Florida, and stay on the beach there without food while being attacked by salespeople who felt you owed then.

The main draw that season on the GM floor was the Pontiac Grand Prix. We had one Grand Prix on the lot, and it was sold. In a pinch you could sell a car you didn't have. I'd seen that done. You sold the car, then ordered it. Or else you hoped that after they'd imagined the new car, accommodated themselves to the expense, you could switch vehicles. But this was a risky maneuver, and I hadn't supposed we would actually advertise a car we didn't have. Joe had a Grand Prix pictured in the display ad, bold as sin, with the price $17,997 listed, crossed out, and below that the words *make an offer.*

Joe explained that even if we'd actually had one, we wouldn't have wanted to sell a Grand Prix for $17,997. That's where the words *make an offer* came in. 'The customer is going to insist that we bargain, and we won't bargain. And he certainly won't pay $17,997, since we've already drawn a line through that price. So he can't buy the car at all,' Joe explained. 'He'll shoot himself in the foot.'

Opening day of the big weekend, we all came in early and met with Jeffrey Stern. Like Ahab hammering his gold piece to the mast, Stern waved a hundred-dollar bill in front of us and said it was going to the man who made the first sale. Then, as at a football game, we huddled, put our fists into the circle, and all roared. I can't remember now if it was Danny Johnson or Bentley Rusk, but somebody refused.

Despite the free time-share in Florida, despite the fictional Grand Prix, the weekend went badly at GM. Few people came in, and they weren't buying.

I had one customer who said he wanted something in leather, but then was horrified when he saw the sticker price on the Pontiac Sunfire, which was the most economical (read, cheap) new vehicle in our lot. Danny had a man who came in and said, 'Money is no object,' but then when it was time to put a couple hundred dollars down, he said he first had to check with his wife about the color. 'He'll never come back,' Danny told me. 'Neither of them will.'

'Money is no object' became a running joke.

'Benny,' Danny would say whenever he caught my eye, 'I want something in leather. You got anything in leather?'

'Money is no object,' I'd say back.

We were in the heart of winter now, and after the great Presidents' Day sale fizzled, the morale went pop. One morning I walked in from the Masters lot with Mark Y, the former IBMer. I said I didn't know how to bury money in a lease. He said he'd show me how. So I put away my coat, checked in, and then set up with him at a cubicle far from the managers' desks.

Mark asked how I was getting along with Jeffrey Stern. I said not well. He said that Jeff was in a foul humor because he had been

moved from Toyota. He said that Joe P. had promised Alvin
Wegman he would do for GM what he'd done for Toyota.

'And he didn't?'

'Toyota still sells one hundred and forty cars a month. GM sells
thirty.'

'Thirty cars a month?' I asked.

'That's right. Sometimes less.

'You should quit,' he said. The obvious question here was 'If I
should quit, then shouldn't you?' I didn't ask. He said he'd show
me on paper how bad it was.

We'd all been getting a draw (unearned advance on expected
commissions) of three hundred dollars a week, with the understanding that this would explode when we actually began to sell.

Mark Y led me through the pay plan. The bulk of the salesmen's
earnings come from gross profit. The gross profit is the difference
between the car's invoice and the price it sells for. Salesmen were
entitled to 20 per cent of gross profit until they hit the bogey,
which changed from month to month, but had been set at $5,300
the previous month. When a salesman hit the bogey, the profit
went up over 40 per cent; but since only one salesman had done so
last month, Mark and I agreed that we could put this consideration
aside for the moment. He got out a notebook and a ballpoint pen.
Car salesmen like to perform simple equations in order to make
their arguments. There's a magic in those numerals.

He said that actually most of us were earning less than three
hundred a week. He said we might end up owing the dealership
money. He wrote down the figures as he explained. Twenty per
cent of $6,000 was $1,200 a month, or about $300 a week. Since
the average markup was $1,000, a salesman needed to sell six cars in
order to chalk up $6,000 in gross profit.

'There are ten salesmen on the floor. Each one of them needs to
sell six cars a month in order to meet his draw. Or our absolute
minimum, if we were all going to meet draw, would be to sell sixty
cars a month. We are selling thirty cars a month. You do the math.'

He said that the dealership expected each salesman to meet his draw, and if he didn't, he had to pay back the money he owed. He told me that Claudia had already quit. He said she'd quit because of the pay plan. He said she'd gone to a lot in the Bronx. She'd get $250 a week there no matter what, plus 20 per cent of profits, plus a car. I still don't know if Mark was trying to give advice to a young man he liked or just trying to get me off the floor so that a higher percentage of the limited profits would be his. He said that Bentley Rusk hadn't been coming in because he had a draw of six hundred dollars a week, and business was so bad last month that he owed Wegman money – and Wegman was trying to collect.

First, Mark said, there were too many salesmen. Also, there was now a free-standing preowned department. In the old days the GM salesmen could also sell preowned cars. If you'd gotten a customer who turned out not to be able to afford a new car, you could have sold him a used car. The average profit on used cars was three thousand dollars. Now, if you got somebody who couldn't afford a new car, you had to pass that customer off to the preowned department.

I said I didn't believe Wegman was going try to collect back the money they'd paid me. But he said it was in the pay plan: I should look it up.

I went back to my cubicle and looked up my pay plan. The second paragraph read as follows:

Note: If sales consultants draw exceeds earned commissions for three consecutive months, a conference shall be scheduled with general and general sales managers. This condition may constitute just cause for termination of employment. If the aforementioned occurs, each sales consultant understands and accepts their obligation to satisfy its debts with the Wegman organization even if it survives employment.

Badly written, but easily understood.

I hadn't signed my pay plan, but I didn't consider this legality much of a protection. I woke up in the middle of the night thinking about it. It was fun selling cars, and I didn't expect to make a fortune, but I also didn't expect to have to write my employer a check.

The next day Danny Johnson took me aside. I suspected that he and Mark Y had been talking. Danny also said I should quit. I said I didn't want to quit. I said I liked the job. 'It's fun,' I said. 'Fun's all right,' Danny said, 'but you can't take fun to the bank.'

I asked Danny why he was still there, if I should quit. He said that he, too, might quit. He said the old pay plan was much better. I asked how the old pay plan had worked, and Danny got out his ballpoint pen and steno pad. He said that under the old pay plan a salesman was entitled to $150 a week no matter what. He wrote down '$150'. After that he was entitled to 20 per cent of profit, plus 5 per cent off the back end. He wrote down '20% × X' and then '5% of Y'.

I asked what the back end was, and he said this was the profit made in Finance and Insurance on options and warranties. He said that under the old pay plan he always made five hundred dollars a week. He wrote down '$500 a week'.

He said that having the percentage of profit rise when we hit our bogey made the new plan look good, but nobody hit the bogey.

He wrote down 'bogey' and then crossed it out. He turned his steno pad around and presented it to me in exactly the way we were supposed to present our computations to a prospect. The new pay plan was rotten, he told me. 'Benny, the job looks good on paper,' he said. 'World War Two looked good on paper to Hitler. And look how it come out.'

There was an air of gloom about the GM showroom. Stern kept trying to cheer us up with little training sessions. One morning he got out a buy order, and we all had to practice filling it out, then turning the document around and tossing the pen to the prospect. There was a magic in the way this maneuver was completed, he told us. Maybe so, but first you needed your ups. If there was nobody in the showroom, then it didn't matter how skillfully you could force a close.

If Willy Loman had had a bad sales district, then so did we.

The cliché has the drill sergeant pick out the toughest green recruit and beat him in a fair fight while the platoon watches in awe. But I was the least-threatening recruit at a number of jobs, and the drill sergeant often picked me out to be made an example of.

Stern was constantly on my case. 'Ben,' he'd call to me from across the room, 'you're not making phone calls.' Whenever I strayed out of my office to talk with a colleague, he'd catch me. His comments were a constant goad.

Then we had a murderously slow day. I don't believe we had one genuine up. We were all depressed. Especially Rick Kaiser. He didn't actually reach for his Glock, but Rick said, 'I feel like shooting somebody.'

Every time I got out of my cubicle, Jeffrey Stern would come darting over and say, 'Ben, you haven't made all your phone calls.'

This ticked me off on two counts: (1) I had made many phone calls; (2) I seemed to be one of the only sales consultants on the floor who made any phone calls at all.

I'd put my head down, though, retire to my desk, and phone a couple of people. Sometimes I cheated, of course. I'd begged a couple of friends to come in, filled out sheets on them so that I could phone them every day and get credit for it. Meanwhile, the cold calling wasn't working. Most people just wouldn't come into the showroom, and I had to beg so desperately for those who did that the chances of selling them a car were slim indeed. I already owed them when they stepped through the door.

Other salesmen came regularly into my cubicle for clementines. And to ask the Magic 8 Ball if they had a chance with Cindy Crawford.

Danny came in after he and Bentley had been out smoking.

'I'm sorry I don't smoke,' I said. 'It would give me something to do. A profession.'

Danny nodded. 'I have a nice big White Owl for you,' he said, and laughed. Rick laughed, and Victor laughed. So I knew I'd been insulted. So I said, 'I should warn you, Danny, that when I smoke a big cigar, I bite down hard.'

Everybody laughed again.

'Money is no object,' Danny said, and we all laughed.

Stern appeared. 'Ben,' he said, 'you're not making your phone calls.'

'Look at my sheet,' I said. 'I made my phone calls.'

So Jeffrey turned on his heel and walked out into the center of the showroom. He picked up a phone and pressed Page. 'All GM salesmen on me,' he said. 'All GM salesmen on me.'

When we got there, and most of us didn't have to go very far, he said, 'Since you people don't want to make phone calls, we're going to do a little work on product knowledge.'

He led us all over to the Cadillac Catera. 'Ben is going to do the walk around,' he said. 'Danny is going to be the customer.'

Everybody else formed a circle around the car.

'Welcome to Wegman Auto,' I said. 'My name is Ben Cheever, and yours?' My voice was choking with rage.

'Danny,' said Danny, 'Danny Johnson.'

'What brings you here today, Mr. Johnson?'

'I'm not going to buy a car,' Danny said. 'I'm only shopping.'

'Fine,' I said. 'Have you purchased a car from Wegman in the past, or is this your first visit?'

Danny said it was his first visit.

I found myself remembering what I wasn't supposed to say about the Catera – that the engine was built by Opel, that it was a small car for a Cadillac. I could feel Stern watching me.

'The car has a hundred and ninety horsepower,' I said.

'Two hundred,' Danny said.

'Two hundred horsepower,' I said.

Stern broke in. 'How many litres does the engine have?'

I said, 'Let me check,' and started to walk around to the window sticker.

'Buzz!' Stern said. 'Wrong! You're supposed to know the specifications on every car in this showroom.' Everybody was looking. Everybody was quiet. 'Everybody should know the specs on every car in the showroom.'

I turned around and walked up to Stern. He was furious, sticking out his chin at me. I was furious as well. 'Nobody knows all the fucking specifications on every car in this showroom,' I said.

'You *should*,' Stern said, and he gave me his trademark wolfish grin.

'All right, then,' I said, and I began to jab at the shoulder of his double-breasted jacket with my hand. 'Fire me! Fire me now for not knowing what nobody knows!'

I don't recall exactly what happened next. Stern seems to have led me into an office and closed the door. Then we were both shouting.

Me saying, 'Nobody makes their fucking calls but me, and you're always on my ass.'

Him saying, 'I don't want this to be a good showroom. I want this to be the best fucking showroom.'

Me saying, 'You think I don't want to sell cars? I want to sell cars more than I want anything else in the world.' Which was true at the moment.

There was some more yelling. Then I said something about having fun. Having fun, I said, was part of selling cars.

Stern didn't think so. He did think you needed passion to sell cars. 'You need fire in the belly,' he told me. 'I'm glad to see you have fire in the belly.' A phone rang for him. I waited. Then I went back out into the showroom. Silence.

I walked back to my cubicle. I sat there trembling. Five minutes later, Stern came out of the office and walked the floor. I was scheduled to go off duty at six P.M. He came over to my cubicle at 5:42 P.M. and asked, 'You off at six?'

I said I was.

'You can go now,' he said.

So I did. I went back into the lunchroom and put on my coat. When I passed Victor's cubicle, he wouldn't even look up. I walked out through the showroom. Everybody was at his desk.

Nobody was talking. Nobody was on the phone. When I passed Danny, he called out to me in a hoarse whisper. 'Money is no object,' he said.

I came to work the next day. Stern wouldn't speak with me. He didn't ask me to make my calls, either. I sat at my desk. I made my calls.

Two days later, we had our Saturday-morning meeting. Stern got us all in one cubicle and went from man to man, giving profit figures, some congratulations, and some criticisms. Victor had had bad luck, he said, but Victor would be OK. I assumed I wouldn't be OK. I assumed I would be fired. He'd use me to show the others who was boss. When he got to me, though, he wasn't angry anymore. He reached out and grabbed my shoulder with his hand. 'Benny, here, done phenomenal!' he said.

For the month of February, I had a higher gross profit than any of the other new salesmen. I wasn't anywhere near the bogey, but I had more than four thousand dollars in gross profit. It's shaming to admit, but this counts as one of the half-dozen happiest moments of my life. My heart was racing, my pulse roaring in my ears. I could feel tingling in the soles of my feet.

Talking with Rick Kaiser afterwards, I said I thought Victor was way ahead. After all, he'd sold the first car.

'Victor,' said Rick, 'he sells cars like old people fuck.'

Now it turned out that it wasn't just the cars I'd sold, or even the deals I'd arrived at that made my profits high that month. The buyer and I would agree on a price, but in more than one case, the lease-and-loan figures we presented him with were for a higher price. So for instance, I might agree to sell a car for twenty-eight thousand dollars and actually sell it for thirty thousand without the buyer ever suspecting the change, which was hidden from him, since all he saw were the monthly payments. This pushed up the profits without the buyer's knowing it. It also pushed up the profits without *my* knowing it. So if you're ever leasing or financing a car and the salesman gives a price for the car and also a monthly payment, do the math yourself.

These are not bad men, but they are liars. Professional liars. I had a pair in once who wanted to buy a Grand Prix we'd advertised. The car they were looking at had been sold, but Gary said we had another Grand Prix on the lot at a comparable value. The buyers took Gary at his word. So did I. It happened that they didn't buy. I went home that evening and did the math myself. I saw that we were charging two thousand dollars more than the advertised price. When I came back to work, I asked Gary about this. 'That's why I said comparable value,' he told me. 'I didn't say the same price. I said *comparable* value.'

But Bentley Rusk was the champ. That man could lie on a dime. And with brio. Remember, I told you how Claudia wasn't exactly a beauty? How the GM customers who liked her seemed to think she should get married? So one day a couple of customers came in who had seen Claudia and liked her. They wanted to buy a car from Claudia. They came on to the showroom floor and asked for her.

But now Claudia was gone. She was at a different dealership. I remember thinking, *What to say? Can't lose them to a different dealership.*

Bentley was right there, shaking hands, beaming.

'Oh, Claudia,' he said, 'she's on a sort of sabbatical. Taking six months off. Gone out to Colorado. And you know what?' he asked them.

'What?' they asked.

'I believe she's going to get married,' he said, and winked. 'Now buy the car from me, and I'll see to it that Claudia gets whatever she's got coming.'

I'm sorry, but that man was a genius.

I was definitely not a genius, but I *had* learned the patter, had learned never to laugh at a customer or even smile in disbelief. So when an elderly gentleman appeared and said he wanted to look at a car – any car – with a compass in it, I didn't see anything funny about it. He'd heard that there was an Oldsmobile minivan with a compass in it. That was the Silhouette. I didn't say, 'I once bought a compass for my car, and it didn't work.' I didn't say, 'If you're interested in minivans, I like the Pontiac Montana better.' Our only Silhouette was up at Prep, so we drove there together. Unfortunately, this van had a sunroof, which changed the configuration of the interior, leaving no room for a compass. My new customer, Jefferson Trowbridge, looked like a dry well.

Soft-spoken, neatly dressed and groomed, Trowbridge was easy to like. He told me he had just bought a new Cadillac Catera in January. Now it was March, so the prospects weren't good, but I stayed hopeful. 'There's a switch in there,' Joe P. had told us. 'You need to be able to find that switch and turn it on.'

I asked Trowbridge how he liked the Catera. 'It's not really a Cadillac,' he said.

'Sure it's a Cadillac,' I said. 'I'd be fired if I admitted that it wasn't a Cadillac.' He told me he was eighty-eight years old. I told him that the Catera is made by Opel in Germany and has the same engine as the Saab 900. He didn't seem to care about litres.

Back at the showroom, we settled into my cubicle. He didn't want a clementine. He had no questions for the Magic 8 Ball. I got the precise spelling of his name, and his phone number. Then I asked if (a) he would like me to order him an Oldsmobile Silhouette with a compass or if (b) he wanted to look at one of the Cadillac sedans we had on the lot – one of which almost certainly had a compass.

He chose b. If we had any Cadillacs with compasses, he'd look at one of those. So I got the keys to a burgundy Cadillac DeVille sedan, and we went and sat in it. There was a compass in the rearview mirror. The DeVille sedan was blocked in by another car, so I couldn't take him for a test-drive. He did like the vehicle.

He said he'd like to trade in the Cadillac Catera and get the Cadillac DeVille. How much would that cost?

I went over to Gary. This was way too good to be true. 'He's interested,' I said. Gary fiddled with his computer for a while and then came back and said the exchange would cost ninety-five hundred dollars.

Not my idea of good news for Mr. Trowbridge. If you're lost at sea, a compass is vital, but nine thousand, five hundred dollars seemed a lot to pay for such an instrument when you were just off the highway in Westchester County. Still, I remembered what Joe P. had told us: 'There are no natural-born salesmen. It's the triumph of training over instinct.' Walking back to the cubicle, I tried to stand up straight, something else that has never come naturally to me. 'We can make the trade immediately,' I said, and beamed. 'The car you like is free and clear. We can run the papers, switch the plates. Spot-deliver it. You can have the exact vehicle you want. You can drive home in it this afternoon. It'll only cost you ninety-five hundred dollars.'

Jefferson blanched, and he let a couple of beats go by. 'That sounds all right,' he said, 'but I'll need to think about it.'

I waited a couple of hours for Trowbridge to drive home to his place in Millbrook and settle in. Then I called. 'Did you think about it?'

'It sounds good to me,' he said, 'but you know I hate to pay taxes. If you can absorb the taxes, we've got a deal.'

So I said I'd get right back to him, but all the managers were having a powwow. I signaled to Gary, but he wouldn't come out of the circle. I waited fifteen minutes and called Trowbridge again. 'I don't know yet,' I said. 'I just didn't want you to think I'd forgotten you. Can I call you in half an hour?'

Trowbridge said he was going out to dinner. I said I'd call him after dinner. 'By the time I get back from dinner, you're going to be heading home to bed,' he told me.

'Not today,' I said. 'I work the iron today. Open to close. I'll be here until nine P.M.' So he said I could call him at 7:15 P.M. The meeting broke, and Gary said the taxes on $9,500 were $640.

'He'll make the deal,' I said, 'but he wants us to eat the taxes.'

'We'll split them,' Gary said. 'Tell him we'll split the taxes.'

I tried to call Trowbridge again, but there was no answer. I kept trying until the place closed at nine P.M. At home the next morning, I told Janet I was going to insist that we pay the taxes. 'He's a sweet guy,' I said. 'It's a sweet deal for us. I'll tell Joe he insists. Even if he doesn't insist, I'll tell Joe he does.'

'Ah,' said J, 'the Robin Hood of car sales.'

As soon as I got in the next day, I began to call Trowbridge. No answer. *Sure,* I thought, *he's going to pay ten thousand dollars for a compass on a car he hasn't even taken for a test drive. He's probably over at Ford now looking at a Lincoln with a thermometer.*

But he did call. He said he was going to visit a tailor in Mount Kisco, and on the way back he'd stop in. I told him the taxes were $640 and we'd split them. He went for it.

Rumors of a big sale always spread mysteriously through the showroom. Somebody I'd met only once or twice patted me on the back and said, 'You can't retire yet.' Everybody seemed to know that Benny was selling a thirty-eight-thousand-dollar Coupe DeV-ille at sticker price and taking in trade a Catera that was also virtually new. There was joy in Muddville. 'It's a good deal,' Gary told me. 'We can go a month without a deal like this. We can go a year without a deal like this.'

After the buy order is signed, the options, insurance, and deal with the bank are all completed in Finance and Insurance. A key man in F and I was picked to work the sale.

'There are fat profits here,' the F-and-I ace told me. 'We can make this a one-payment lease and not charge him anything. In fact, we can make it into a one-payment lease and give him a check for ten thousand dollars. It'll look like we're generous.'

'How would that work?' I asked.

He explained that we'd take possession of Trowbridge's old car, but lease him the new one for two years. The customer wouldn't really own the new car, and in two years he'd have to buy it, or surrender it. The value of leasing a car for two years is substantially less than the value of full ownership. Since the deal was a one-pay lease, it would appear as if the customer were buying the car, but actually he wouldn't be. He would only be renting it for two years, while we would be getting the full value of the car he already owned. So we could cut him a check for ten thousand dollars.

We were taking in the Catera, which was valued at twenty-six thousand dollars, although we fully expected to sell it for more. In return, we were giving Trowbridge two years' use of a car whose sticker price was thirty-eight thousand dollars.

I said that sounded fine as long as it was explained. 'He's eighty-eight years old,' I said.

I was given the manual for the sedan. I set the clock, tried the radio, and tried the heat. I learned how to adjust the seat and mirror. I couldn't figure out the compass. I thought it had to be set, and I didn't know how to set it. I asked around. Nobody else seemed to know, either. Would the compass queer the deal? Would Trowbridge show up at all?

He arrived, all right, smiling and full of apologies for being late. I brought him over to the ace in F and I. Then I went and sat in my cubicle and watched them through the glass partition. My phone rang. Would I join them in F and I, please?

It turned out Jefferson Trowbridge didn't have the title on his car. It used to be that ownership on a car in New York State could be transferred with the registration, but now cars have titles. We needed the title to make the deal.

I stepped back into the showroom, dizzy with the blow. Victor had already heard. He looked up at me from behind the walls of his cubicle as I passed. 'You're screwed,' he said.

Gary was at my desk and signaled violently for me to cross the room and join him there. 'Will you drive him?' he asked, as soon as I got into the cubicle. 'Will you drive him home and get the title?'

I said Millbrook was an hour away. That would be a two-hour drive, at least. 'Should I do that?'

'You'd better do it,' Gary said. 'He might forget. He might die.'

So when Trowbridge came on to the floor, I stepped forward, said I'd drive him to Millbrook and back, if that was OK. He thought this would be fine, although he certainly didn't want to inconvenience me. I said I didn't mind. I thought the Catera might be fun to drive, although I didn't say that.

So we got in the car and headed north. We talked about the diminution of the race. I said it was extraordinary what the great men of old were capable of. I told Trowbridge that I had a particular admiration for Lord Nelson. 'You know they sent him to sea expecting him to die young, release his family of the burden of support? He becomes the greatest naval commander of all time. When his right arm was cut off aboard the *Theseus,* after the failed landing at Tenerife, he felt that the knife was cold. Afterwards he insisted that all surgeons under his command heat their instruments. He didn't want his men to feel the cold knife.'

Jefferson Trowbridge had heard of Lord Nelson. He was a little shy about admitting it, but said that his greatest hero was the man he'd been named after, Thomas Jefferson. I said that I, too, was an admirer of Thomas Jefferson. Wasn't there a famous Kennedy quote? I asked.

Trowbridge knew it. At a dinner honoring Nobel Prize-winners, JFK had said, 'I think this is the most extraordinary collection of talent, of human knowledge, that has ever been gathered together at the White House, with the possible exception of when Thomas Jefferson dined alone.'

I said I knew that Jefferson had been one of the foremost architects of his time. 'Not to mention writing the Declaration of Independence.'

Trowbridge remembered that his namesake had been a spectacular gardener. 'His attention to detail in all things was extraordinary,' I said. 'He once counted the number of peas in a pint measure.' Then, of course, there was the Louisiana Purchase, and the Lewis and Clark expedition. Trowbridge hadn't seen *Jefferson in Paris.* I had. I hadn't visited Monticello. He had. Jefferson Trowbridge hadn't read the John Adams biography *Passionate Sage* by Joseph Ellis. I had. He seemed to have at hand most of the facts I'd gleaned from that excellent book. Yes, I knew that both men died on the same day, the Fourth of July. He knew that Adams's last words were 'Thomas Jefferson still survives.'

Trowbridge himself lived in a retirement community that had once been a girls' school. His unit had its own entrance and garage. The apartment was neat and bright. He had a candlestick display. 'She collected these,' he said, 'so I brought them up here.' Trowbridge then told me that he still said good morning to his late wife's picture every day, and good night to it before he went to sleep.

They had had no children. This was important to me. No lawyer offspring lurking in the wings.

My prospect found the title. We drove back to Wegman Auto. The burgundy DeVille was parked right out in front of the main door, still dripping from the car wash. There were two men out in the sun, drying the new car with rags. When we pulled in, they rushed over to the Catera, removed the plates, and put them on the new DeVille. Ordinarily, the salesman performs this chore himself, but the entire dealership seemed to have been galvanized.

'That's your car,' I said. 'Want to take it for a ride?'

Trowbridge didn't see the need, but I insisted. 'We have to make sure it's not broken. We need to adjust the seats and mirrors.'

So he captained the car around the circle of roads commonly used for a test-drive. I showed him all the gadgets. Everything worked splendidly. Everything but the compass.

'I think it has to be set up,' I said. 'If you have trouble with it, come back, and we'll fix it.'

He didn't seem to mind. He liked the roomy feeling of the car.

I led him back to F and I and made the pass-off to our ace in that office. Then I retreated to my cubicle. Rick Kaiser leaned over the partition. 'You're going to make four or five thousand on the deal,' he said. 'You're going to be salesman of the month.'

I sat at my desk and watched anxiously as the man in F and I did his magic. The offices were all glass, and I could see Trowbridge inside. He seemed to be nodding and smiling. Then my phone rang.

'Mr. Trowbridge is ready,' I was told. 'Why don't you come in and take him out to his car?'

I walked over to F and I. Trowbridge had all his papers in his hand. He was beaming. 'You know what?' he said. 'They actually gave me a check.'

'Really?' I said, as if this were a big surprise.

'That's right. I got a new car and also a check.'

'Good,' I said, 'I'm glad.'

'You want to see it?' he asked.

'Sure,' I said. So we stopped walking, and he showed me the check.

The check was for two hundred dollars. I couldn't believe my eyes. I looked again. Two hundred dollars. But F and I had told me the old man was getting ten thousand dollars. *What happened to the other ninety-eight hundred*? I wondered. I felt ill. I walked Trowbridge to the car. He got in. He said he was pleased to have met me. I said that I was pleased to have met him. 'I'm tickled,' he told me. 'I still don't know how I got the car and didn't have to pay a thing.' He drove off.

I walked back into the showroom. The man at F and I was on the phone, of course, so I went to Gary's desk. 'That guy was supposed to get a check for ten thousand dollars,' I said. 'How did that turn into two hundred?'

Gary thought I should calm down. Anyway, he was busy.

'Tomorrow,' he said.

When I came to work the next day, Gary was still busy. I went and stood in front of his desk. I wasn't going away until I had the sale explained. Gary was very cool. He said all right, he'd draw up the figures for me.

He got out a yellow legal pad and a calculator. (These men can't talk without a calculator.) In order to make the trade come out to ninety-five hundred plus half the tax, as we'd originally offered, we had to let the Cadillac go for cost, Gary said. Which was all right, since there was a two-thousand-dollar bonus for selling a new Deville. But since the car was leased, not sold, we weren't entitled to that two thousand. Now we had no profit. So we took two thousand out of the ten-thousand-dollar check that Trowbridge had coming. 'Or *you* wouldn't have earned *anything*,' Gary said.

I had no way of proving that this was a fairy tale, but it sure sounded like one. Otherwise, why was everybody in the dealership so excited? Salesmen who made a profit of two thousand dollars changed their own license plates.

Trowbridge spent seven thousand more on the back end, Gary told me. That's what the guy at F and I had done with my old friend. Gary said I should be pleased, because I was going to get 5 per cent of what was sold in the back end. I asked what had been sold in the back end. Well, for starters, there was an extended warranty. That cost twenty-five hundred dollars.

'An extended warranty?' I said. 'Cadillacs come with a fifty-thousand-mile, bumper-to-bumper warranty. He's only leasing for two years. That's robbery.'

'Not necessarily,' Gary said. 'What if he keeps the car?'

Next I talked with the man in F and I. He, too, wondered what I was so upset about. 'He's rich. He told me he makes a hundred and seventeen thousand dollars a year in interest.'

'Because he's rich, we have to rob him?' I asked. 'You know that if he was poor, you would have robbed him anyway,' I said, and got a smile.

I was angry, but I knew that to complain about how we'd treated the old man would throw up a wall between me and the people I worked with. So I tried to make a stink about how *I'd* been robbed, as clearly I *had* been robbed.

'I caught a big fish,' I said. 'You gave me the head and tail.'

Gary just sat there and took it. Danny Johnson tacked over to listen. I gestured in his direction. 'You wouldn't have robbed Danny like that,' I said. Gary didn't say anything.

Danny was wise to me. He knew why I was upset. 'You can't be a salesman, Benny,' he said, 'and expect to go to heaven.'

Nor did I become salesman of the month. When I got paid, my bonus for that month was $986.77. They also let me keep my $300-a-week draw. If they had deducted the $2,200 draw, I would have owed *them* money. The draw was forgiven for all the new salesmen, Gary told me. 'Until you get your feet under you.' So my four-week total was $2,186.77. This broke down to $546.69 a week.

More than $500 a week. That was what they'd been earning in the good old days, according to Danny Johnson. That's what he'd told me during his Hitler speech. So I felt like a star, until I multiplied $546.69 out by 52. My estimated annual income was $28,427.88 a year – provided I took no vacation.

Wegman would not keep forgiving the draw, either. In which case I'd be robbing old men for $246.69 a week.

They'd already stopped forgiving Bentley Rusk his draw, which was why he'd quit. Rick Kaiser had threatened to quit, and I suspected that this was over the same issue.

In the future, I could count on earning $246.69 for a fifty-hour week or a shade under five dollars an hour. Five dollars and fifteen cents was minimum wage at the time.

I kept wondering about the classified ad that had brought us all in. What about those people earning '$75,000 +, No experience necessary'? Where were *they*? I was at the cashier's window one afternoon, when one of the Toyota studs appeared. He was wearing a handsome leather jacket. I asked him, 'Is leather required?'

'What?'

'For you guys in Toyota, is leather required? I notice you all wear leather.'

'We're sort of outlaws,' he said.

I said, 'There were fourteen people in class with me. Guess how many of them wanted to go to work at Toyota?'

'I don't know,' he said.

'Fourteen,' I said. 'You're not outlaws.'

He shrugged.

'How did you get into Toyota?' I asked.

So then he asked me if I'd had other car-sales experience. I said I hadn't. He said he had been a car salesman in Kissimee, Florida. 'Joe wanted me to be in GM,' he told me, 'but I said, "I'd love to come sell Toyotas for you, Joe. If I can't do that, I'll sell them for your competitor. Which would you prefer?" So he put me in Toyota.'

'And you like it?'

'I love the job. You want to go outside, you can go outside. You want to be inside, you can be inside. None of that boring desk work. I was the number two salesman last year, sold two hundred cars. I made sixty thousand dollars.'

This was a whole lot more than I was earning, but it wasn't '$75,000 +', either. Not that I wouldn't have leapt at a chance to move across the street to Toyota. I asked Joe repeatedly for a transfer.

I also asked for Nissan, and supposedly that transfer was being considered. I didn't want to go to Preowned. The guys in Pre-owned were having even less fun than the guys in GM.

This was another area that had been profitable before the new pay plan. The average markup on a used car was three thousand dollars, but the people I knew who'd gone there said it wasn't working out the way they'd hoped. Ralph, the former mechanic with the curly hair and the Lotus, told me he sometimes actually lost money on a sale.

Wegman had juiced the department by offering a thirty-day money-back guarantee. This may have drawn in more customers, but each salesman had to contribute four hundred dollars for each car he sold in order to cover the expense. The salesman also had to pay $213 to get the car cleaned. Plus, there was a ninety-day parts-and-labor guarantee, and the salesman was supposed to cover *that* out of his commission. Repair orders often came to one thousand dollars, and sometimes they went so high they ate up the entire commission.

Jeffrey Stern had gotten himself moved back to Toyota. Jeffrey's transfer seemed to indicate that the plan to increase GM profitability had been abandoned. So now we had a new general sales manager. This was an older man from F and I.

Victor Amato and I were lounging outside of our cubicles on the first day after the new GSM was promoted. Let's call the new GSM Tom Pullman. We were wondering what sort of manager Pullman would turn out to be. We knew he was highly religious and that his daughter had been very sick recently.

'He's a phony,' Victor told me.

'What do you mean, "he's a phony"?'

'He's got that terrible wig.'

'How do you know it's a wig?'

'You can't tell?'

'No. I can never tell. Women can always tell about wigs. That's why I won't wear one, but I can never tell. How can you be so sure?'

'Look at his fucking hairline. You can't tell?'

'No. I just thought he had great hair.'

'My second father-in-law had that exact same wig. I know, because when they laid him out in the coffin, it got knocked off, and I had to put it back on him.'

Tom was determined, of course, to turn us around, raise morale, sell GM cars as if they were Toyotas. His first Saturday-morning meeting, he gave us all a sheet of paper with a paragraph of writing on it. We were supposed to find all the *f*s on the sheet. I found three. Most everybody found three. The former IBM engineer found seven. Then Tom explained to us that there were eleven *f*s on the page. He showed us where they were.

Same was true of customers, he told us. 'There may not seem to be many customers,' he said, 'but they're out there if you look.'

Then he pulled from his wallet a tattered version of a poem titled 'Don't Quit', and made a Xerox of it for every GM salesman. He said that he'd found this poem years ago, when he was in despair, and that it had been an inspiration ever since. You couldn't read the whole poem anymore, but the lines I could see went like this:

> Success is failure turned inside out,
> The silver tint of the clouds of doubt.

I guessed he could have gotten a new copy of the poem at Hallmark, but I didn't say so. This object in his wallet had taken on totemic significance.

Then he had a meeting with each of his salesmen. These were held in one of the glassed-in offices ordinarily occupied by the F-

and–I people. As soon as I sat down with him, I said I thought I was going to leave.

He wanted to know why. I said that I figured out how little money I was making. I said I liked the job and the people, but that the work was too hard for so little money. I said I'd wait until the end of the month to make my final determination.

He said that with such a negative attitude, I was condemning myself to failure. I said that that wasn't true. 'I'll work hard,' I said. 'See how it comes out.'

'But your attitude is negative,' he said.

I said, 'Many successful people have negative attitudes.'

At the end of the month, I prepared to quit. I felt wretched about it. I felt that I was betraying Gary. I went and stood outside to consider. John was standing in front of the showroom. Remember John? He also came from the *Reader's Digest*. He wore a lot of gold chains. John was very upset. He was chain-smoking.

I asked him what the matter was. He said he'd been fired. He said he'd come back to talk with them about it, and they wouldn't even do that for him.

So that settled it. I figured that if they could fire John, then I could also quit.

I went back inside. I pulled up the chair in front of Gary's desk. I told him I was going to leave. His face fell. He told me it was winter. 'Nobody buys cars in the winter,' he told me. 'The winter is always slow,' he said. 'Spring and summer, that's when people buy cars. I don't want you to leave.'

'That's kind of you,' I said.

He said I should wait. Sales were looking up.

I went back to my cubicle to pack. Rick Kaiser wasn't surprised. He had seen it coming. But Victor Amato was shocked. 'I never thought you'd do this,' he said.

I went back to Gary and asked if he wanted my Magic 8 Ball.

'No, thank you,' he said. 'I'd rather wing it. I'd rather not know the future.'

I told Gary again how sorry I was. I knew he'd done a lot of work with me.

'It's not that,' he said. 'It's just that I think you can sell cars.'

Right before I left, Joe P. showed up. 'You want to go to Nissan?' he asked.

I shook my head.

'Toyota?' I asked.

This time Joe shook his.

Almost two years later, in the fall of 1999, I went back to the GM showroom. The place had been remodeled. At first, I thought that nobody I knew was still there. Then I spotted Gary. Still in a double-breasted jacket. Still with his tiny black shoes. I found him hunched over a phone. I patted him on the shoulder. He looked up, blinked a couple of times in recognition, and went back to his call.

I waited until he got off the line.

We shook hands. 'Everybody's gone,' I said.

He nodded.

I asked if he remembered me.

He nodded again.

'I have to make another call,' he said.

I nodded, and he went back to the phone.

There was a cappuccino machine in the lunchroom. But it was the kind you had to put money in, not at all what we'd imagined, or asked for.

I went across the street to Toyota. Lorretta was there, beaming, laughing, glad to see me – but Loretta is always glad to see everybody. She asked what I'd been doing with myself. I told her I'd been writing books. She asked if I had any with me. I said I didn't. She said I should come by sometime and show her one. I said I would do that.

I asked how Robert Garcia was. She told me that Garcia had been promoted to manage an entire dealership, then fired.

I could see Tom Pullman – the one with the good attitude and the bad wig – working in the background. He came over and said hello.

When I asked Lorretta about Victor, she told me Victor was back in the painting business. She said that once in a while he'd come in.

'He's the same?' I asked.

'The same,' she said, and smiled.

Al Wegman had cleaned house. The mighty had fallen. Joe P. had been fired. 'Came out with his box in his arms and everything,' she said.

Loretta told me that Al Wegman had remarried and that his new, young wife was running a tighter, more efficient ship. Loretta thought things were looking up. A couple of weeks later, I saw Loretta again, this time at a local restaurant. When I asked her how it was going under the new and improved management at Wegman, she told me she'd been fired.

After a section of this story had appeared in *The New Yorker,* a number of people called or wrote to compliment it. Many of them had the feeling, though, that this world would vanish soon. This sort of barbarism is outdated, they told me. It wouldn't survive the Internet.

But early in the spring of the year 2000, well into the new millennium, I found this advertisement in the classified section of the local newspaper. It was for Wegman Auto.

Sales/Auto NO EXPERIENCE

MALE & FEMALE

WORKING A JOB? START BUILDING A CAREER!

One of New York's most progressive and highest-paying auto dealers now seeks salespeople without experience. We need 10 motivated people to teach how to sell cars and make big $$$$$$

EARN FROM

$45,800 TO OVER $80,000

your first year!

Epilogue

AOL, JCPENNEY, LUCENT TECHNOLOGIES, AND SARAH LEE
were among the well-known companies that announced massive
staff cutbacks at the beginning of this year. 'Laid Off: How Safe Is
Your Job?' was a *Newsweek* cover headline in February.

The story was also hot back in 1996. A growing public awareness
of mass white-collar firings had crystallized around a seven-part
New York Times series. Forty-three million jobs had vanished since
1979, according to the book in which the articles were collected:
'And while many more have been created, increasingly, the jobs
that are disappearing are those of higher-paid, white-collar workers, and many of the new jobs pay much less than those they
replaced.'

I have friends who were savaged by the economic turmoil. Many
of the stories had happy endings, but not all of the stories had happy
endings. Often I lost touch with the people whom I'd met when
they had held jobs they were later fired from, or positions that had
melted away.

I took the course for Burns Security with an older guy who said
that he'd been a phone-company executive. Probably he was using
the word *executive* loosely, but who knows? I spoke with one
engineer who seemed to have lost his job as the result of being too
exacting in his inspections on the assembly line while working for a
defense contractor. He has since tried his hand at a variety of jobs,
including that of freelance lemonade vendor. He was never hired as
an engineer again. I worked with several people who told me they
had fallen from well-paid positions at IBM, one lost her job because

of an R. J. Reynolds restructuring. A handful had been fired from
the *Reader's Digest*. How far they'd actually fallen is a matter of
conjecture. While showing me how to operate the freight elevator
at CompUSA, my friend and mentor Bill told me that – before he'd
lost his money – he'd planned to spend the rest of his life sailing and
taking graduate courses. I believed him then. I believe him now.
The Tufts graduate at the auto mall was convincingly refined; once
when I was in Manhattan, I thought I saw him on Fifth Avenue
near the offices of the Norton Publishing Company. Fear clutched
at my heart. *My God, he's writing a book,* I thought. *I bet his comes out
before mine does.*

About a year into this project, I was alarmed to look up and
discover that my subject had vanished. Unemployment had fallen
and dot.com millionaires were now the focus of our attention.
Companies were still shedding workers, but nobody seemed to
mind particularly, or nobody minded except the workers themselves. Which recalls a joke: What's the difference between a
depression and a recession? When your next-door neighbor loses
his job, it's a recession. When you lose *your* job, it's a depression.

The heightened vulnerability of white-collar employees may
lose our attention as it loses novelty, but fewer and fewer people are
safe. Regular mass firings, long common in some blue-collar
professions, are now also apt to occur to those with higher salaries
and higher expectations. It is no longer axiomatic that a worker
who does his job brilliantly will get to keep it. What if the company
is bought by another company, and they already have somebody at
the job you do so well? Many public corporations are driven now
by the need to please investors before pleasing employees, or even
customers.

'The point is, ladies and gentlemen, that greed – for lack of a
better word – is good,' says Gordon Gecko in the 1987 Oliver
Stone movie, *Wall Street*. 'Greed is right. Greed works. Greed
clarifies, cuts through and captures the essence of the evolutionary
spirit. Greed in all of its forms – greed for life, for money, for love,

knowledge – has marked the upward surge of mankind, and greed – you mark my words – will not only save Teldar Paper, but that other malfunctioning corporation called the USA.'

I suppose that's the justification for millions of fractured lives, but even a tough guy like Oliver Stone ends his movie with Gecko headed for jail.

When I think of Americans who went to jail, I like to recall, instead, Socialist presidential candidate Eugene Debs. Sent to prison in 1918 for trying to obstruct the draft, Debs delivered a speech which began, 'Your honor, years ago I recognized my kinship with all living beings, and I made up my mind that I was not one bit better than the meanest on earth. I said then, and I say now, that while there is a lower class, I am in it; while there is a criminal element, I am of it; while there is a soul in prison, I am not free.'

Most Americans would applaud Debs and condemn Gecko, but both philosophies are alive and well in America. We like to say that money is the bottom line, but is it? Don't we expect justice as well?

Ours is a nation conceived and dedicated to the proposition that all men are created equal.

The problem here is that all men aren't created equal. Am I getting old, or is every belief system built around a shared falsehood? Maybe facts just aren't stirring enough to march behind. Can you imagine a cult built around a shared faith in gravity?

America is driven by this noble falsehood. I wouldn't have it any other way. Stirring and instructive nonsense, but nonsense nevertheless. We aren't equal. We don't all have the same capabilities, the same chances, or the same luck. We don't even have the same inclinations.

And yet our belief has led us to great good and even greater prosperity. Because we believe in equality, we have striven for equality under the law. In business and in society, we have attempted a meritocracy. We mean for the race to be fair. It's not fair, but it's certainly a race.

The trouble then is not in the American Dream, but in our assumption that we've already made it real. We're not there yet.

Not by a long shot. We mustn't give up. In the meantime we can't ever forget that the woman serving us from the other side of the counter has a story, too. The American Dream is part nightmare. What goes up may also come down. Someday you and I might find ourselves saying, 'Yes, sir, how can I help?' Or even, 'Who's the lucky person buying a car today?'

I had a horrible time researching this book, a horrible, glorious time. Getting the jobs was like plunging into cold water on a hot day. It was frightening to jump. It felt great to get wet.

We often take our possessions and status as essential to life. The job, the neighborhood, a taste in wine can all seem as vital as the air we need to breathe. The good news is that if you lose your job, you won't lose your life.

The bad news is that there are people who will act as if you've died.

A woman who had worked down the hall from me as an editor found me selling computers and accepted my apparent economic disaster with breathtaking equanimity. The last time she'd seen me, I'd been in a suit, an employee with more tenure than she had and the same number of stripes on my sleeve.

There I was, out under the fluorescent lighting at CompUSA, wearing khakis and my red polo shirt complete with Superstore name tag. 'Oh, so you're into this now,' she said, and beamed.

Once through the barbed wire of humiliation, I often enjoyed the work. It was fun to sell computers. I loved selling cars.

In February of 1996 I had a higher gross profit than any other new salesman on the GM floor. 'Benny, here, done phenomenal.' That's what the general sales manager said. And I was absurdly pleased. My heart was racing, my pulse roaring in my ears. I could feel tingling in the soles of my cowboy boots.

I'd switched classes, a transition I was reminded of at a Manhattan dinner party shortly after I'd participated in the fleecing of Jefferson Trowbridge. I got drunk and told the table all about it. 'They made him pay twenty-five hundred dollars for an extended warranty, when the car's regular coverage ran for fifty thousand miles, and he was only leasing the Cadillac for two years,' I explained, and chuckled.

I was expecting applause. I got a deadly silence instead. When my dinner companions spoke up, they were angry. They were horrified that I had participated in such a transaction. 'I'm surprised at you.'

'Car salesmen have to rob,' I said defensively. 'Otherwise, we don't get paid. They're like pirates. You wouldn't condemn a pirate for leading a boarding party.'

I didn't exactly carry the day.

I forget what we talked about next. 'Where did this excellent wine come from? It's really very good. Would you like a Cohiba?'

I was telling rich people about robbing rich people. If I'd told a hilarious story about refusing to pay a plumber or having a waiter fired, I would have found a much more sympathetic audience.

I'm still proud of my stint on the GM floor.

'The winter is always slow,' Gary had said when I told him I was going to quit. 'Spring and summer, that's when people buy cars. I don't want you to leave.'

My competence was affirmed. But then the greatest affirmation of self is the one that puts competence aside.

A friend who came to Cosi when I was working there shocked me by saying it made him sad to see how slow I was. 'They must think you're some old white guy out of the Bowery,' he told me.

Thank God for Andrea, then. Remember Andrea? She was my manager. Andrea was halfway through her complimentary sandwich when I went down to her basement office to say good-bye.

'So I have to know,' I said. 'Has anybody ever been slower?'

There was a pause as she chewed her sandwich. She swallowed. 'Plenty of people are slower,' she said. 'A million people are slower. Nobody else is so kind.'

Andrea's a sweetheart, but there are a lot of people out there kinder than I was, men and women who see a value in life and in other people that goes beyond class and even beyond skill. Life is precious. They see this and they make it so. For me, that's the bottom line.

The job I had the highest hopes for and liked the least was at Nobody Beats the Wiz in Scarsdale. But even there I made friends. I was part of something.

I knew Ralph Palmer of the muttonchop whiskers liked me better than he liked Souflé, but I didn't know we were friends until late one night when he opened up about his dog. Ralph had owned a purebred sheepdog once: 'A dog like that is worth hundreds of dollars,' he told me. Ralph found the animal at a pound. The children loved the dog. The pet was so smart, it pretended to be stupid, Ralph told me.

'You'd throw a tennis ball one way, and he'd run the other way. Just to make us laugh.'

For each job, I dove underwater and came up in a different universe. In this case, the oversized Wiz vest was my pass. I remember going out for my lunch break once, and seeing a huge old man in an electrician's green uniform buying a bouquet of flowers.

'You're in trouble,' I said, and chuckled.

'No, no,' he said, and smiled back at me, 'it's a birthday.'

My Wiz vest made that exchange possible. If I'd been wearing my ordinary uniform – penny loafers, jeans, and a sweater – and I'd said, 'You're in trouble' to that same man, and in that same deli, he might have swatted me like a fly.

I remember buying a BB rifle for my eldest boy at the Sports Authority in White Plains, and thinking afterwards, *Gosh, that salesman was friendly. I've never had such a positive experience.* Then I realized that I was wearing my khakis and CompUSA polo shirt with name tag. He thought I was one of them, not the affluent, blue-jeans-wearing, former longhair I usually appear to be, and am.

So holding these jobs has given me perspective, a new understanding of how large the world is, and how fortunate I have been in it. I've grown to respect the people on the other side of the counter. What I feel for them now is much more than respect.

I'm also a little less frightened about losing everything, although I still seem to frighten easily.

For instance, I'm always in a fever before I leave a job. It's hard to explain. I've never been able to explain it to myself actually, but I was nearly as anxious about leaving CompUSA and the auto mall as I was about leaving a corporation that I'd been at for more than a decade. Quitting a job is like leaving a woman. It's like abandoning a part of yourself. Sounds silly, but I can never sleep. The day I quit the Wiz, I was terrified. I was certain my boss was going to send me up to Loss Prevention (which is what they called security) and have me interrogated. For what? I don't know, exactly. A failure of loyalty.

I was so frightened, I got dressed up for work. I put on dark shoes, suit pants, and a necktie. I planned to quit that morning, but if my manager insisted that I stay, I'd work for one more day. I'd give up the small point to win the larger one.

But my manager didn't ask me to stay. 'I'm sorry it didn't work out,' he said. 'Have a nice life,' he said.

When I walked out of the store, I was relieved, of course, but also surprised that I had meant so little to them all. I was surprised and unexpectedly disappointed.

Suddenly released, I was in no rush to get home, so I drove up Central Avenue instead. I felt sad, abandoned. Winter on Central Avenue is a study in gray. There are many different shades of asphalt. The signs on the stores are more garish than cheering. This is not the sort of landscape you go to when you need your spirit affirmed. I looked for a place to stop. I settled on Barnes & Noble. I told myself that I needed to buy a book.

Inside the store I found two salesgirls talking to each other. I had a question. I tried to get their attention. I was a customer now, though. I was one of those people who is always right. They weren't particularly interested in me.

I was interested in them, though. So it's not just respect I feel for hourly workers. It's not just admiration for their perseverance and humor. I miss their company. I miss my friends.

ACKNOWLEDGMENTS

There are two great difficulties with an acknowledgment page. The first is that the very act of acknowledgment seems to suggest that something has been accomplished. Haven't you ever read an acknowledgment page and thought, *What's all the celebration about? Nothing happened here.* So forgive me for going on. This isn't about me, but the people who have been kind or helpful, or both.

The second great difficulty with acknowledgment pages is that they are all so damn cheerful. Every woman cherishes her husband, every writer his publisher. Or her publisher as the case may be. The children, if mentioned, seem to have spent years tiptoeing around in felt slippers, presenting trays of tea and toast to the invalid genius. *Who are these people?* Acknowledgments often leave me with the impression that I've been lied to.

Not that I don't harbor some positive feelings. I do want to thank Adam Bellow, who bought the proposal when it was called *Square One* and the book hadn't a friend in the world. Then Karen Rinaldi, who saved it when Adam left the Free Press and the manuscript fell into unsympathetic hands. She and Panio Gianopoulos haven't just been smart and enthusiastic: they've been good company. Karen's one of those rare editors who seems interested in publishing only the books she would like to read. She's married to the writer Joel Rose. This helps. Panio's a writer, too, so Karen's surrounded. Panio's always funny. Often brilliant.

Karen came up with the title. If you don't like the title, blame Karen.

Then I want to thank Kathy Robbins. She can change the world with a shrug. I also want to thank her husband, Richard Cohen. He's a writer, too, and therefore always sympathetic. Also David Halpern, who works for Kathy and has done this book and its author many services.

Once a week I meet with four other writers and we read to each other from works-in-progress. Terry Bazes, Marilyn Johnson, Esmeralda

Santiago, and Larkin Warren are in the group, and it's thrilling not to be alone.

Terry Bazes has taken extra time away from his own excellent novel to struggle with me on this book and I'm deeply grateful. Any spelling or grammatical errors should be blamed on Terry.

Ruth Reichl gave me a much-needed boost by assigning the 'Cosi Sandwich Bar' piece for *Gourmet,* and editing it lovingly when it came in. Chip McGrath was wonderful about the 'Borders Books and Music' piece, and ran it in *The New York Times Book Review.* Henry Finder encouraged the 'Auto Mall' piece and then edited it deftly for *The New Yorker.*

I've done a lot of research, but I'm afraid my personality pokes through the text a lot. Those of you who don't like what you see can blame my wife. If it weren't for her tender affection and endless support, I wouldn't exist as a man, or a writer.

If the book is hard on her, this should be taken in the spirit of fun. We're always kidding each other. She laughs easily, and often makes me laugh when I need it most. My life really began the day we met.

Which doesn't mean that I'll give her a break here. If there are any shortcomings in the text, you should blame my wife and children. My life is evenly split between work and family, and when I stayed out late at a job, or was preoccupied at home, there were recriminations.

'Perfection of the life or of the Work,' Yeats asks, forgetting the mass of men who make a shambles of them both.

I recall one Sunday in particular, when I was at the auto store, and J brought the boys to visit her parents on Long Island. Andrew, my younger son, got his head stuck between the rungs in the back of a chair. His head had to be soaped in order to be withdrawn, and feelings ran high that I should have been there for the crisis, not swanning around a car showroom.

The support system that has made it possible for me to write is vast and complicated, but these are some of the names that come immediately to mind. Both John (fifteen) and Andrew (twelve) have been champions of my work. Mostly they don't read it, which may help them to sustain their enthusiasm. My mother, Mary Cheever, has been consistently enthusiastic. Peter Boyer and Kari Granville have listened patiently to my litany of complaint. My mother-in-law, Lucille Maslin, has been endlessly supportive. Maggie Fox-Moore goes out of her way to give me time to work.

My sister once said, 'Friends co-sign each other's shit,' and she's had most of the tricky passages in this book read to her over the phone. She told me they were brilliant. If they're not brilliant, blame Susan.

Rafe Yglesias heard every page of this book over the phone and then read the final text. I asked him repeatedly if there was anything I should change or shorten. He told me to leave it alone. So if it's bad, blame Rafe.

Barry Malzberg has published dozens of novels. He read this book and said he liked it. The man ought to know better.

Bill Maxwell didn't survive to see this manuscript, but he was enthusiastic about everything else I've written, and it's entirely possible that without his encouragement, I would have gone into another line of work by now. So if I disappoint you, blame William Maxwell.

E-mail has greatly enlarged my world, and I have several friends with whom I correspond frequently, and whose support has been essential. First among these is Lucy Waletzky, the neighbor with whom I drive to the Union Church for the nine A.M. service, the Reverend Dr. F. Paul DeHoff presiding. Paul's vision of Christianity is intensely compelling and so generous that it includes me. The book's spiritual failings should be blamed on Paul.

The other e-mail correspondents on whom I rely for encouraging words and guidance include Douglas Brayfield, Peter Canning, Ted Zeigler, Linda Lee, and Eleanor Swink. Alec Wilkinson and Annabel Davis Goff both looked at the preface for me and made encouraging sounds.

Ben Gerson, Katherine McNamara, Caroline Miller, Steve Katz, Victor Novasky, Richard Snow, and Robin Whitten have all been friends to my work at one time or another. Gail Hochman sold the first novel. Lee Goerner bought it.

Michael Singer and Gerald Krovatin, Esquire, have been friendly in ways that I mistook for licence. You needn't blame them, but when the book is attacked, I will.

You can't blame Laura Shaine Cunningham, Anna Quindlen, or Robert Benton for the preface, though, because they all told me it might be lightened up and shortened considerably. Janet agreed. She thought the book's opening unnecessarily confrontational, even gloomy.

But I'm a gloomy guy and this – God help us – is a gloomy subject.

A NOTE ON THE AUTHOR

Benjamin Hale Cheever was born in New York
City. He has been a newspaper reporter, an
editor at *Reader's Digest* and is the author of three
novels: *The Plagiarist, The Partisan*, and
Famous After Death. He edited *The Letters of John
Cheever*, and has taught at Bennington College
and The New School for Social Research.
His work has appeared in *The New York Times,
The Nation*, and *The New Yorker*.

A NOTE ON THE TYPE

The text of this book is set in Bembo. This type was first used in 1495 by the Venetian printer Aldus Manutius for Cardinal Bembo's *De Aetna*, and was cut for Manutius by Francesco Griffo. It was one of the types used by Claude Garamond (1480–1561) as a model for his Romain de L'Université, and so it was the forerunner of what became standard European type for the following two centuries. Its modern form follows the original types and was designed for Monotype in 1929.